P9-CML-693

Focus on GRAMMAR

1

THIRD EDITION

Irene E. Schoenberg
Jay Maurer

ALWAYS LEARNING

PEARSON

**FOCUS ON GRAMMAR 1: An Integrated Skills Approach, Third Edition
Teacher's Resource Pack**

Copyright © 2012, 2006, 2003 by Pearson Education, Inc.
All rights reserved.

Pearson Education, 10 Bank Street, White Plains, NY 10606

Staff credits: The people who made up the *Focus on Grammar Teacher's
Resource Pack* team, representing editorial, production, design, and
manufacturing, are, Iris Candelaria, Dave Dickey, Christine Edmonds,
Nancy Flaggman, Ann France, Shelley Gazes, Lester Holmes, Stacey
Hunter, Pamela Kohn, Theodore Lane, Christopher Leonowicz, Jennifer
McAliney, Lise Minovitz, Jennifer Raspiller, Mary Perrotta Rich, Debbie
Sistino, Ken Volcjak, Marian Wassner, and Adina Zoltan.

Contributing writers (Level 1): Carol Chapelle, Nan Clarke, Evelyn Fella,
Leslie Grant, Bethany Gray, Joan Jamieson, Xiangying Jiang, Hsin-Min Liu,
Ruth Luman, Kathleen Smith, Gabriele Steiner, BJ Wells, and Kevin
Zimmerman.

Cover image: Shutterstock.com
Text composition: ElectraGraphics, Inc.
Text font: New Aster

ISBN 10: 0-13-248414-5
ISBN 13: 978-0-13-248414-5

Printed in the United States of America

1 2 3 4 5 6 7 8 9 10—V001—16 15 14 13 12 11

CONTENTS

ABOUT THE TEACHER'S RESOURCE PACK

This Teacher's Resource Pack offers a multitude of ideas for working with the material for the new edition of *Focus on Grammar 1: An Integrated Skills Approach*. The Teacher's Resource Pack includes:

- a **Teacher's Manual** (including General Teaching Notes, Unit Teaching Notes, Student Book Audioscript, and Student Book Answer Key)
- a **Teacher's Resource Disc** (including interactive PowerPoint® grammar presentations, placement test, reproducible Unit and Part assessments, and test-generating software)

THE TEACHER'S MANUAL

The Teacher's Manual includes the following sections:

- **General Teaching Notes** (pages 1–13) provide general suggestions for teaching and assessing the activities in the Student Book. A Strategies for Teaching Grammar section offers a quick reference for some of the most common and useful grammar teaching techniques. A Frequently Asked Questions section answers some of the most common issues that teachers encounter.
- **Unit Teaching Notes** (pages 14–137) provide step-by-step instructions on how to teach each unit and supplementary "Out of the Box Activities." They also include suggestions on when to use activities and tests from **www.myfocusongrammarlab.com**, assignments from the workbook, and materials from the Teacher's Resource Disc.
- The **Student Book Audioscript** (pages 138–147) includes scripts for the Listening and Pronunciation exercises in the Student Book.
- The **Student Book Answer Key** (pages 148–167) includes answers for the exercises in the Student Book.

THE TEACHER'S RESOURCE DISC

The Teacher's Resource Disc includes additional teaching resources and a complete assessment program:

Teaching Resources

- **PowerPoint® Presentations** of all Grammar Charts for each unit in the Student Book offer an alternative teaching tool for introducing the grammar presentation in the classroom. For select units, animated theme-based grammar presentations provide interactive follow-up practice activities for the contextualized instruction of grammar.

Assessments

- **Placement Test** in PDF format can be printed and used to place students into the appropriate level. Along with this 40-minute test is an audioscript and an answer key in PDF format, and audio as MP3 files.
- **Part and Unit Tests** in PDF format can be printed and used in class. These include Part Pre-Tests, Part Post-Tests, and Unit Achievement Tests. Also included are assessment audioscripts and answer keys in PDF format, and audio as MP3 files.
- **Test-Generating Software** provides thousands of questions from which teachers can customize class-appropriate tests.

GENERAL TEACHING NOTES

These notes are designed to guide you in teaching and assessing the recurring sections of the Student Book. Experimenting with the various options will enliven your classroom and appeal to students' different learning styles.

In the following section and in the Unit Teaching Notes, the icon ⏱ indicates an optional step you may wish to include if time permits.

The **Part Overview** previews the grammar and themes covered in each unit.

⏱ Part Pre-Tests

Before beginning each part, you may want to have students complete a diagnostic test. There are two options.
1. You can use the Part Pre-Tests to help you determine how well students know the material they are about to study in the next part of the Student Book. Since the material is usually new, students often score low on these tests. Each test takes about 50 minutes and includes about 60 items. The test begins with a listening exercise, includes several contextualized grammar exercises, and ends with an editing exercise. The tests are offered in two formats:
   - automatically graded tests at **www.myfocusongrammarlab.com**
   - reproducible tests on the Teacher's Resource Disc in this manual
2. You can use the Test-Generating Software on the Teacher's Resource Disc to create customized Part Pre-Tests of any length. The test items focus on grammar.

The **Grammar Overview** portion of the Unit Overview (offered in this Teacher's Manual) highlights the most important grammar points of each unit. It also points out common grammar trouble spots for students. You may also find it helpful to preview the Grammar Charts and Grammar Notes in the Student Book before teaching each unit. The **Unit Overview** previews the unit theme.

Step 1: Grammar in Context

Each unit opens with a reading selection designed to raise students' interest and expose them to the target grammar in a realistic, natural context. The selections include newspaper and magazine excerpts, websites, newsletters, advertisements, conversations, and other formats that students may encounter in their day-to-day lives. All of the texts are recorded and available on the audio program or at **www.myfocusongrammarlab.com**.

Before You Read (5 minutes)

This prereading activity creates interest, elicits students' knowledge about the topic, and encourages students to make predictions about the reading.

Suggested Procedure
1. Have the class look at the illustrations.
2. Ask students to respond to the questions. Ask these questions in a conversational way, instead of reading them from the book.

Option A
- Have the class read the questions in pairs or small groups and discuss their answers.
- Call on pairs to share their ideas with the class.

Option B
- Have students prepare questions about the topic in pairs.
- Call on pairs to share their questions and write them on the board.

Read (15–20 minutes)

Depending on the needs of your class, have students complete the reading in class or at home. Encourage students to read with a purpose and to read the passage once or twice without stopping to look up new words.

Suggested Procedure

1. Write the comprehension questions from the Unit Teaching Notes on the board. Establish a purpose for reading by going over the questions with the class. Have students think about the questions as they read the passage and listen to it.
2. Play the audio and have students follow along in their books. Have them underline any new words.
3. Have students read the passage again silently, looking for answers to the questions.
4. (!) Have students discuss their answers with a partner or in small groups.
5. (!) Put students in pairs or small groups to discuss the reading. Invite them to respond to the reading in a way that is meaningful to them: What was most interesting? What did they learn?

Option A (At Home / In Class)

- Write the comprehension questions on the board for students to copy or prepare them as a handout for students to take home.
- Go over the questions as a class and clarify as needed.
- Have students read the passage and answer the questions at home.
- (!) Have students write a few additional questions about the reading.
- Have students discuss their answers in pairs or small groups.
- (!) Have students take turns asking and answering the questions they prepared at home.
- Follow steps 4–5 in the Suggested Procedure for Read above.

Option B (In Class)

- Have students work in pairs. Divide the reading in half and have each student in the pair read one half.
- Have students summarize the information in their half of the reading for their partner.
- Follow steps 3–5 in the Suggested Procedure for Read.

After You Read (10–20 minutes)

A. Practice

Depending on the needs of your class, you may want to point out vocabulary or expressions in the reading that may be problematic for your students before they begin the oral practice. You will find some suggestions in the Unit Teaching Notes.

Suggested Procedure

1. Have students read the opening passage silently.
2. Group students according to the number of roles in the opening reading or conversation.
3. Have students read the passage aloud in pairs or groups a minimum of two times so that each student has an opportunity to read each of the roles. For example, in Unit 1, page 2 of the Student Book, the opening reading is essentially a monolog. Students would work in pairs and practice reading twice. The first student in the pair would read the entire passage, and then the second would read. Alternatively, students could take turns reading each section and then switch. In Unit 16, page 147 of the Student Book, there are three speakers in the opening conversation. Students would work in groups of three and read three times, changing roles after each practice.
4. Circulate as students are practicing reading aloud. Make corrections as needed. You might also want to note particular challenges students are having and design a mini-lesson that you can do later in the unit based on those challenges.
5. (!) Invite groups or one person from different groups to perform the reading for the class.

B. Vocabulary

Suggested Procedure

1. Have students look over each of the vocabulary items.
2. As students listen to and repeat the words, have them look at the vocabulary pictures and words in the Student Book.
3. Have students designate a page in their notebooks for Vocabulary, either unit by unit or for all vocabulary items that are new to them.
4. (!) Have students work in pairs or groups to compare words that are new to them and share their knowledge about them with each other.
5. (!) Have them write the word, part of speech, meaning, and a sample sentence.

C. Vocabulary

Suggested Procedure
1. Have students find and circle the target words in the opening text.
2. Elicit or explain the meanings of any new words.
3. Have students complete the vocabulary exercise individually or in pairs.
4. Call on volunteers to read their answers aloud.

D. Comprehension (5 minutes)

These post-reading questions help students focus on the meaning of the opening text. In some cases, they may also focus on the target grammar without explicitly presenting the grammar point.

Suggested Procedure
1. Have students answer the questions individually.
2. Have students compare answers in pairs.
3. Call on volunteers to read their answers aloud.

Step 2: Grammar Presentation

There are many ways to teach the material in the Grammar Presentation. As a general rule, the more varied and lively the classroom activities, the more engaged students will be— and the more learning will occur. Approaching grammar from different angles and trying out different classroom management options can help increase student motivation. The Strategies for Teaching Grammar on page 10 provide some guidelines to keep in mind when presenting a new grammar point. In addition to these strategies and the procedures outlined below, you can find specific suggestions for presenting the unit's grammar in the Unit Teaching Notes.

Grammar Charts (5–10 minutes)

The Grammar Charts provide a clear reference of all the forms of the target grammar. Students also become familiar with grammatical terminology. The charts also enable you to pre-teach some of the Grammar Notes that follow. You may want to use the charts in the PowerPoint® presentations on the Teacher's Resource Disc to help direct all of your students' attention to the same focus point. Select presentations also include colorful graphics, animations, and interactive practice activities that reinforce the grammar point.

Suggested Procedure
1. Using the examples from the charts and/ or the PowerPoint® presentations, draw students' attention to important features by pointing them out or asking questions.
2. Confirm students' understanding by engaging them in some recognition activities. Try one or two activities from Strategies 3, 4, 5, or 6 (page 10).
3. Get students to manipulate the new structures through substitution or transformation drills. See Strategy 7 (page 10) for an example of a transformation drill.
4. Encourage students to make sentences that are personally meaningful using the new grammar.

Option A
- Have students study the Grammar Charts at home.
- In class, follow step 1 in the suggested procedure above.
- Move directly to the Grammar Notes section. Carry out steps 2, 3, and 4 in the suggested procedure above using the notes together with the charts.

Option B
- Assign individual students responsibility for presenting a topic to the class by combining the information in the charts and the relevant notes. You may want to give them large pieces of paper and markers to prepare posters.
- Meet with students individually. Allow them to practice their presentations, and provide any coaching needed.
- Call on students to present their topics to the class. Encourage questions from the class.
- Choose appropriate practice activities from Strategies 4–8 (page 10) or move directly to the Grammar Notes section.

Grammar Notes (20–30 minutes)

These notes provide helpful information about meaning, use, and form of the grammatical structures that students have encountered in the opening text and Grammar Charts. They include the following features to help students understand and use the forms.
- Where appropriate, timelines illustrate the meaning of verb forms and their relationship to one another.
- *Be Careful!* notes alert students to common errors among English-language learners.
- *Usage Notes* provide guidelines for using and understanding different levels of formality and correctness.
- References to related structures are provided below the notes.

Suggested Procedure

1. Have students read each note at home and/or in class.
2. For each note, write examples on the board and elicit or point out the key features of the form (see Strategy 1, page 10).
3. If possible, demonstrate the meaning of the grammatical form(s) by performing actions (see Strategy 6, page 10).
4. Model the examples and have students repeat after you so that they become comfortable with the appropriate stress, intonation, and rhythm.
5. Engage students with the grammar point by choosing appropriate activities, for example:
   - Elicit examples of the target structure.
   - Confirm students' understanding by having them categorize examples or perform actions that illustrate the structure (see Strategies 5 and 6, page 10).
   - Provide controlled practice with quick substitution or transformation drills (see Strategy 7, page 10).
   - Encourage students to make personally meaningful sentences using the new grammatical forms.
   - Use the Focused Practice exercises in the Student Book.
6. You may want to repeat steps 2–5 for each Grammar Note.

Option

- Photocopy one set of Grammar Notes for each group of three or four students in your class. Cut them up so that the notes and their corresponding examples are not attached.
- Divide the class into groups of three or four students and give a set of cut-up notes to each group.
- Give students their task:
  1. Match the examples with the correct notes.
  2. Attach the notes and corresponding examples to a sheet of newsprint (a large piece of paper).
  3. Have students create more examples for each note.
- Circulate to ensure that students are on the right track, and provide help as needed.
- Have students post their results around the room, and invite groups to look at each other's work.
- Regroup as a class to answer questions.

Identify the Grammar (5–10 minutes)

This optional activity helps students identify the target grammatical structures embedded in the context of the opening text. This helps students learn the form, meaning, and usage of the target grammar point and helps you make a smooth transition from the Grammar Presentation to Discover the Grammar in Focused Practice.

Suggested Procedure

1. Choose an example of the target grammar from the opening text and write it on the board.
2. Point out that the target grammar is presented in boldfaced type in the opening text. Elicit more examples from students and write them on the board.
3. Ask students to identify the form, meaning, or usage of the grammar in the examples. Have them refer to the Grammar Charts and Grammar Notes if needed.

Step 3: Focused Practice

The exercises in this section provide practice for the structures in the Grammar Presentation. You may want to have students complete the corresponding exercise immediately after you have presented the relevant Grammar Note. Another option is for students to complete one or more of the exercises at home, using the cross-references to the Grammar Note(s) for support.

If you decide to have students complete the exercises in class, you can keep them motivated by varying the order of the exercises and/or the way you conduct them. Following are various ways of conducting the exercises.

After students complete the Student Book practice, you may want them to go to **www.myfocusongrammarlab.com** for automatically graded grammar exercises or to the workbook for traditional grammar exercises. You may want to assign these to be completed in class or as homework.

Discover the Grammar (5–10 minutes)

This opening activity gets students to identify the target grammar structures in a realistic context. It also sometimes checks their understanding of meaning. This recognition activity raises awareness of the structures as it builds confidence.

Suggested Procedure

1. Go over the example with the class.

2. Have students complete the exercise individually or in pairs.
3. Elicit the correct answers from the class.

Controlled Practice Exercises (5–10 minutes each)

Following the Discover the Grammar activity are exercises that provide practice in a controlled, but still contextualized, manner. The exercises proceed from simpler to more complex and include a variety of exercise types such as fill in the blanks, matching, and multiple-choice. Exercises are cross-referenced to the appropriate Grammar Notes so that students can review as necessary. Students are exposed to many different written formats, including letters, emails, websites, charts, and graphs. Many exercises are art-based, providing a rich context for meaningful practice.

Options

• Have students complete the exercises in pairs.
• If the exercise is in the form of a conversation, have students practice the completed exercise in pairs and role play it for the class.
• When going over answers with students, have them explain why each answer is correct. For example, have them point to the appropriate rule in the Grammar Charts or Grammar Notes.
• Whenever possible, relate exercises to students' lives. For example, if an exercise includes a timeline, elicit from students some important events that have happened in their own lives.

Editing (10 minutes)

All units include an editing exercise to build students' awareness of incorrect usage of the target grammar structures. Students identify and correct errors in a contextualized passage such as a student's composition, a journal entry, or an email. The direction line indicates the number of errors in the passage.

Suggested Procedure

1. Have students read the passage quickly to understand its context and meaning.
2. Tell students to read the passage line by line, circling incorrect structures and writing in the corrections.
3. Have students take turns reading the passage line by line, saying the structures correctly.

Alternatively, read the passage aloud to the class and have students interrupt you with their corrections.

4. There are usually examples of the correct usage of the structures in each editing exercise. After students have identified the errors, point out the correct usages and ask why they are not errors.

Step 4: Communication Practice

These in-class exercises give students the opportunity to use the target structure in communicative activities. These activities help develop listening and speaking fluency and critical thinking skills, as well as provide opportunities for students to "own" the structures. As with the Focused Practice exercises, you may wish to vary the order of these activities to keep student motivation high.

Since there are many different exercise types in the Communication Practice section, specific ideas and guidelines are provided in the Unit Teaching Notes. Following are general suggestions for the main types of exercises. (Note: See the FAQs on pages 11–13 for more information about setting up pair work and group work.)

Following the relevant Student Book practice, you may want your students to go to **www.myfocusongrammarlab.com** for automatically graded Listening, Pronunciation, Speaking, or Writing exercises and activities. The Pronunciation exercises provide additional practice with the pronunciation feature from the Student Book; the Listening, Speaking, and Writing exercises and activities are on related topics.

Listening (10 minutes)

The first or second exercise in each Communication Practice section deals with listening comprehension. Students hear a variety of listening formats, including conversations, phone calls, voicemail messages, news reports, and interviews. After listening, students complete a task that focuses on the form or meaning of the target grammar structure. The recordings for the listening exercises are on the audio program and at **www.myfocusongrammarlab.com**, so students can complete the exercises outside of class.

Suggested Procedure
Before Listening
1. Explain the situation or context of the listening passage. Provide any necessary cultural information, and pre-teach any vocabulary students may need to know. Since some of these words and phrases may appear in the listening, not in the exercise itself, refer to the audioscript at the back of this manual as necessary.
2. Ask students to read the exercise questions first so that they know what to listen for.

First Listening Task
1. Play the audio. Have students listen with their pencils down.
2. Play the audio again. Have students listen again and complete the task.
3. You may want to let students listen as many times as necessary to complete the task.

Second Listening Task
1. See steps 1–3 from the first listening task for general instructions.
2. Have students compare their answers in pairs or small groups.

After Listening
1. Elicit answers for the exercise items and write them on the board. Answer any questions the students may have.
2. ⏱ Students listen a final time and review the passage.

Option A
• Rather than play the audio, read the audioscript aloud.
• Speak with a lot of expression and at a natural pace. Change positions and tone of voice to indicate who the speaker is.
• Draw stick figures on the board and label them with the characters' names. Then point to the appropriate character as you change roles.

Option B
• Make photocopies of the audioscript and hand it out to students.
• Play the audio recording and have students read along with it in chorus. Explain that this exercise will help them to hear and practice the rhythms, stresses, and clusters of English sounds.

Option C
Have students listen and complete the exercise at home or in a language lab.

Pronunciation (10 minutes)
The first or second exercise in each Communication Practice section deals with pronunciation. The pronunciation exercise generally focuses on the grammar presented in the unit or a difficult sound that appears in the opening text. It also prepares students for the speaking activities that follow. The recordings for the pronunciation exercises are on the audio program and at **www.myfocusongrammarlab.com**, so students can practice the exercises outside of class.

Suggested Procedure
First Task
1. Go over the instructions and point out the Pronunciation Note.
2. Play the audio.

Second Task
1. Play the audio. Have students close their eyes and notice the pronunciation feature.
2. ⏱ Play the audio again. Have students listen again and follow along in their books.

Third Task
1. Play the audio again.
2. Have students repeat in pairs or small groups. Circulate and monitor their pronunciation.
3. ⏱ Call on students to practice in front of the class.

Games (10–20 minutes)
Games are designed to encourage communication among students. In these activities, students compete in pairs or small groups to complete a task such as guessing something or winning points.

Advantages of Games
• They can create a fun and stress-free environment.
• They involve friendly competition and keep students engaged.
• They can improve students' ability to speak in a communicative way.

Suggested Procedure
1. Go over the instructions to make sure students understand the task.
2. Have students model the example or provide one of your own.
3. Have students carry out the instructions. Circulate and help as needed.
4. ⏱ Go over answers as a class or ask who won.

5. ⏱ Note any incorrect uses of grammar. After students complete the task, write the sentences on the board and have students correct them.

Surveys / Interviews (10–20 minutes)
In these classroom speaking activities, students ask and answer interesting and meaningful questions about their personal preferences, opinions, feelings, and experiences.

Advantages of Surveys / Interviews
- They are fun and motivating for most students.
- By broadening the world of the classroom to the students' real lives, surveys and interviews allow students to use a wider range of language than less open-ended activities.
- Interviews can help students build confidence in their ability to ask and answer extemporaneous questions.
- Interviews provide students with an opportunity to learn about each other.

Suggested Procedure
1. Review the task so students understand what is required.
2. Model the survey or interview with a student in front of the class.
3. Divide the class into the suggested groupings and give them a fixed time limit for completing the task. If you have a mixed-level class, you may want to vary the groupings based on the specific activity. Sometimes you may want groups to have both higher- and lower-level students. Other times you may want groups to be homogeneous.
4. While students are working, circulate among the pairs or groups to answer students' questions and help them with the activity.
5. Have students share what they have learned about each other with the class.

Discussions (10–20 minutes)
In these classroom speaking activities, students express their ideas about a variety of topics. These activities include Picture Discussions and other types of discussions.

Advantages of Discussions
- They help students move from speaking accuracy to speaking fluency.
- They help students develop critical thinking skills as they explore the pros and cons of an issue.
- They help students build confidence in their ability to express their opinions on a variety of topics.

Suggested Procedure
1. Go over the instructions so students understand the task.
2. Elicit or present useful language and write it on the board.
3. Have two or three students model the example discussion.
4. Divide the class into the suggested groupings and give them a fixed time limit for completing the task.
5. Circulate while the students discuss the topic. Help with language or monitor their grammar as needed.
6. Ask volunteers from each group to summarize the discussion or conclusions.
7. ⏱ Write any sentences with incorrect grammar you noticed on the board. Have the students correct them as a class.

Writing (15–25 minutes)
These activities give students the opportunity to develop their writing skills and provide additional practice using the target grammatical structures. There are a variety of realistic formats, including paragraphs, essays, letters, and journal entries. The themes are related to material covered in the unit so that students already have some preparation for the writing task.

Suggested Procedure
Prewriting (in class)
1. Go over the instructions with the class.
2. Brainstorm ideas for the assignment with the class and write them on the board.
3. Encourage students to include grammar and vocabulary from the unit in their assignment.

Writing and Editing (at home)
1. Have students compose a draft of the writing assignment at home.
2. Have students use the Editing Checklist to correct their work.

Wrap-Up (in class)

1. Have students submit the draft to you or share it with a partner in class.
2. Give students a score on the draft. You can comment on the following features:
   - Content: Has the student responded appropriately to the task? Are the main points well supported?
   - Organization: Is the flow of ideas logical and effective?
   - Accuracy: Are there any major errors in the grammar points taught in the unit?
3. ⏱ Depending on your class's needs, you may want to have students complete a second draft at home. When you check these drafts, point out any further areas needing correction, concentrating especially on errors in the target grammar point or grammar points from a previous unit.

Option A

Have students share their final drafts in class. For example:
- Post students' work on the class bulletin board.
- Publish their work on a website or in a class magazine.
- Have students exchange papers with a partner.
- Have students read their papers aloud in small groups or to the class.

Option B

Have students put the final drafts of their written work in a folder, or portfolio, which you can review at the end of the course. This will allow your students and you to see the progress they have made.

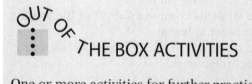

OUT OF THE BOX ACTIVITIES

One or more activities for further practice (in the Teacher's Manual only) can be found at the end of every unit in the Unit Teaching Notes. These activities offer additional communicative practice with the target structure of the unit. Most can be done in class with no before-class preparation. The activities often involve a combination of skills, such as grammar and speaking or grammar and writing.

Unit Review

The last section of each unit of the Student Book is a review feature that can be used as a self-test. These exercises test the form and use of the grammar content presented and practiced in that unit. They give students a chance to check their knowledge and to review any problematic areas before moving on to the next part. An answer key is provided at the back of the Student Book.

Suggested Procedure

1. Have students complete the exercises at home and check their answers in the Answer Key.
2. During the next class, go over any remaining questions students may have.

Option

- Have students complete the exercises in class. Give them a time limit of 10 minutes and circulate as they work.
- Have students use the Answer Key to check and correct their answers in pairs. Or you can go over the answers as a class.

⏱ Unit Achievement Tests

After the Unit Review, you may want to have students complete an achievement test. There are two assessment options.

1. You can use the **Unit Achievement Tests** to help you assess students' knowledge of the specific grammatical topics presented in the unit. If students have mastered the material presented in the unit, they should answer most of the questions correctly. Each test takes about 30 minutes and includes about 30 items. The test begins with a listening exercise, includes two or three contextualized grammar exercises, and ends with an editing exercise. The tests are offered in two formats:
   - automatically graded tests at **www.myfocusongrammarlab.com**
   - reproducible tests on the Teacher's Resource Disc in this manual.
2. You can use the **Test-Generating Software** on the Teacher's Resource Disc to create customized Unit Achievement Tests of any length. The test items focus on grammar.

⏱ Part Post-Tests

At the end of each part, you may want to have students complete an achievement test. There are three assessment options.

1. You can have students go to **www.myfocusongrammarlab.com** for an automatically graded review. Students can complete the review on a computer in class, at home, or in a language lab. Each review takes about 25 minutes and includes about 30 items. The test focuses on grammar.

2. You can have students take the **Part Post-Tests** to help you determine how well students have mastered the material they have studied in that part of the Student Book. If students have mastered the material presented in the part, they should answer most of the questions correctly. Each test takes 50 minutes and includes about 60 items. The test begins with a listening exercise, includes several contextualized grammar exercises, and ends with an editing exercise. The tests are offered in two formats:
   - automatically graded tests at **www.myfocusongrammarlab.com**
   - reproducible tests on the Teacher's Resource Disc in this manual.

3. You can also use the **Test-Generating Software** on the Teacher's Resource Disc to create customized Part Achievement Tests of any length. The test items focus on grammar.

From Grammar to Writing

The From Grammar to Writing section at the end of the Student Book integrates grammar presented in the units. It also goes beyond the grammar in the unit and gives additional information about writing in English. This information may include mechanics (e.g., punctuation, capitalization), cohesion (e.g., compound sentences, time clauses), format (e.g., business letters, reports), and rhetoric (e.g., expressing an opinion).

Each section gives students a specific writing task and begins with prewriting strategies. These strategies may include the use of graphic organizers, such as charts, outlines, and Venn diagrams. Students are also given example texts that serve as models for the writing task. Text types include both formal and informal writing, such as personal letters, business letters, essays, summaries, emails, and descriptive paragraphs. The section concludes with peer review and editing.

Depending on your class's needs, you may want to have students go to an additional From Grammar to Writing exercise at **www.myfocusongrammarlab.com**.

Suggested Procedure

Prewriting

1. Explain the prewriting task. Where appropriate, provide a model for students on the board or on an overhead.

2. Have students complete the prewriting task in pairs or small groups. Circulate and answer any questions.

Composing and Correcting

1. Go over the instructions to make sure students understand the task.

2. Have students complete the writing assignment at home.

3. In class, complete the peer review portion of the task. Circulate while students are working together to make sure they are on task and to provide appropriate feedback. (See Suggested Procedure for Writing on pages 7–8 for examples.)

4. ⏱ Have students revise their writing and turn in the second draft to you.

Strategies for Teaching Grammar

1. Develop awareness

- Ask questions that help students become aware of the form of the structure. For example, for the imperative (Student Book page 78), read an affirmative command in the opening conversation, such as "Drive to the corner," and ask the class to name the verb. (*Drive*) Ask students what form it is. (*the base form*) Ask students what "base" form means. (*the simple form without an ending*) Ask students: "Do you see a subject?" (*no*) Explain that in the imperative we understand that the subject is "you." Ask: "How do we form the negative in the imperative?" (*Add* Don't *before the base form*.)
- Compare information in the Grammar Charts. For example, for the simple past (Student Book pages 60, 70, 210, 221, 230) there are Grammar Charts for the past of *be* and for other verbs. Ask: "How many forms are there for the simple past of be?" (*two*: was *and* were) "How do you form the negative with *be* in the simple past?" (wasn't, weren't) "How many forms are there for the negative with other verbs?" (*one*: didn't + *base form*) Ask: "Do you use the base form for past *yes / no* questions with be?" (*no*) "Do you use the base form for past *yes / no* questions with other verbs?" (*yes*)

2. Present meaning
Show the meaning of a grammatical form through a classroom demonstration. For example, to illustrate the use of present progressive, you could show a picture of a person pushing a grocery cart. (*He / She is shopping.*)

3. Identify examples
Ask students to go back to the Grammar in Context section and label examples in the reading passage with the grammatical terms in the Grammar Charts.

4. Generate examples
Find examples from the reading or elsewhere that could fit into the Grammar Charts. An interesting way to do this is to photocopy and enlarge the Grammar Chart. White out the targeted structures and replace them with blank lines for each missing word. Make copies and distribute them to students in pairs or small groups. Have students fill in the blanks, using examples from the reading. Then generate more examples. Books can be open or closed, depending on the level of challenge desired.

5. Show understanding by categorizing
Check comprehension of a grammatical principle by asking students to label multiple examples appropriately. For example, students can label verbs "present" or "future" or they can label examples "correct" or "incorrect."

6. Show understanding by performing actions
Ask students to show their understanding of the meaning of a grammatical form by following instructions or devising a demonstration. Ask students, for example, to think of and perform a set of actions that they could describe using the present progressive.

7. Manipulate forms
Have students manipulate the examples in the Grammar Charts to practice the form. Drills such as substitution or transformation help students to build fluency. For example, in Units 31 and 32 (Student Book pages 300 and 309) you might put one form on the board (*He is going to leave soon.*) and then elicit other forms by saying, "Negative" (*He isn't going to leave soon.*), "Yes/no question" (*Is he going to leave soon?*), "Short answer, affirmative" (*Yes, he is.*), "*Wh-* question, *when*" (*When is he going to leave?*), and so on to get students to produce the other forms rapidly.

8. Personalize
Ask students to provide personal examples. For example, on page 89 of the Student Book, students see the example, "I come from Brazil." Ask students where they're from. (*I come from Chile.*)

9. Repeat, reinforce
Students need to be exposed to new grammar many times in order to internalize it completely. You can first present a new structure on the board, then point it out in the book, then have students use it in an informal oral exercise, then do a written exercise in pairs, and finally review the same structure in homework. Varying the content and focus of these activities will keep students interested, and the grammar will be reinforced almost automatically.

FREQUENTLY ASKED QUESTIONS (FAQs)

1. When should I have students work in pairs or groups rather than individually or as a whole class?

Varying your classroom organization to suit particular activity types will result in more effective and more interesting classes. Many students are not accustomed to working in pairs or groups, so it is important to use these groupings only when they are most beneficial.

- **Whole-class teaching** maximizes teacher control and is especially good for:
  — presenting information, giving explanations and instructions
  — showing material in texts and pictures or on audio or video recordings
  — teacher-led drills (such as substitution or transformation) or dictations
  — reviewing answers or sharing ideas after students have completed an activity
  — enabling the whole class to benefit from teacher feedback to individuals
- **Students working individually** allows quiet, concentrated attention and is most effective for:
  — processing information or completing a task at students' own pace
  — performing writing tasks

For objective exercises such as fill-in-the-blank, matching, multiple-choice, and editing, vary your class organization to keep student motivation high. Students can sometimes complete these exercises individually, and sometimes they can work with a partner.

- **Students working in pairs** maximizes student speaking time, breaks up the routine and "teacher talk," and is ideal for:
  — information-gap activities
  — role plays and interviews
  — writing and/or reading dialogues
  — predicting the content of reading and listening texts
  — comparing notes on what students listen to or see
  — checking answers
  — peer assessment

Pair work can also be very effective for completing objective exercises such as fill-in-the-blank, matching, multiple-choice, and editing.

- **Students working in groups** creates ideal conditions for students to learn from each other and works well for:
  — generating ideas
  — pooling knowledge
  — writing group stories
  — preparing presentations
  — discussing an issue and reaching a group decision

2. How should I set up pair work and group work?

Here are a few different techniques:

- **Streaming.** Grouping students according to ability or participation has certain advantages.
  — **ability:** Grouping weaker and stronger students together allows more able students to help their less fluent classmates.
  — **participation:** If you see that some students participate less than others, you could make a pair or group of weak participators. By the same token, you can also put especially talkative students together.
- **Chance.** Grouping students by chance has many benefits, especially if it results in students working with varied partners. You can group students by chance according to:
  — **where they sit:** Students sitting next to or near one another work in pairs or groups. This is the easiest option, but if students always sit in the same place, you will want to find other ways of grouping them.
  — **the "wheels" system:** Half the class stands in a circle facing outward, and the other half stands in an outer circle facing inward. The outer circle revolves in a clockwise direction, and the inner circle revolves in a counterclockwise direction. When you tell them to stop, students work with the person facing them. This is a very effective way to have students engage in meaningful repetition, such as asking the same question of many different partners.
  — **assigned letters:** Assign each student a letter from A to E. Then ask all the As to form a group, all the Bs to form a group, and so on.

— **birthdays:** Students stand in a line in the order of their birthdays (with January at one end and December at the other). The first five students form one group, the second five students another group, and so on.

— **native language:** If possible, put students in groups or pairs with others who don't share a native language. This helps create an "English-only" classroom.

3. How can I make activities more successful?

Before the activity:

• **Motivate students and explain the purpose.** Make it clear that something enjoyable or interesting is going to happen. Explain the rationale for the activity. Make sure that students understand the purpose of the activity is to practice what they learned and encourage them to participate.

• **Provide clear directions.** Explain what students should do in every step of the activity. Have students paraphrase or demonstrate the task to be sure they understand it.

• **Demonstrate.** Show the class what is supposed to happen in an activity. This might involve asking a student to demonstrate the activity with you or having two students role-play in the front of the room.

• **Provide a time frame.** It is helpful for students to know how much time they have and exactly when they should stop. Approximate times are given for all the activities in this Teacher's Manual.

For open-ended activities, such as writing exercises, you will also want to:

• **Stimulate thinking.** When there are choices for students to make, it is often helpful to set up small-group and/or whole-class brainstorming sessions to define the focus and/or content of their task.

• **Prepare language.** Review grammar and vocabulary that students may need to complete the task. This can be done as a follow-up to a brainstorming activity where you elicit ideas and write key language on the board.

During the activity:

• **Observe students.** Walk around the room watching and listening to pairs or groups.

• **Provide assistance as needed.** See FAQ 5 for suggestions on giving feedback and correcting errors.

After the activity:

• **Elicit student responses.** For some activities, you may ask for volunteers or call on students to share some of their ideas with the class. For other types of activities, a few pairs or groups can be asked to role-play their discussions to demonstrate the language they have been using.

• **Provide feedback.** In many cases, this is most conveniently done in a whole-class setting. It may be preferable, however, for you to meet with individuals, pairs, or groups. While the principal focus in a grammar class is language use, it is also important to acknowledge the value of students' ideas. See FAQ 5 for suggestions on feedback and error correction.

4. What can I do to encourage students to use more English in the classroom?

It is perfectly natural for students to feel the need to use their first language in an English class. There are a number of actions that teachers can take to promote the use of English.

• **Set clear guidelines.** Some teachers in monolingual classes find that activities such as providing vocabulary definitions, presenting a grammar point, checking comprehension, giving instructions, and discussing classroom methodology are best done in the students' native language.

• **Use persuasion.** Walk among the students during speaking activities and say things like "Please speak English!" or "Try to use English as much as possible." This helps to ensure that students will speak English most of the time.

5. What's the best approach to giving feedback and correcting errors?

Here are two considerations:

• **Be selective in offering correction.** Students can't focus on everything at once, so concentrate first on errors relating to the target grammar point and grammar points from units previously studied, as well as any errors that interfere with communication. Whether you respond to other errors depends on your judgment of students' readiness to take in the information. If you see a teachable moment, seize it! Rather than correct every error individual students make in the course of activities, it is generally preferable to note commonly occurring mistakes and give a short presentation for the whole class at the end of the activity.

- **Recasting.** If a student makes an error—for example, "I *didn't came* to class yesterday because I was sick"—you can recast it as, "You *didn't come* to class yesterday because you were sick?" The student ideally notices the difference and restates the original sentence: "Right. I didn't come to class yesterday because I was sick." This process can be effective because the student has the opportunity to self-correct an error that is still in short-term memory. As a variation, you can restate but stop, with rising intonation, right before the potential error: "You didn't . . . ?"

6. What can I do to accommodate different learning styles?

Focus on Grammar recognizes different styles of learning and provides a variety of activities to accommodate these different styles. Some learners prefer an analytical, or rule-learning (deductive), approach. Others, especially younger learners, respond best to an inductive approach, or exposure to the language in meaningful contexts. Indeed, the same students may adopt different styles as they learn, or they may use different styles at different times.

As teachers, we want to help the students in our classes who prefer to follow rules become more able to take risks and to plunge into communicative activities. We also want to encourage the risk-takers to focus on accuracy. *Focus on Grammar* provides the variety to ensure that students achieve their goal: to learn to use the language confidently and appropriately.

UNIT TEACHING NOTES

PART I OVERVIEW

This is / These are; SUBJECT PRONOUNS; NOUNS

UNIT	GRAMMAR FOCUS	THEME
1	*This is / These are*; Subject Pronouns	An Apartment
2	Singular and Plural Nouns.; Proper Nouns; *A* and *An*	Things in the Kitchen

Go to **www.myfocusongrammarlab.com** for the Part and Unit Tests.

Note: PowerPoint® grammar presentations, test-generating software, and reproducible Part and Unit Tests are on the *Teacher's Resource Disc*.

UNIT 1 OVERVIEW

Grammar: *This is / These are*; SUBJECT PRONOUNS

Unit 1 focuses on the meanings and uses of *This is / These are* in statements and questions. It also introduces subject pronouns and their meanings and use in statements.

• *This is / These are* are used to introduce and talk about people and things near the speaker; both are used in statements and questions.

• Subject pronouns replace a subject noun.

Theme: AN APARTMENT

Unit 1 focuses on language that is used for basic introductions of people and things and descriptions of an apartment.

Step 1: Grammar in Context (pages 2–4)

See the general suggestions for Grammar in Context on page 1.

Before You Read

• Have students discuss the pictures in pairs. Then call on pairs to discuss their answers.

• You may want to point out that *pets* specifically refers to animals that live in a home with people. *Animals* is a more general term. It could be used in a more general way or in the context of a farm. *We have two pets, a dog and a cat. My uncle has a lot of different animals on his farm—cows, horses, chickens, and pigs.*

Read

• To encourage students to read with a purpose, write on the board:
  1. Where is Steve's apartment? *(Seattle)*
  2. Is it big or small? *(small)*
  3. Who is Pam? *(a bird)*
  4. Who is Kip? *(a cat)*
  5. Who is on the left in the family picture? *(Steve's parents)*
  6. Who is in the middle? *(Steve's sister and her husband and children)*

• Have students read the text. (OR: Play the audio and have students follow along in their books.)

• Have students discuss the questions in pairs or small groups.

• Call on pairs or groups to share answers with the class.

After You Read

A. Practice

• Have students practice the opening reading in pairs. Then call on two or three students to read it for the class.

B. Vocabulary

• Play the audio and have students repeat each word or phrase. Encourage them to use the pictures to figure out the meaning.

• Have students write new words and their meanings in their notebooks.

C. Vocabulary

• Go over the example with the class. Explain that the answer *(son and daughter)* means *children*.

• Have students complete the exercise individually. Then have them compare their answers in pairs.

• Call on pairs to read their answers aloud.

D. Comprehension

- Go over the example with the class. Have students look at the opening reading on page 2. Have them point to the picture with the example answer. (The first picture—*It's small but comfortable.*)
- Have students complete the exercise individually. Then have them compare answers in pairs.
- Call on pairs to share their answers with the class.
- Have students continue to correct the false statements in pairs. Call on pairs to read the false statements and their corrected statements.

Go to **www.myfocusongrammarlab.com** for an additional reading, and for reading and vocabulary practice.

Step 2: Grammar Presentation (pages 4–5)

See the general suggestions for Grammar Presentation on page 3.

Grammar Charts

- To explain *This is / These are* and subject pronouns, write on the board:
  <u>This is</u> my apartment in Seattle. <u>It's</u> small but comfortable.
  <u>These are</u> my pets. <u>They're</u> wonderful.
- Underline the target structures.
- Point to the example of *This is*. Ask: "How many apartments is Steve talking about?" *(one)*
- Point to the example of *These are*. Ask: "How many pets is Steve talking about?" *(two—a cat and a bird)*
- Point out that *This + is* is used to introduce or talk about singular nouns. *These + are* is used to introduce or talk about plural nouns.
- Point to the sentence with *It's*. Ask: "What does the pronoun *it* refer to?" *(apartment)* "What does the pronoun *they* refer to?" *(pets)*
- Point out that pronouns take the place of nouns. They must match the nouns they are replacing in number (i.e., singular or plural). Also point out that the pronouns in these examples are the subjects of the sentences.
- Point out that *it's* and *they're* are both contractions: a shortened form of two joined words. Ask students the meanings of these two contractions. *(it's = it is; they're = they are)*
- To explain questions with *This is / These are*, write on the board:
  <u>Is this</u> your apartment?
  <u>Are these</u> your pets?

- Underline the target structures.
- Explain that the verb goes first to form questions with *this is* and *these are*.

Grammar Notes

Note 1

- Have a student come to the front of the room. Introduce the person to the class. Say: "This is my student _____ ."

Note 2

- Now have another student join the first one. Introduce them to the class. Say: "These are my students _____ and _____ ."
- Have students practice using *this* and *these* in pairs with objects they have with them (e.g., notebooks, books, pencils, and pens). Circulate, making corrections as necessary.

Note 3

- To review the structure for questions, hold up a book and ask: "Is this my book?" *(Yes, it is.)* Then hold up another book and ask: "Are these my books?" *(Yes, they are.)* Repeat the process and have students repeat the questions and answers after you say them.
- Hold up a student's book and ask: "Is this my book?" *(No, it isn't.)* Then hold up two students' books and ask: "Are these my books? *(No, they're not.)*
- Have students practice in pairs with various objects.

Note 4

- To review subject pronouns, talk about yourself and students in the class to demonstrate first-person, second-person, and third-person singular and plural pronouns. *(I'm a teacher. You're my students. He's Pedro.)*
- Have students practice in groups of three and say similar sentences with subject pronouns.

⏱ **Identify the Grammar**: Have students identify the grammar in the opening reading on page 2. For example:
  <u>I'm</u> Steve Beck.
  This is my apartment . . .
  <u>It's</u> small . . .

Go to **www.myfocusongrammarlab.com** for grammar charts and notes.

Step 3: Focused Practice (pages 5–6)

See the general suggestions for Focused Practice on page 4.

Exercise 1: Discover the Grammar

- Have students complete the exercise individually. Then have them compare their answers in small groups. Go over the correct answers as a class.
- Call on students to explain what two words each contraction represents.

Exercise 2: *This* and *These*

- Have students complete the exercise individually and compare answers in small groups.
- Call on students to read their answers aloud.

Exercise 3: Subject Pronouns

- Have students complete the exercise individually. Then have them compare answers in pairs.
- Have each pair work together to rewrite the contractions in the exercise in their long forms.

Exercise 4: Editing

- Go over the example with the class. Ask: "How many friends?" *(one—Pedro)* "Do we say *these* to introduce only one person?" *(no)* Make sure students understand that *This* is the correct word for this sentence.
- Have students complete the exercise individually. Go over the correct answers as a class. Then have them practice the corrected conversations in pairs.

Go to **www.myfocusongrammarlab.com** for additional grammar practice.

Step 4: Communication Practice (pages 7–8)

See the general suggestions for Communication Practice on page 5.

Exercise 5: Listening

- Pre-teach *on the left*, *in the middle*, and *on the right*. Say: "Look at the person on the left. Do you think he's a student or a teacher?" Ask similar questions about the other people in the picture.
- Have students listen and complete Parts A and B. Correct their answers. Then play the audio again as a dictation, pausing as necessary. Have students work in small groups to compare their answers. Call on groups to write the sentences on the board and correct as necessary.

Exercise 6: Pronunciation

A
- Play the audio and go over the example with the class.
- Play the rest of the audio and have students complete the exercise. Then go over the answers as a class.

- Play the audio again and have students repeat each sentence, pausing as needed.

B
- Show students how to do the activity. Read one of the choices in the first item aloud. Ask: "Is this sentence a or sentence b?"
- Have students complete this activity in pairs. Then have them rewrite the statements as questions and the questions as statements.
- Have students change partners and repeat the exercise, using the new sentences they wrote.

Exercise 7: Introduce Yourself

A
- Divide the class in half. Have one group read A's lines aloud and the other read B's. Then have groups change roles.
- Have students continue to practice the conversation in pairs.

B
- As a variation, have students work in pairs and introduce each other to another pair.

Exercise 8: Talk about Photos

- Model the activity for the class with a student, then have them complete the exercise. (Note: Photos from popular magazines such as *People* will also work well for this activity.)

Exercise 9: Writing

- Have students complete the exercise and correct their writing using the Editing Checklist. Then have them exchange papers and check each other's work and rewrite their own sentences.

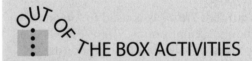

THE BOX ACTIVITIES

Speaking

- Walk around the room and have each student drop a personal object into a bag. Make sure that there are some plural objects, such as glasses or keys. Make sure the class does not see what each student puts in.
- Call on students to come up, take an item from the bag, and try to locate its owner. Model this dialogue:

  S1: Marta, is this your lipstick?
  Marta: Yes, it is. [S1 returns the lipstick to Marta.]
  S2: Yuko, are these your keys?
  Yuko: No, they aren't.
  S3: Thong, are these your keys?
  Thong: Yes, they are. [S3 returns keys.]

Speaking

- Have students draw a diagram of their house, apartment, or room. Encourage them to add details such as plants, furniture, and posters or paintings on the walls.
- Have students share their diagrams in pairs or small groups. Have them talk about them using statements and questions with *This is* and *These are*. For example:
  S1: This is my apartment. It's very small.
  S2: Is this your bedroom?
  S1: No, it's not. It's the kitchen.

Reading, Speaking, and Writing

- Make a copy of a map of a continent that is unfamiliar to the students. Erase or cross out the name of the countries.
- At the top or on the back, add a word box containing the names of all the countries you erased. Then make enough copies of this handout for every two or three students.
- Have students work in pairs or small groups. Have them work together to write in the name of each country on the map. Model a sample exchange with a student.
  S1: This is Mali.
  S2: OK. Is this Sierra Leone?
  S3: No, it's not. It's Ghana.
- **Note:** If you are in the United States, this activity would also work well with a map of the section of the United States you are in, such as New England or the Northeast, the Midwest, the West Coast, and so on.

Go to **www.myfocusongrammarlab.com** for additional listening, pronunciation, speaking, and writing practice.

Note:
- See the *Focus on Grammar Workbook* for additional in-class or homework grammar practice.

Unit 1 Review (page 9)

Have students complete the Review and check their answers on Student Book page UR-0. Review or assign additional material as needed.

Go to **www.myfocusongrammarlab.com** for the Unit Achievement Test.

Grammar: SINGULAR AND PLURAL NOUNS; PROPER NOUNS; *A* AND *An*

Unit 2 focuses on the meanings and uses of singular and plural nouns, proper nouns, and *a* and *an*.

- *Common* nouns are words that name people, places, things, or ideas.
- Singular nouns refer to only one.
- Plural nouns refer to more than one.
- *Proper* nouns are the names of people and places on a map. They always start with a capital letter.
- *A* and *an* are words that come before singular nouns. They are not used with plural nouns.

Theme: THINGS IN THE KITCHEN

Unit 2 focuses on language that is used to name things in a kitchen.

Step 1: Grammar in Context (pages 10–12)

See the general suggestions for Grammar in Context on page 1.

Before You Read

- Have students compare their lists in groups. Then have them combine their lists into a single list on the board.
- Keep the list on the board for reference as the class works through this unit.

Read

- To encourage students to read with a purpose, write these questions on the board:
  1. What is Elena asking Judy about? Why? *(She's asking about things in the kitchen because she wants to learn English.)*
  2. What does Judy want Elena to do at the end of the conversation? *(teach her Portuguese)*
- Have students look at the pictures on pages 10–11 in small groups to predict answers to the questions.
- Have students read the conversation. Then have the class discuss answers to the questions.
- If any of the kitchen items in the conversation are not in the list on the board, have students add them.

After You Read

A. Practice
- Read the opening conversation aloud and have students repeat. Encourage them to copy your intonation and pronunciation.
- Have students practice the conversation in pairs. Encourage students to look at each other, not the book, so that the conversation sounds natural.
- Have students change partners and practice the conversation again. Call on pairs to role-play parts of the conversation for the class.

B. Vocabulary
- Play the audio and have students repeat each word or phrase. Encourage them to use the pictures to figure out the meaning.
- Have students write new words and their meanings in their notebooks.

C. Vocabulary
- To show students how to complete the activity, write on the board:
  A _____ is in my kitchen.
  An _____ is in my kitchen.
  _____ are in my kitchen.
- Model the activity by talking about things in your kitchen, using the language on the board. For example, say: "An oven is in my kitchen. A refrigerator is in my kitchen. Forks, knives, and glasses are in my kitchen."
- Have pairs talk about their kitchens. Have students compare answers in pairs.
- Call on pairs to read their answers aloud. Compare them to the list the class generated in the Before You Read activity above.

D. Comprehension
- Remind students that the opening conversation is on pages 10–11.
- Have students complete the exercise individually and then compare answers in pairs or groups of three.

Go to **www.myfocusongrammarlab.com** for an additional reading, and for reading and vocabulary practice.

Step 2: Grammar Presentation (page 13)

See the general suggestions for Grammar Presentation on page 3.

Grammar Charts
- To explain singular and pural nouns, write on the board:
  This is a fork.   These are forks.
  It's an oven.   They are ovens.

- Point to *this* and *it* in each of the sentences. Ask students how many people or things *this* and *it* refer to. *(one)* Point to *these* and *they* in each of the sentences. Ask students how many people or things *these* and *they* refer to. *(more than one)*
- Explain that *singular* nouns name one person, place, thing, or idea and that *plural* nouns name more than one person, place, thing, or idea. Ask students, "Which are the singular nouns in the sentences?" *(fork, oven)* and "which are the plural nouns?" *(forks, ovens)*.
- Ask students what the difference in form is between *fork* and *forks* (an *-s* has been added to *forks*). Point out that the *-s* at the end of *forks* and *ovens* indicates that they are plural.
- To explain *a* and *an*, review the vowels in English (*a, e, i, o, u,* and sometimes *y*). Point out that all other letters are consonants.
- Go back to the first sets of sentences you wrote on the board. Ask students why they think *a* is used before *fork*, but *an* is used before *oven*.
- Point out that we use *a* before a singular noun that begins with a consonant sound. We use *an* before singular nouns that begin with a vowel sound.
- To explain proper nouns, write on the board: My roommate Elena is from Brazil.
- Ask students why *Elena* and *Brazil* start with a capital letter (*Elena* is the person's name and *Brazil* is the name of the country she's from).
- Point out that a proper noun always begins with a capital letter.

Grammar Notes

Note 1
- Ask students how adding *-s* to nouns changes the meaning (*-s makes a singular noun plural*).
- Write these sentences on the board:
  This is a glass.   These are glasses.
- Ask students why they think *-es* has been added to *glass* to form the plural. Point out that because *glass* ends in *-ss*, *-es* is added to form the plural and adds an extra syllable to the plural form. The addition of this syllable makes pronunciation of the plural form easier.
- Write these words on the board: match, brush, box. Ask students how to form the plurals of these words (add *-es*). Point out that for words that end in *-s, -ch, -sh, x,* and *z, -es* is added to form the plural.

Note 2

- Have students read Note 2. Point out that these articles are never used with plural nouns.
- Emphasize that the use of *a* or *an* depends on the initial sound of the word, not the initial letter. Sometimes the initial letter may be a consonant (as in *hour*), but the initial sound is a vowel sound. In this case, the *h* in *hour* is silent.
- You may also want to point out that the use of *a* or *an* makes pronunciation easier. It's much easier to say *an oven* or *an hour* than it is to say *a oven* or *a hour*. Likewise, it is easier to say *a fork* than *an fork*.

Note 3

- You may want to point out to students that irregular plurals are shown in a dictionary.

Note 4

- Point out to students that the names of languages are also proper nouns and should be capitalized, as in the dialogue they read on pages 10–11: *Not so fast. Now in Portuguese.* Also emphasize that *a* and *an* are not usually used before proper nouns.

🕐 **Identify the Grammar**: Have students identify the grammar in the opening conversation on pages 10–11. For example:
  a toaster
  an oven

Go to **www.myfocusongrammarlab.com** for grammar charts and notes.

Step 3: Focused Practice (pages 14–15)

See the general suggestions for Focused Practice on page 4.

Exercise 1: Discover the Grammar

A
- Have students complete the exercise. Then go over the answers as a class.
- Have students make the singular nouns plural *(knives, kitchens)*. Remind them that *knife—knives* is one of the irregular plural nouns in Note 3 on page 13. Then have them make the plural nouns singular *(apple, fork)*.

B
- Have students complete the exercise individually. Then go over the answers as a class.
- Ask students which words take the article *a* and which take *an*. Have them repeat the words with their indefinite articles *(an apple, an egg, a knife, etc.)*.

C
- Have students work in pairs to write a list of ten common and proper nouns.
- Have pairs compare lists and check to make sure all of the proper nouns are capitalized.

Exercise 2: Singular and Plural Nouns

- Have students complete the exercise individually. Then have them compare answers in pairs.
- Review the exercise with the class. Call on students from each pair to provide correct answers.
- Have pairs practice the conversation.

Exercise 3: Articles

- Review the exercise as a class. Call on students to provide the correct answers and to explain why each choice is correct.

Exercise 4: Editing

- Go over the example with the class. Ask: "Is *apples* singular or plural?" *(plural)* "Do we use *a* before plural nouns?" *(no)*
  Make sure students see that the article *a* needs to be crossed out to make the sentence correct.
- Have students complete the exercise and work in pairs to check their answers. Call on pairs to write their corrections on the board and explain the corrections they made.

Go to **www.myfocusongrammarlab.com** for additional grammar practice.

Step 4: Communication Practice (pages 16–17)

See the general suggestions for Communication Practice on page 5.

Exercise 5: Pronunciation

A
- Play the audio. Have students read along as they listen to the Pronunciation Note.

B
- Have students complete the exercise. Then have them work in pairs to take turns pronouncing words from the list in random order. As the speaker pronounces the word, the listener identifies the number of syllables.
- **Note:** As a variation, students can complete this exercise as a class activity. You (or a student) can pronounce the words, and students can hold up one, two, three, or four fingers to show the number of syllables they heard.

C
- Have students work in groups of two or three to compare their answers. Then have them take turns pronouncing each of the words in the exercise.

Exercise 6: Listening

A
- Have students complete the exercise. Then go over the answers as a class.

B
- Have students complete the exercise. Then play the audio again as a dictation, pausing as needed to give students time to write.
- Call on students to write their sentences on the board. Have students discuss whether the sentences on the board are correct. Then use the audioscript on page 138 to check their answers.

Exercise 7: Name Things from A to Z
- Go over the examples with the class. Quickly review the letters of the alphabet and write them on the board. Make sure students understand that they will name a thing for each letter, but the letters in the article (*a / an*) do not count. For example, *a bed* goes with the letter B.
- Have students complete the activity. Go over the answers as a class. Write students' answers on the board by the corresponding letters.
- Have students practice saying the nouns in singular form with *a / an* and in plural form.

Exercise 8: Memory Game
- Go over the example with the class. Make sure students understand how to do the activity.
- For variation, have the whole class form one large circle. Student 1 names one thing; student 2 repeats what student 1 said and adds an item. Continue around the circle, with the next student repeating all of the items that have been named and adding one more. When someone misses, start the process again with a different student.

Exercise 9: Writing

A
- Have students fold their papers lengthwise, so that the paper has two long columns. Have them complete Part A on the left-hand side of the paper.

B
- Have students correct their work using the Editing Checklist.

C
- Have students draw their pictures for each sentence on the right-hand side of the paper across from each sentence.
- Have students work in pairs and exchange papers, looking only at the pictures their partner drew.
- Have students write a sentence that goes with each of their partner's pictures. Then have them compare the sentences they wrote with their partner's sentences on the left-hand side of the paper.

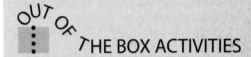

OUT OF THE BOX ACTIVITIES

Writing and Speaking
- Have students work in pairs. Give each group pictures (from magazines, newspaper ads, or the Internet) of various items found in a kitchen or of different foods. Be sure that some are singular and some are plural.
- Have each group categorize the items into two groups: singular and plural. Have each pair make a list of the items in each category.
- Have two pairs work together, taking turns talking about the items on their lists, using the sentence patterns they have learned:
  This is a(n) _____ .
  These are _____ .

Reading and Writing
- Provide students with a simple text that contains errors related to the unit grammar, such as the one below.
  This is myrna. She is from bogota, colombia. She has two sisters—hilda and marta. They all study english at a university in chicago. marta also studies french. She wants to live in france someday. hilda speaks spanish, english, and a little german. hilda and her boyfriend wolfgang plan to marry and live in germany. myrna loves the united states, but she has a boyfriend in bogota, so she wants to live there.
- Have students correct the text individually. Then have them compare answers in pairs or small groups.

Go to **www.myfocusongrammarlab.com** for additional listening, pronunciation, speaking, and writing practice.

Note:

• See the *Focus on Grammar Workbook* for additional in-class or homework grammar practice.

Unit 2 Review (page 18)

Have students complete the Review and check their answers on Student Book page UR-0. Review or assign additional material as needed.

Go to **www.myfocusongrammarlab.com** for the Unit Achievement Test.

From Grammar to Writing (page FG-1)

See the general suggestions for From Grammar to Writing on page 9.

Go to **www.myfocusongrammarlab.com** for an additional From Grammar to Writing Assignment, Part Review, and Part Post-Test.

PART II OVERVIEW

Be: Present; *That Is / Those Are*; POSSESSIVE ADJECTIVES

UNIT	GRAMMAR FOCUS	THEME
3	Present of *Be*: Statements	Meeting People
4	*That is / Those are*; Possessive Adjectives	Sightseeing in Seattle
5	Present of *Be*: Yes / No Questions; Questions with *Who* and *What*	A Wedding
6	Present of *Be*: *Where* Questions; Prepositions of Place	Giving Addresses

Go to **www.myfocusongrammarlab.com** for the Part and Unit Tests.

Note: PowerPoint® grammar presentations, test-generating software, and reproducible Part and Unit Tests are on the *Teacher's Resource Disc*.

UNIT 3 OVERVIEW

Grammar: PRESENT OF *Be*: STATEMENTS

Unit 3 focuses on the meanings and uses of the present of *be* in statements.

• The present of *be* has three forms for affirmative and negative statements: *am, is,* and *are*.

• Negative statements with *be* in the present are formed by using *be* + *not*.

• Sentences have a subject and a verb. The subject of a sentence is a noun or pronoun.

• Contractions, or short forms, are used in speech and informal writing. There is one contracted form for affirmative statements with *be*; negative statements with *be* usually have two contracted forms.

Theme: MEETING PEOPLE

Unit 3 focuses on language that people use when they meet someone new.

Step 1: Grammar in Context (pages 20–22)

See the general suggestions for Grammar in Context on page 1.

Before You Read

A

• Have students complete the exercise in pairs.

• Call on pairs to share their answers with the class. Make corrections as needed.

B

• Have students make a list of other things they know about Australia in small groups.

• Call on a student from each group to share the group's list with the class.

Read

• To encourage students to read with a purpose, write on the board:

 1. Is Amy a man or a woman? *(woman)*

 2. Are Amy and Jenny on vacation? *(Yes, they are.)*

 3. Are Amy and Jenny from Seattle? *(No, they're from Australia.)*

 4. Is Seattle dirty? *(No, it's clean.)*

• Play the audio and have students follow along in their books.

• Have students discuss the questions in pairs or groups of three.

• Call on pairs or groups to share answers with the class.

After You Read

A. Practice
- Read the opening conversation aloud and have students repeat. Encourage them to copy your intonation and pronunciation.
- Have students practice the conversation in groups of three. Circulate as students practice the conversation.
- Call on students from different groups to read each person's part in the conversation and perform it for the class.

B. Vocabulary
- Play the audio and have students repeat each word. Encourage them to use the pictures to figure out the meaning. Have students write new words and their meanings in their notebooks.
- Point out that most of these vocabulary items are opposites, or antonyms. Have students generate a list of the pairs of antonyms and have a student record it on the board (*clean / dirty; delicious / awful; friendly / unfriendly; popular / unpopular; great / terrible; good / bad; expensive / reasonable* or *cheap*).
- Have students work in pairs to practice saying the pairs of words to each other. Have partners take turns being speaker and listener. The listener closes his or her eyes as the speaker says a word. The listener has to say the correct opposite.
- For variety, you can do this as a whole-group activity.

C. Vocabulary
- Go over the example with the class.
- Have students complete the exercise individually. Then have them compare answers in pairs.
- Call on pairs to share answers with the class.

D. Comprehension
- Go over the example with the class. Make sure students understand that *Seattle* is the correct word. Have students look at the opening conversation on page 20 and say the lines that gave them the answer. (*They're here on vacation; Jenny and I love Seattle.*)
  — Explain that only one of the underlined words is correct; the rest are incorrect. Have them complete the exercise individually, then go over the answers as a class.
  — Read the corrected paragraph aloud as students repeat. Then have them practice the paragraph in pairs.

Go to **www.myfocusongrammarlab.com** for an additional reading, and for reading and vocabulary practice.

Step 2: Grammar Presentation (pages 22–23)
See the general suggestions for Grammar Presentation on page 3.

Grammar Charts
- Point to items in the chart and ask students questions to help them notice the grammar:
  — What is the only word used with *am?* (*I*) Is *I* singular or plural? (*singular*)
  — What words are used with *is?* (*He, she, it, Seattle*) Are these words singular or plural? (*singular*)
  — What words are used with *are?* (*We, you, they, Jenny and Amy*) Are these words singular or plural? (*plural*)
  — How are contractions formed? (*Some letters in the original two words are removed and replaced with an apostrophe.*)
  — How do we make *be* negative? (*We add* not *after* be.)
  — What are the two different contractions for *you, he, she, it, we,* and *they + not?* (*you're not / you aren't; he's not / he isn't; she's not / she isn't; they're not / they aren't*)

Grammar Notes

Note 1
- Point out that *am* is only used with the pronoun *I.*
- Ask students if *are* is used with singular or plural pronouns or nouns. (*It is used with both.*) Ask students if *is* is a singular or plural form. (*It is only used with singular nouns or pronouns.*)
- Say some pronouns or names (e.g., *I, they, Steve, you, Mark and Amy*) and have students say the form of *be* that goes with each one.

Note 2
- Read the example sentences aloud and have students repeat. Point out that negative statements use the word *not,* not the word *no,* and it goes after the *be* verb (not before).
- Say: "I am not a student. I am not from Canada." Have students say similar sentences in pairs.

Note 3

- Some students may benefit from a visual representation of the information in this note. Draw the following on the board:

Subject	+	Verb	
Noun	Pronoun		
Amy	She	is	my cousin.

- Select several sentences from the conversation on page 20 and write them on the board.
- Have students work in pairs or small groups to identify the subjects and verbs. Have them also say whether the subject is a noun or pronoun. Call on students from each group to mark the sentences on the board and discuss them as a class.

Note 4

- Have students work in pairs or groups to complete the chart below:

Pronoun	Affirmative	Contraction	Negative	Contraction(s)
I	I am	I'm	I am not	I'm not
You				
He				
She				
It				
They				

- Say a full form (e.g., *I am, she is not)* and have students say the contracted form (*I'm; she isn't*). Have students practice the same way in pairs.

🕐 **Identify the Grammar**: Have students identify the grammar in the opening reading on page 20. For example:
   They**'re** here on vacation.
   So you**'re not** from around here?
   We**'re** from Australia.
   The people **are** friendly.

Go to **www.myfocusongrammarlab.com** for grammar charts and notes.

Step 3: Focused Practice (pages 23–25)

See the general suggestions for Focused Practice on page 4.

Exercise 1: Discover the Grammar

- Go over the example with students. Have students complete the exercise and compare answers in small groups. Then as a class, review the correct answers.
- Have students work in pairs to make the affirmative statements into negative statements and the negative statements into affirmative.

Exercise 2: Affirmative Statements

A
- Go over the example with students. Ask: "Is Amy a man or a woman?" (*a woman*) "Is Amy one person or more than one person?" (*only one*) Make sure students understand why the correct answer is *She is*.
- Have students complete the exercise individually and then check their answers in pairs.
- Call on students to read their answers aloud.

B
- Have students write the sentences with contractions. Then have them practice saying them in pairs.

Exercise 3: *Be*: Negatives and Contractions

A
- Go over the example with students. Write the sentence *I am a teacher* on the board. Say: "I am a teacher. So the sentence is true." Put a checkmark next to the sentence. Then ask a strong student: "Are you a teacher?" When the student answers *no*, say: "_____ is not a teacher. So the sentence is false." Have the student write *I am not a teacher* on the board.
- Have students complete the exercise individually and compare answers in pairs.
- Call on students to read their answers aloud. Call on other students to change the first-person sentences to third-person (e.g., *Juan is not a new student*).

B
- Have students complete the exercise. Then have pairs of students take turns reading the statements with negative contractions and providing the alternate if there is one.

Exercise 4: Present of *Be*

- Go over the example with the class. Have students complete the exercise individually. Then go over the correct answers as a class.
- Have students practice reading the letter aloud to a partner.

Exercise 5: Editing

- Go over the example with the class. Ask: "Where is the verb?" (*There isn't one.*) Make sure students understand that *is* needs to be in this sentence for it to be correct.
- Have students work with a partner to check their answers. Go over the answers as a class.
- Have partners practice reading the corrected versions with each other.

Go to **www.myfocusongrammarlab.com** for additional grammar practice.

Step 4: Communication Practice (pages 25–28)

See the general suggestions for Communication Practice on page 5.

Exercise 6: Pronunciation

A
- Have students look at the sentences on the page. Point out that the sentences on the left are full forms and the sentences on the right are contractions.
- Play the audio once and have students listen. Point out that the full form has two syllables or sounds and the contractions have only one.

B
- Play the audio again, pausing as needed while students repeat.

C
- Explain that students will listen to sentences and check whether they hear full forms or contractions. Have students listen for the number of syllables or sounds.
- Play the first sentence and go over the example with the students.
- Play the rest of the audio. Then play the audio again, pausing as needed, while students complete the exercise individually. Go over the answers as a class.

Exercise 7: Listening

A
- Have students read the three answer choices. Explain that they will listen to a man and a woman talking and check the sentence that matches the conversation.
- Play the audio and go over the answer as a class.

B
- Have students read the sentences and go over any unfamiliar words. Make sure students understand what the "No information" option means and when to choose it.

- Have students complete the exercise individually. Then have them work in small groups to check their answers. Go over the answers as a class.
- Play the audio again as a dictation. Pause when necessary to give students time to write. Call on students to write one line each on the board, and discuss the answers.

Exercise 8: True Sentences about You

A
- Go over the example with the class. Make sure students understand to write sentences that are true for them. They could be affirmative or negative.
- As students complete the exercise, write on the board:
  A: I'm not here on business.
  B: My sentence is the same. I'm not here on business.

  A: I'm not here on business.
  B: My sentence is different. I'm here on business.
- Model the two conversations with students. Have them compare answers in pairs and check *Same* where appropriate. Go over the answers as a class.

B
- Go over the example with the class. Have students write their sentences individually. Then have them read their sentences for the whole class or in groups.
- Have partners read their sentences to each other and work together to rewrite the statements they wrote. If the statement was written with a long form, have them change it to a contraction. If it was a contraction, have them rewrite it as a long form. Have them write negative statements with both forms of the contraction when possible.

Exercise 9: Talk about a City

- Have a pair of students read the example conversation aloud. Point out the phrase *Yes, I agree*. Tell students that the opposite is *I disagree*.
- Write the vocabulary words from page 21 on the board for easy reference as students create their conversations. Challenge them to use as many words as they can and to keep the conversation going for as long as possible.
- Have students complete the activity. Call on pairs to perform their conversations for the class. Have the class keep track of which vocabulary words were used.

Exercise 10: Writing

- Have students complete the exercise individually. Then have partners work together to correct each other's work, using the Editing Checklist as a guide.
- Challenge them to write four more sentences about their city and share them with each other.

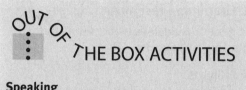

OUT OF THE BOX ACTIVITIES

Speaking

- Have students prepare a thirty-second speech about themselves and their native country using language from this unit. Instruct them to use contractions when possible. For example:
  I'm Tina, and I'm from Kiev. Kiev is the capital of Ukraine. It's a great city, and it's clean. Parts of it are dirty from the accident in Chernobyl. Some food is expensive and some is cheap, but it's all delicious. The people are friendly. One popular sport is wrestling, but I think it's awful.
- Give students time to write their speeches in class. Circulate and help with language as needed.
- Have students practice their speeches in pairs, and instruct partners to listen for correct use of *be* and contractions.
- Have each student speak in front of the class. After each speech, encourage the class to ask follow-up questions.

Reading, Writing, and Speaking

- Provide students with a script of the conversation on page 20. Have them work in groups of three to rewrite the script, substituting real information about themselves and the places in the conversation. Give each group time to practice.
- Have different groups role-play the conversation for the class.

Writing, Reading, and Speaking

- Have each student write a letter similar to the one from Exercise 4 on page 24 to a family member or a friend.
- Have students work in pairs to correct each other's work using the Editing Checklist on page 28.
- Have students change partners and read their letters to each other.

Go to **www.myfocusongrammarlab.com** for additional listening, pronunciation, speaking, and writing practice.

Note:

- See the *Focus on Grammar Workbook* for additional in-class or homework grammar practice.

Unit 3 Review (page 29)

Have students complete the Review and check their answers on Student Book page UR-0. Review or assign additional material as needed.

Go to **www.myfocusongrammarlab.com** for the Unit Achievement Test.

UNIT 4 OVERVIEW

Grammar: *That is / Those are*; POSSESSIVE ADJECTIVES

Unit 4 focuses on the meanings and uses of *That is* and *Those are* in affirmative statements and questions.

- *That is* is used to talk about one person or thing that is not near the speaker.
- *Those are* is used to talk about more than one thing that is not near the speaker.

The unit also introduces possessive adjectives and their meanings and use in affirmative statements and questions.

- Possessive adjectives tell who something or someone belongs to.
- Possessive adjectives have both singular and plural forms.

Theme: SIGHTSEEING IN SEATTLE

Unit 4 focuses on language used on a typical sightseeing trip.

Step 1: Grammar in Context (pages 30–31)

See the general suggestions for Grammar in Context on page 1.

Before You Read

- Have pairs of students complete the exercise.
- Have pairs circulate and talk with other pairs about their answers. Call on students to share their answers with the class.

Read

- To encourage students to read with a purpose, write the following questions on the board:
  1. Is Jenny with Steve and Amy? *(no)*
  2. What are the big buildings? *(stadiums)*
  3. What is the colored building? *(the EMP)*
  4. What is the EMP? *(a music museum)*
- Play the audio and have students read along in their books.
- Have students discuss the questions in pairs or groups of three.
- Call on pairs or groups to share answers with the class.

After You Read

A. Practice

- Read the opening conversation aloud and have students repeat. Encourage them to copy your intonation and pronunciation.
- Have students practice the conversation in pairs. Circulate as students practice.
- Call on students from different groups to read each person's part in the conversation and perform it for the class.

B. Vocabulary

- Play the audio and have students repeat each word or phrase. Encourage them to use the pictures to figure out the meaning.
- Have students write new words and their meanings in their notebooks.

C. Vocabulary

- Write on the board:
  Do you have _____ in your town?
- Have students write each of the words in one column on the left side of a piece of paper. With a student, model asking a question using one of the vocabulary words from C.
- Have students mingle and ask each other questions using each of these vocabulary items. Have them put tally marks next to each item for the *yes* answers.
- Have students compare answers in pairs or small groups.

D. Comprehension

- Remind students that the opening conversation is on page 30.
- Have students complete the exercise and work in pairs to check their answers.
- Call on students to share answers with the class.

E

- Pre-teach the word *initials*. Give examples of famous people and their initials.

- Have pairs read the text and complete the activity. Tell students that the building is mentioned in the opening conversation on page 30.

Go to **www.myfocusongrammarlab.com** for an additional reading, and for reading and vocabulary practice.

Step 2: Grammar Presentation (page 32)

See the general suggestions for Grammar Presentation on page 3.

Grammar Charts

- Call on students to read the sentences in the first chart.
- Ask: "How is *that* similar to *this*?" *(They are both singular.)* "How is *those* similar to *these*?" *(They are both plural.)*
- Ask: "What form of *be* is used with *that*?" *(is)* "What form of *be* is used with *those*?" *(are)*
- Call on students to read the sentences in the second chart.
- Ask: "Which possessive adjectives are singular?" *(my, your, his, her, its)* "Which possessive adjectives are plural?" *(our, your, their)*
- Say a subject pronoun and have students say the possessive adjective that goes with it, e.g., *I—my*. Have students practice in pairs. Challenge them to try it without looking at the grammar charts.

Grammar Notes

Note 1

- Call on a student to read Note 1 aloud to the class.
- Have one student stand near you at the front of the room and have another student stand at the back of the room.
- Say: "This is my student _____," and point to the student near you. Say: "That is my student _____," and point to the student at the back of the room.

Note 2

- Have another student read Note 2 aloud.
- Call on two more students. Have one stand next to the student at the front and the other stand next to the student at the back.
- Say: "These are my students _____ and _____," and point to the students near you. Say: "Those are my students _____ and _____," and point to the students at the back.
- Have the students remain in their places for the next note.

Note 3
- Have another student read Note 3.
- Point to one of the students at the back and ask: "Is that my student _____?" Elicit the answer *Yes, it is.* Then point or gesture to indicate both of the students at the back. Ask: "Are those my students _____ and _____?" Elicit the answer, *Yes, they are.*
- Have students practice the questions and answers in pairs, asking, "Is that our classmate _____?" and "Are those our classmates _____ and _____?"

Note 4
- Call on another student to read Note 4.
- Bring in photos of yourself with groups of people, and have students bring in photos of themselves in groups. You might also use magazine photos of groups. Model sentences with different possessive adjectives. For example: *That's my brother Joe and that's his wife. Those are our parents, and that is their cat.*
- Have students ask you two or three questions about the photo using *Is that* or *Are those* and possessive adjectives. Then have them practice in pairs. They can bring photos to class, use photos on their phones, or use magazine photos.

🕐 **Identify the Grammar**: Have students identify the grammar in the opening reading on page 30. For example:
That's the Space Needle.
Are those people next to them?
That's your university, right?
It's **his** "baby."

Go to **www.myfocusongrammarlab.com** for grammar charts and notes.

Step 3: Focused Practice (pages 33–34)

See the general suggestions for Focused Practice on page 4.

Exercise 1: Discover the Grammar
- Go over the example with the class. Make sure students understand that the answer (*No, they're her books*) is the correct response to the question *Are those your books?*
- Have students complete the exercise and work in pairs to check their answers.
- Then have partners practice asking the questions and giving the answers.

Exercise 2: *That* and *Those*
- Have students complete the exercise individually. Go over the answers to the exercise as a class.

- Have students change statements 1 and 4 to questions. Remind students that questions with *that* and *those* usually require a subject pronoun in the answer. Then have pairs practice asking and answering the questions. Circulate and make corrections as needed.

Exercise 3: Possessive Adjectives
- Go over the example with the class. Make sure the students understand that a picture of one head means the speaker or subject is singular; two heads means it is plural.
- Have students complete the exercise. Then call on students to give their answers.

Exercise 4: Possessive Adjectives
- Have students look at the picture. Read the instructions aloud. Ask: "Who is Judy?" *(the woman on the sofa)* "Who is on TV?" *(Judy's family or friends)*
- Have students complete the exercise individually. Then have them work in pairs to correct their answers. Call on students to share their answers with the class.
- Have students practice reading the text aloud to a partner.

Exercise 5: Editing
- Go over the example with the class. Ask: "Is *keys* singular or plural?" *(plural)* "Do we say *that* with plural nouns?" *(no)* Make sure students understand that *those* is the correct word for this sentence.
- Have students complete the exercise. Then go over the answers as a class.
- Have partners practice reading the corrected versions to each other.

Go to **www.myfocusongrammarlab.com** for additional grammar practice.

Step 4: Communication Practice (pages 35–36)

See the general suggestions for Communication Practice on page 5.

Exercise 6: Pronunciation

A
- Have students listen to and read the Pronunciation Note. Point out that *your* is a possessive adjective and *you're* is the contraction for *you are.*
- Ask students what two other possessive adjectives also sound the same as contractions. *(their / they're; its / it's)*

B
- Play the first sentence and go over the example answer with the class. If necessary, write the sentence on the board and play the sentence again.

- Play the audio and have students complete the exercise. Go over the answers as a class.
- Play the audio again as a dictation. Pause as needed to give students time to write.
- Call on students to write the sentences on the board and discuss the answers as a class. Have students make sure that each possessive adjective and contraction is spelled correctly.

Exercise 7: Listening
- Explain that students will listen to two women, Judy and Jessica, talking about Jessica's pictures. Have students read the questions and answer choices. Explain any unfamiliar vocabulary and make sure students can pronounce the names.
- Have students complete the exercise individually. Then have them work in small groups to check their answers. Go over the answers as a class.
- Give students the audioscript for the exercise and have them practice the dialog in pairs.

Exercise 8: Suggestions and Information
A
- Play the audio. Make sure students understand the meaning of *Let's*.
- Model the conversation with a student. Then model the conversation with a different student, this time substituting one of the activities in the box in B.

B
- Go over the activities and explain any unfamiliar vocabulary. Then have students practice the conversation in pairs.

C
- Play the audio. Then model the conversation with a student as above. Tell students that you can check or confirm information by adding *right?* to the end of a statement.

D
- Have students practice the conversation in pairs. Circulate to monitor the activity and make corrections as needed.

Exercise 9: Game
- Model the example conversation with two students. Then have students play the game.

- For variation, seat students in a large circle. Have each student put two or three personal items in the center. Spread them out so they are clearly visible. Use a pointer (or a ruler or yard stick) and point to an item. Ask a student: "Ling, are those your sunglasses?" The student can answer: "Yes, they are" or point to a different student and say: "No, they're not. I think they're his (or her) sunglasses." If the answer is *yes*, the owner takes the item from the center. Hand the pointer to another student and continue the activity until all of the items are gone.

Exercise 10: Writing
- Have each student tell the class about his or her city. Encourage the other students to ask two to three questions. Model if needed.
- Challenge students to write four more sentences about their photo and share them with each other.
- Have partners work together to correct each other's work, using the Editing Checklist as a guide.

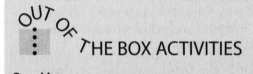

OUT OF THE BOX ACTIVITIES

Speaking
- Have students bring in photos of a vacation or special occasion.
- Divide the class into two groups. Students in one group remain seated at their desks with their photos. The other group of students "visit" each of the other students and ask questions about the photos. Remind students to use *this, that, these,* and *those* in their questions. Seated students answer the questions. Remind them to use possessive adjectives in their answers.
- Set a time limit, and then have the groups change roles.

Writing and Speaking
- Bring in magazine photos of people in groups—one for each one or two students.
- Give a photo to individuals or pairs. Have each person or pair write a story about the people in the photo. Remind students to use *That is / Those are* and possessive adjectives.
- Have students work in pairs or small groups to read their stories to each other.

Go to **www.myfocusongrammarlab.com** for additional listening, pronunciation, speaking, and writing practice.

Note:
- See the *Focus on Grammar Workbook* for additional in-class or homework grammar practice.

Unit 4 Review (page 37)

Have students complete the Review and check their answers on Student Book page UR-0. Review or assign additional material as needed.

Go to **www.myfocusongrammarlab.com** for the Unit Achievement Test.

UNIT 5 OVERVIEW

Grammar: PRESENT OF *Be*: *Yes* / *No* QUESTIONS, QUESTIONS WITH *Who* AND *What*

Unit 5 focuses on the meanings and uses of *be* in *yes* / *no* questions and both affirmative and negative short answers to *yes* / *no* questions.

- In *yes* / *no* questions with *be*, we use the same verb form that we used in statements— *am, is,* and *are*.
- In *yes* / *no* questions with *be*, the verb comes before the subject.
- We often use contractions in negative short answers to *yes* / *no* questions.

The unit also introduces information questions with *Who* and *What*, along with both short and long answers to these types of information questions.

- Begin an information question with *Who* or *What* followed by a form of *be*.
- Use *Who* to ask about people. Use *What* to ask about things or ideas.
- In speaking and informal writing, we often use a contraction such as *Who's (Who is)* or *What's (What is)*.
- Information questions can have short or long answers.

Theme: A WEDDING

Unit 5 focuses on language used at a wedding or other social event.

Step 1: Grammar in Context (pages 38–40)

See the general suggestions for Grammar in Context on page 1.

Before You Read

- Have students complete the exercise and share their answers in small groups.

- Then have the groups suggest other things they think people would say at a social event such as a wedding.
- Call on students from each group to share the ideas with the class.

Read

- To encourage students to read with a purpose, write on the board:
  1. Who is Amanda? *(Steve's cousin)*
  2. Who is Mark? *(Josh's friend)*
  3. Is Mark married? *(No, he's not.)*
  4. Who is with Amanda? *(Kathy)*
- Have students read the conversations and discuss the questions in pairs or groups of three.
- Call on students to share answers with the class.

After You Read

A. Practice

- Have students practice the opening reading in pairs. Call on three pairs to perform the conversations for the class.

B. Vocabulary

- Play the audio and have students repeat each word or phrase. Encourage them to use the pictures to figure out the meaning.
- Have students write new words and their meanings in their notebooks.
- Have students work in pairs to practice the new words. Student A points to a picture, and Student B says the word. Then they switch.

C. Vocabulary

- Have pairs from Part B join another pair to form small groups to complete this activity.
- Go over the instructions and example with the class. Point out that more than one occupation might use an item. For example, a writer and a clerk both might use paper.
- Go over the answers as a class.

D. Comprehension

- Remind them that the opening conversation is on pages 38–39.
- Have students complete the exercise individually. Then go over the answers as a class.

Go to **www.myfocusongrammarlab.com** for an additional reading, and for reading and vocabulary practice.

Step 2: Grammar Presentation (pages 40–41)

See the general suggestions for Grammar Presentation on page 3.

Grammar Charts

- To explain *yes / no* questions, write on the board:
  Steve is here for the wedding.
- Ask students how they would make this statement into a *yes / no* question. *(reverse the position of the subject and verb, then add a question mark)*
- Write the question on the board:
  Is Steve here for the wedding?
- To explain questions with *who* and *what*, write on the board:
  Who is that man with Steve?
  What is his name?
- Ask students what comes after *who* and *what*. *(be or the verb)*
- Elicit answers to each question. *(That's Mark. / Mark.; His name is Mark. / It's Mark. / Mark.)*
- Point out the difference in intonation between *yes / no* and information questions. Use your hand to show the rising intonation in a *yes / no* question and the falling intonation in a question with *who* or *what*.
- Have students repeat several of each type of question to practice intonation.

Grammar Notes

Note 1

- Read the note aloud. Then do a quick transformation drill. Read some statements and have students change them to *yes / no* questions. For example:
  T: I am late.   S: Am I late?
  T: That's Mark.   S: Is that Mark?

Note 2

- Go over Note 2. Point out that contractions are not used in affirmative short answers.
- Ask students different *yes / no* questions and elicit affirmative and negative answers with contractions. For example:
  T: Are you students?   S: Yes, we are.
  T: Is today Tuesday?   S: Yes, it is.
  T: Are you a doctor?   S: No, I'm not.
  T: Is it Friday?   S: No, it's not. / No, it isn't.
- Have students practice asking and answering similar questions in pairs.

Note 3

- Go over Note 3 with the class. Point to a student and ask someone, "Who is that?" Elicit a long answer *(That's Mei)* and a short answer *(Mei)*. Point to a different student and ask: "What is his name?" Elicit a long and short answer.

- Have students practice asking and answering similar questions in pairs.
- Review the contracted forms of the questions *Who's that?* and *What's his name?* Have students practice again using the contracted forms.
- **Note:** You can also use pictures of famous movie stars or musicians for this activity.

🕐 **Identify the Grammar**: Have students identify the grammar in the opening conversations on pages 38–39. For example:
  Are you here for the wedding? **Yes, I am.**
  Who's that man with Steve?
  Is he single? **Yes, he is.**

Go to www.myfocusongrammarlab.com for grammar charts and notes.

Step 3: Focused Practice (pages 41–43)

See the general suggestions for Focused Practice on page 4.

Exercise 1: Discover the Grammar

- Have students complete the exercise and work in pairs to check their answers. Then have each pair write six new *yes / no* questions about people in the class. Have students exchange their questions with another pair and answer each other's questions. Encourage students to ask each other questions to get information if they don't know the answer to a question about someone.

Exercise 2: *Who* and *What*

- Have students complete the exercise. Go over the answers as a class. Then have students practice the conversations in pairs.

Exercise 3: *Yes / No* Questions and Answers

- Have students complete the exercise. Then go over the answers as a class.
- Have students practice asking and answering the questions in pairs. Then have them switch partners and practice again, this time giving the opposite answer, for example, a *no* answer instead of a *yes* answer.

Exercise 4: *Yes / No* Questions and Answers

- Have students quickly read the conversations and the words in the boxes. Ask: "What do you think each conversation is about?" *(A and B are asking and talking about people they see.)*
- Have students complete the exercise individually. Have students compare answers in pairs. Call on a pair to read each conversation. Discuss the answers as a class.
- Have pairs practice reading each role of both conversations.

Exercise 5: Editing

- Go over the example with the class. Make sure students understand why *Are* is the correct word in the question.
- Have students complete the exercise individually. Call on students to write their edited items on the board. Discuss the answers as a class.
- Have students practice the corrected conversations in pairs.

Go to **www.myfocusongrammarlab.com** for additional grammar practice.

Step 4: Communication Practice (pages 44–46)

See the general suggestions for Communication Practice on page 5.

Exercise 6: Pronunciation

A
- Have students read and listen to the Pronunciation Note. Say the questions in the note again and have the class repeat them to practice intonation.

B
- Have students complete the exercise. Then go over the answers as a class. Play the audio again for clarification as needed.
- Play the audio again as a dictation. Pause as needed so students have enough time to write.
- Call on students to write their sentences on the board. Discuss them as a class.

C
- Have students complete this part and then work in pairs. Have them take turns asking and answering the questions from Part B. Circulate and correct intonation as needed.

Exercise 7: Listening

A
- Explain that students will listen to two people talking at a wedding. The people are asking about other guests at the wedding. Have students read the questions. If needed, practice pronouncing the names in the questions.
- Have students complete the exercise and check their answers in pairs.

B
- Have students complete the exercise. Call on students to provide answers for the class. Discuss any differences.
- Play the audio again as needed.

Exercise 8: Talk about Occupations

A
- Play the audio.
- Have students repeat each word and phrase in the box after you.

B
- Explain the exercise. Then have the students complete it as a class. Go around the room and give help as needed.

C
- Go over the instructions. Model the conversation with a student. Give the students a minimum number of people to ask about as they complete the exercise. Have students take turns asking and answering the questions in the conversation.

Exercise 9: Game

A
- Have three students write the names of writers, actors, and singers on the board as the class brainstorms names.

B
- Go over the instructions and have students complete the task.

C
- Model the activity for the students. Have a student write the questions you ask on the board. Keep this list on the board for reference.

D
- Have students complete the game.
- **Note:** For variation, you may want to call the game "Who Am I?" Have the person who is asking the questions use the first-person.

Exercise 10: Writing

A
- Go over the instructions.
- Point out that there are seven items in the box but students need to write only five questions.
- Call on students to say each of the words and phrases aloud. Correct pronunciation as needed.

B
- For variation, you may want to have students work in pairs to correct each other's work using the Editing Checklist.
- Then have students practice reading their questions aloud in pairs.

C

- Have students record the answers as they interview their classmates.
- Give each student an opportunity to introduce his or her classmate to the group. Allow students to use their notes as needed.

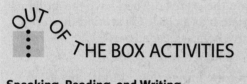

OUT OF THE BOX ACTIVITIES

Speaking, Reading, and Writing

- Have each student interview someone outside of the class. You may want to assign this for homework or give students a specific amount of class time in which to complete the interview. To prepare for the interview, have them write five to seven questions to ask. Remind students to take notes during the interview.
- When they return to class, have students work in small groups to tell each other about the person they interviewed.

Writing and Reading

- Have the class form a circle with their desks or clipboards so they can write.
- Assign each student a word to use to begin a question: *Are, Is, Am, Who,* or *What.* Have students write their word at the top of their paper. Each student writes one question with his or her word.
- Students pass their papers to the right. Each student writes an answer to the question, and then writes a new question using that same word. Students pass their papers to the right again and write an answer to the new question.

Go to **www.myfocusongrammarlab.com** for additional listening, pronunciation, speaking, and writing practice.

Note:

- See the *Focus on Grammar Workbook* for additional in-class or homework grammar practice.

Unit 5 Review (page 47)

Have students complete the Review and check their answers on Student Book page UR-0. Review or assign additional material as needed.

Go to **www.myfocusongrammarlab.com** for the Unit Achievement Test.

UNIT 6 OVERVIEW

Grammar: PRESENT OF *Be: Where* QUESTIONS; PREPOSITIONS OF PLACE

Unit 6 focuses on the meanings and uses of *be* in questions with *where*.

- Use *where* to ask questions about the location.
- *Where's* is the contracted form of *where is*. It is used in speech and informal writing.

The unit also introduces prepositions of place and ordinal numbers.

- Prepositions of place tell about the location of places and things.
- Use ordinal numbers for names of streets and floors in a building.

Theme: GIVING ADDRESSES

Unit 6 focuses on language that describes the locations of buildings and addresses.

Step 1: Grammar in Context (pages 48–49)

See the general suggestions for Grammar in Context on page 1.

Before You Read

- If students have trouble thinking of another address to talk about, they can talk about their own addresses. You can also give them a list of some famous addresses, for example, 1600 Pennsylvania Avenue (the White House) or 10 Downing Street (the address of the British Prime Minister).

Read

- To encourage students to read with a purpose, write these questions on the board:
  1. Who are Mark and Judy? *(probably Yuko's friends)*
  2. What is Mark's email about? *(Yuko's birthday party)*
  3. What floor is Yuko's apartment on? *(the second floor)*
  4. Is Mark sure about Yuko's address? *(No, he's not. / No, he isn't.)*
- Go over the questions with the class. Have students think about these questions as they read and listen to the email messages.

- Have students read the messages and work in pairs to answer the questions on the board. Discuss the answers as a class.

After You Read

A. Practice
- Have pairs practice reading the email messages aloud.
- Circulate, helping with vocabulary, pronunciation, and intonation as needed.

B. Vocabulary
- Have students listen to and repeat the vocabulary words. Then have them repeat them as you say them aloud. Encourage them to use the pictures to figure out the meaning. Have students write new words and their meanings in their notebooks.
- Explain that ordinal numbers are related to cardinal numbers. Ordinal numbers tell about the position or order of things. The ordinal number *first* is related to the cardinal number *one; second* goes with *two*, etc.
- Write the cardinal numbers one through ten on the board. As you point to each one, have students say the ordinal number that goes with it. Continue the activity, randomly pointing to the cardinal numbers.

C. Vocabulary
- If students are not familiar with the area around your school, have them talk about different places in their neighborhoods.

D. Comprehension
- Have students look at the illustration and say the street names, businesses, and house numbers aloud.
- Have students complete the exercise in pairs. Remind students that the opening reading is on page 48. Go over the answer as a class.

Go to **www.myfocusongrammarlab.com** for an additional reading, and for reading and vocabulary practice.

Step 2: Grammar Presentation (pages 50–51)

See the general suggestions for Grammar Presentation on page 3.

Grammar Charts
- Have students read the questions and answers in the chart aloud.
- Point out that *Where's* is the short form of *Where is*.
- Have students look at the map. Read the sentences aloud and have students repeat.

- Ask: "What kind of place comes after *on*?" *(a street or a floor)* "What comes before and after *between*?" *(names of buildings or places)* "What comes after *next to* and *across from*?" *(names of buildings or places)*

Grammar Notes

Notes 1–2
- Read the notes aloud. Have students work in pairs to write six to eight questions with *where* using the map on page 50.
- Call on pairs to ask other pairs their questions.

Notes 3–4
- Go over Notes 3 and 4 with the class.
- Call on a few students to write their addresses on the board. If they don't want to write their real addresses, they can make them up. Be sure to have them state what floor they live on if it's an apartment building.
- Have students work in pairs to take turns talking about the locations in different ways. For example:
  Alejandro lives at 116 Seashore Drive, 2nd floor, Surrey, North Carolina.
  He lives on Seashore Drive.
  He lives on the second floor.
  He lives in Surrey. He lives in North Carolina.
  He lives in the United States.
  He lives in North America.

🕐 **Identify the Grammar**: Have students identify the grammar in the opening reading on page 48. For example:
  Where's her new apartment?
  Her apartment is **on** First Avenue. . .
  I think it's **at** 10 First Avenue. . .
  It's **across from** a library. . .

Go to **www.myfocusongrammarlab.com** for grammar charts and notes.

Step 3: Focused Practice (pages 51–53)

See the general suggestions for Focused Practice on page 4.

Exercise 1: Discover the Grammar
- Have students complete the exercise individually. Then go over the answers with the class.
- Have students work individually to write three to four questions with *Where* about the maps on pages 49 or 50.

- Have them work in pairs to take turns asking and answering their questions, using the answers in Exercise 1 as a model. Model the activity with a student if needed. For example:
  A: Look at the map on page 49. Where's the supermarket?
  B: It's on First Avenue between Jackson and Main. It's on the corner.

Exercise 2: Prepositions of Place

- Have students complete the exercise. Then go over the answers as a class.
- Point out that Apt. 2A is most likely on the second floor. Ask students on what floor Apt. 3B would be. *(third floor)*
- Give each student a 3" x 5" index card. Have students design a business card for themselves, using the business card on page 52 as a model. As a class, help students generate questions that would require the answers in Exercise 2 and clues for the answers. Write them on the board. For example:
  Where does _____ live? *(say the city and state)*
  What street does _____ live on? *(say the name of the street)*
  Where is his/her apartment (or house)? *(say the address)*
  What floor is it on? *(say the floor number or say: "It's a house.")*
- Have students exchange cards. Then have them circulate to ask and answer the questions using the information on the card. Model the activity before students begin if needed.

Exercise 3: Using a Map

- Go over the map with the class. Say the names of places, businesses, and street names and have the students point to the places on the map. Pre-teach *north, south, east, west*, as well as *northeast*.
- Have students complete the exercise. Then go over the answers as a class.
- Have students work in pairs to take turns asking and answering the questions.

Exercise 4: Questions about Location

A
- Say the sentences in the box and have students repeat them. Then have students complete the exercise.

B
- Play the audio. Go over the answer as a class.

- Have students work in pairs to practice the conversation. Have Partner A be the man and Partner B be the woman.
- Have the A students form new pairs with different B students. Have them change roles and practice the conversation again.
- Give students time to find the position of the man and woman on the map.

Exercise 5: Editing

- Go over the example with the class. Ask: "What is the full form of *Where's*?" *(where is)* "Which goes with *you—is* or *are*?" *(are)* Make sure students understand that *Where* is the correct word for the question.
- Have students complete the exercise. Then go over the answers with the class. Have students practice the conversations in pairs.

Go to **www.myfocusongrammarlab.com** for additional grammar practice.

Step 4: Communication Practice (pages 54–55)

See the general suggestions for Communication Practice on page 5.

Exercise 6: Listening

A
- Play the audio and have students complete the exercise. Then elicit the correct answer.

B
- Have students look at the map on page 52. Explain that they will listen to people ask about places on the map. Students will listen and complete the items on the board.
- Review the compass points on the maps. Pre-teach *northeast* and *go down [a street]*. Choose an intersection from the map on page 52, and point out the northeast, northwest, southeast, and southwest corners. Explain that *go down* can mean movement in any direction away from the place the speaker is standing.
- Have students complete the exercises. Then go over the answers as a class. Replay the audio as needed.

Exercise 7: Pronunciation

A
- Have students listen to the Pronunciation Note.

B
- Have students listen to the numbers in Part B. Then play the numbers again and have students repeat them.

- Write the numbers from the Pronunciation Note on the board. Point to different ones and have students say them.

C
- Have students complete the exercise and check their answers in pairs.
- Give students the audioscript and have pairs practice the conversations.

Exercise 8: Locations in a Building
- Read the names on the sign aloud and have students repeat. Explain *Family Medicine, Nail Salon, Spa, Passport Office,* and any other unfamiliar words.
- Model the example with two students. Then have students complete the exercise in groups of three. Circulate and make corrections as needed.

Exercise 9: Locations in a Neighborhood
- Model the example conversation with a student. Read the list of places in the directions and write them on the board.
- Have students complete the exercise. Then have pairs work together to brainstorm a new set of places in the area.
- Have two pairs work together and practice the conversation again, using the list of new locations that each pair created.

Exercise 10: Writing

A
- Go over the instructions and the example with the class. Point out that each student needs to write about three different places. Have students complete the exercise.

B
- Have students correct their work using the Editing Checklist. Call on students to tell the class about one of their favorite places. Encourage students to ask clarifying questions using prepositions of place. For example, *Is it next to the park? Is it on First Avenue?*

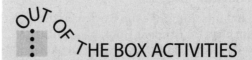

OUT OF THE BOX ACTIVITIES

Writing, Reading, and Speaking
- Go over how addresses are written in the United States (or the country where you are).
- Have students practice writing their complete mailing addresses on an index card or slip of paper. If they do not want to reveal this information, have them make up an address. Students should <u>not</u> include their names.
- Put the papers in a bag or basket and have each student take one. Have each student ask questions to match the address with the person. For example: *Who lives in _____? Who lives on _____? Who lives at _____?*

Writing, Listening, and Speaking
- Have each student draw a map of his or her neighborhood with street names and names or numbers of buildings. They should label some but not all of the buildings. Under the map, have students list the names (or numbers) of the unlabeled buildings. For example, *my house, drugstore, library, supermarket, park, bus stop,* etc.
- Have students work in pairs and ask each other about the unlabeled places on their maps. For example:
  S1: Where's the drug store?
  S2: It's on Mason Street between First and Second Avenue. It's next to the Asian food store.
  S1: Here? (pointing)
  S2: No. Here, across from the gym.

Go to **www.myfocusongrammarlab.com** for additional listening, pronunciation, speaking, and writing practice.

Note:
- See the *Focus on Grammar Workbook* for additional in-class or homework grammar practice.

Unit 6 Review (page 56)

Have students complete the Review and check their answers on Student Book page UR-0. Review or assign additional material as needed.

Go to **www.myfocusongrammarlab.com** for the Unit Achievement Test.

From Grammar to Writing (page FG-1)

See the general suggestions for From Grammar to Writing on page 9.

Go to **www.myfocusongrammarlab.com** for an additional From Grammar to Writing Assignment, Part Review, and Part Post-Test.

PART III OVERVIEW

Be: PAST

UNIT	GRAMMAR FOCUS	THEME
7	Past of *Be:* Statements, *Yes / No* Questions	Movies and Other Pastimes
8	Past of *Be: Wh-* Questions	Travel and Leisure Activities

Go to **www.myfocusongrammarlab.com** for the Part and Unit Tests.

Note: PowerPoint® grammar presentations, test-generating software, and reproducible Part and Unit Tests are on the *Teacher's Resource Disc.*

UNIT 7 OVERVIEW

Grammar: PAST OF *Be*: STATEMENTS, *Yes / No* QUESTIONS

Unit 7 focuses on the meanings and uses of *be* in the past in affirmative and negative statements as well as *yes / no* questions. It also provides information about the use of contractions in answers to negative questions.

- The past of *be* has two forms: *was* and *were.* Use *was* with singular nouns and most singular subject pronouns *(I, he, she, it).* Use *were* with plural nouns, *you* (either singular or plural), and plural subject pronouns *(we, they).*

- Use *was* or *were* + *not* to make negative statements about the past. We often use the contractions *wasn't* and *weren't* in speaking and informal writing.

- To make a *yes / no* question, put *was* or *were* before the subject.

- To make short answers, use a subject pronoun + *was, were, wasn't,* or *weren't.*

- For long answers, use *yes* or *no* and then give more information.

Theme: MOVIES AND OTHER PASTIMES

Unit 7 focuses on language that is used to talk about going to the movies or enjoying other pastimes.

Step 1: Grammar in Context (pages 58–59)

See the general suggestions for Grammar in Context on page 1.

Before You Read
- Have students discuss their answers in groups. Call on groups to share their answers with the class.

Read
- To encourage students to read with a purpose, write these questions on the board:
  1. Who was at Kathy's house last night? *(Josh and Amanda)*
  2. Was Kathy home? *(No, she wasn't. She was at the movies.)*
  3. Was the movie good? *(Yes, it was. It was funny and exciting.)*
- Play the audio and have students follow along in their books. Have students discuss the questions in pairs or groups of three. Call on students to share answers with the class.

After You Read

A. Practice
- Read the conversation aloud and have students repeat.
- Have the students practice the conversation in pairs. Then have them find a new partner and switch roles.

B. Vocabulary
- Play the audio and have students repeat each word or phrase. Encourage them to use the pictures to figure out the meaning.
- Have students write new words and their meanings in a notebook.

C. Vocabulary
- Write on the board:
  A: What's a funny / scary / interesting / boring / exciting movie?
  B: I think _____ is funny / scary / interesting / boring / exciting.
- Model the conversation on the board with a student. Use the adjective and movie title from the example in the book. *(exciting: Harry Potter and the Half-Blood Prince)* Have students complete the exercise in pairs.
- Call on pairs to share their answers with the class.
- Remind students that in earlier units, some of the vocabulary items were antonyms, or opposites. Have students identify the opposites in this vocabulary set *(interesting / boring; exciting / boring; asleep / awake)*.

D. Comprehension
- Go over the example with the class. Have students point to the picture or line in the opening conversation that gives the answer. *(In the picture, Kathy is talking on the phone at home in bed.)*
- Have students complete the exercise on page 58 individually. Then have them compare answers in pairs. Call on pairs to share their answers with the class.
- Have students continue to work in pairs to correct the false statements. Call on pairs to read the false statements and their corrected statements.

Go to **www.myfocusongrammarlab.com** for an additional reading, and for reading and vocabulary practice.

Step 2: Grammar Presentation (pages 60–61)

See the general suggestions for Grammar Presentation on page 3.

Grammar Charts
- Have students read the examples in the first chart. Point out that singular nouns as subjects go with *was* (except for *you*), and plural subjects (as well as *you*) go with *were*. Give examples from the reading: *Kathy was at the movies last night. Josh and Amanda were at Kathy's house last night.*
- Have students read each of the example sentences in the second chart.
- Say a name or subject (e.g., *I, Kathy, you, Josh and Amanda, they*) and have students say the negative form of *be* that goes with it. Elicit the full form and the contracted form. Have students practice in pairs.
- Read the questions and answers in the third chart aloud and have students repeat.
- Write on the board:
  Was / Were _____ at the movies last night?
- Say a pronoun or name and have students use the pronoun or name in the question on the board. For example:

T: she	Ss: Was she at the movies last night?
T: Paulo and Diego	Ss: Were Paulo and Diego at the movies last night?

- Have students practice in pairs. For the first few minutes, have them give affirmative short answers. Then have them give negative short answers. Have the students switch roles.

Grammar Notes

Note 1
- Point out again that *was* is used with all singular subjects except *you*. *Were* is used with all plural subjects and *you* singular and *you* plural.

Note 2
- Point out to students that using *be* + *not* in the past is the same as what they learned about *be* + *not* in the present. *Not* follows *was* or *were* in negative statements.
- Make statements with *was* and *were* about students in the class, famous people, or the students' countries. Some statements should be true and others false. Have students call out *true* or *false* after each statement. If the statement is false, call on a student to correct the statement. For example:
  T: Pablo Picasso was from France.
  S: He wasn't from France. He was from Spain.

Notes 3–4

- Ask students how forming *yes / no* questions with *be* in the past is the same as forming questions with *be* in the present. (*In both past and present yes / no questions, the subject follows the verb.*)

- Point out that unlike negative short answers with *is* and *are* in the present, past negative short answers have one form, not two. For example, we can say *No, he's not./ No, he isn't.* There are only two negative contractions for *be* in the past: *wasn't* and *weren't*.

🕐 **Identify the Grammar**: Have students identify the grammar in the opening conversation on page 58. For example:

I stopped by your house last night but you **weren't** there.

Or **were you** asleep?

I guess we **were** there about 9:00.

Go to **www.myfocusongrammarlab.com** for grammar charts and notes.

Step 3: Focused Practice (pages 61–64)

See the general suggestions for Focused Practice on page 4.

Exercise 1: Discover the Grammar

A

- Go over the example with the class. Have the students circle the subjects and underline the past forms of *be* for all the items. Then have students compare answers in pairs.

- Have students check their answers then complete the rest of the exercise by matching the questions and answers. Go over the answers as a class.

- Have students practice the questions and answers in pairs.

B

- Have students read the email. Ask students how they think Ken and Judy know each other—are they friends, co-workers, a couple, or something else?

- Have students complete the exercise individually. Then go over the answers as a class.

- Write Ken's questions with past forms of *be* on the board. Have students imagine they are Judy from the email. Have them think of responses to Ken's questions. For example:
  Where were you?   *I was at the movies.*
  Were you out?   *Yes, I was.*

Exercise 2: *Was* and *Were*

- Have students look at the pictures and say the words under the pictures.

- Have students complete the exercise and check their answers in pairs.

- Have pairs continue to work together to write questions for each answer. You may want to model the first one by writing it on the board. For example, write: *Where were Jessica and Tim last night?*

- Have partners take turns asking the questions they wrote and reading their answers.

Exercise 3: Affirmative and Negative

- Have students complete the exercise individually. Then have them check their answers in pairs.

- Have each pair practice the conversation twice so that each partner has the opportunity to practice both speakers' lines.

Exercise 4: Questions and Answers

- Have students complete the exercise. Then discuss the answers as a class.

- Call on pairs to read each conversation.

Exercise 5: Editing

- Go over the example with the class. Ask: "Why is Kathy sorry? What happened?" (*Kathy was at Mark's house but he wasn't there.*) Make sure everyone understands why *wasn't* makes more sense in the sentence than *was*.

- Have students complete the exercise individually. Call on students to write their corrected sentences on the board.

- Have students practice reading the letter in pairs.

Go to **www.myfocusongrammarlab.com** for additional grammar practice.

Step 4: Communication Practice (pages 64–66)

See the general suggestions for Communication Practice on page 5.

Exercise 6: Pronunciation

A

- Read the instructions aloud. Play the first sentence and go over the example with the class.

- Have students listen once and write *A* for affirmative and *N* for negative. Pause as needed. Then play the audio again and have students circle the words they hear.

- Have pairs work together to check their answers. Have them check the letters they wrote (*A* or *N*) and make sure they match the verbs they circled.

- Play the audio again to clarify answers as needed.

B
- Model the activity with a student. Make sure that the person listening to the sentences has his or her book closed.
- Have students complete the exercise. When one person finishes all of the sentences, have students change roles so that both of them have the opportunity to speak and listen to all of the sentences.

Exercise 7: Listening
- Have students look at the picture. Teach the term *answering machine*. Tell students they will listen to an answering machine message. Have students read the statements. Make sure students understand when to check the box for *No information*.
- Play the audio and have students complete the exercise. Play the audio as many times as necessary.
- Have students complete the exercise individually. Then have students form small groups to check their answers. Go over the answers as a class.

Exercise 8: Ask and Answer
- Have students look at the picture of a schedule on the right of page 65. Ask: "What time is morning?" *(6:00 A.M. to 12:00 P.M.)* "What time is afternoon?" *(12:00 P.M. to 6:00 P.M.)* "What time is night?" *(6:00 P.M. to 12:00 A.M.)*
- Model the conversation with a student. Have students choose a word or phrase from the parentheses to complete the questions. Explain that there is no wrong answer; students should choose any word they want.
- Have students do the exercise in pairs and switch roles. Then have them do the exercise again with new partners, but have them make different choices in the questions and answers. For example, if a student asked his first partner *Were you at home yesterday?*, he might ask his new partner *Were you at work last night?*
- Call on a few pairs to perform their conversation for the class.

Exercise 9: Describe an Event
- Have students repeat each of the words in the box as you say them. Model the activity with a student. You take the A part.
- Have students complete the exercise. Then brainstorm a list of questions that they could ask to get more information. For example, in the example conversation, B might ask another question: *Were you with a friend?* or *Was the theater crowded?*

- Have students form new pairs and repeat the activity, but tell them that this time B must ask at least one more question and A must answer it.
- Call on a few pairs to role-play their conversations for the class.

Exercise 10: Writing
- Have students complete the exercise. Have students work in pairs to exchange papers and correct each other's work using the Editing Checklist. Call on pairs to read their papers to the class.

OUT OF THE BOX ACTIVITIES

Listening and Speaking
- Put students in groups and have them each discuss a movie or show they recently saw. Write on the board:
  I saw _____.
  This movie / show was about _____.
  The star was / stars were _____.
  It was awful / pretty bad / OK / pretty good / wonderful.
  The story was _____.
  The acting was _____.
  The special effects were _____.
  The music was _____.
- Review any unfamiliar vocabulary. Then use the sentences to model a review for your students. Use a movie or show you recently saw.
- Give the students a few minutes to think of ideas. Then have them describe their movie or show in small groups. The other students listen and ask follow-up questions. Circulate and provide help and correction as needed.
- Put students in pairs and have them describe a movie or show they heard about.

Go to **www.myfocusongrammarlab.com** for additional listening, pronunciation, speaking, and writing practice.

Note:
- See the *Focus on Grammar Workbook* for additional in-class or homework grammar practice.

Unit 7 Review (page 67)

- Have students complete the Review and check their answers on Student Book page UR-1. Review or assign additional material as needed.

Go to **www.myfocusongrammarlab.com** for the Unit Achievement Test.

UNIT 8 OVERVIEW

Grammar: PAST OF *Be*: *Wh-* QUESTIONS

Unit 8 focuses on the meanings and uses of the past of *be* in *Wh-* questions.

- *Wh-* questions begin with *where, when, what, who, how,* or *how long.* These words ask for information.
- In informal conversation, answers to *Wh-* questions are usually short.
- Use *where* to ask about location. Use *who* to ask about people. Use *how* to ask about a description, and use *how long* to ask about a period of time.

Theme: TRAVEL AND LEISURE ACTIVITIES

Unit 8 focuses on language that is used to talk generally about travel and leisure activities.

Step 1: Grammar in Context (pages 68–69)

See the general suggestions for Grammar in Context on page 1.

Before You Read

- Have groups of students talk about their last vacation. Then call on students to share with the class.

Read

- To encourage students to read with a purpose, write these questions on the board:
  1. Where was Mark's vacation? *(in Spain)*
  2. How long was he there? *(ten days)*
  3. How was the weather? *(hot and sunny; cool at the beach)*
  4. Who was Mark's guide? *(Kathy—Amanda's friend from the wedding)*
  5. What city was Mark in? *(Barcelona)*
- Have students look at the three pictures on page 68. Have them work in small groups to predict answers to the questions on the board. Call on groups to share their predictions. Write them on the board.
- Have students read the conversation. Discuss answers to the questions as a class.

After You Read

A. Practice

- Read the opening conversation aloud and have students repeat. Encourage them to copy your intonation and pronunciation.
- Have students practice the conversation in pairs. Encourage the students to look at each other, not the book, and try to sound like they are having a real conversation.
- Have students change partners and practice the conversation again. Call on pairs to act out parts of the conversation for the class.
- You may find that students have trouble pronouncing *vacation* and *delicious*. Explain that *-tion* is pronounced /shun/ and *–cious* is pronounced /shus/.

B. Vocabulary

- Play the audio and have students repeat each word or phrase. Encourage them to use the pictures to figure out the meaning.
- Have students write new words and their meanings in their notebooks.
- Draw a horizontal line on the board and write the words *hot, warm, cool, cold,* and *freezing* along the line as a continuum. Tell students that there are two antonym pairs among these adjectives and have them guess what they are (*hot / cold; warm / cool*).

C. Vocabulary

- Model the example with a student. Then model the example with another student and substitute different days of the week and weather words. If needed, write the days of the week on the board for reference.
- Have pairs complete the exercise. Then have each pair make a chart of answers about the weather for each day of the previous week.
- Have partners take turns asking and answering *yes / no* questions with *be* about the weather in pairs. For example, *Was it sunny on Tuesday? Was Wednesday cold? Were Saturday and Sunday rainy?*

D. Comprehension

- Go over the example with the class. Have students find the line in the opening conversation on page 68 that gives the correct information. (*How long were you there? Ten days.*)
- Have students complete the exercise individually and then compare answers in pairs or groups of three.

- Discuss the answers as a class by asking questions with the target grammar to elicit the answers. For example, ask: "Was Mark in Spain for seven days? Was the weather sunny and cool? Was it hot at the beach?"

Step 2: Grammar Presentation (page 70)

See the general suggestions for Grammar Presentation on page 3.

Grammar Charts

- Read the *Wh-* questions and answers aloud and have students repeat.
- Write these words on the board: person or people, location, time period, description.
- Have a student read the first question in the chart. Then ask the class what information the question is asking for. Elicit one of the words on the board *(location)*.
- Continue the activity for each of the questions in the first chart.
- Have a student read the question in the second chart. Then have two other students read the long answer and the short answer.
- Point out that there are two possible short answers for questions such as these. We can answer with a subject and the verb as in *Mark was*. We can also answer with the subject only: *Mark*. Explain that short answers are very common in spoken English and that each one is equally acceptable.

Grammar Notes

Note 1

- Do a simple chain drill. Have students form a circle. Have them ask the next person about his or her weekend. That person gives short answers. Encourage them to use a variety of short answers. For example:
  S1: How was your weekend?
  S2: Great!

  S2: How was your weekend?
  S3: Interesting.

Notes 2–5

- Read each note and have students repeat the example questions and answers.
- Make three columns on the board with these headings: *Question Words, Was/Were,* and *Person, Place, or Thing.*
- Elicit from students the various question words from Notes 1–5 and write them in the *Question Words* column.

- Elicit from students the two past forms of *be: was* and *were*. Write those in the second column.
- Have the class brainstorm a list of people, places, or things they could ask about and write those in the third column. For example:

Question Words	*Was / Were*	Person, Place, or Thing
Who Where How When How long	was were	your vacation your mother your roommate the test the books the game the concert the dance the weather

- Have students work in pairs, small groups, or as a class to ask and answer as many different questions as they can using the chart on the board. Circulate and make corrections as needed.
- For variation, do this as a written activity for pairs. Have each pair write ten to twelve questions. Then have them exchange questions with another pair and write answers for the questions. Call on students to share some of their questions and answers with the class.

Note 6

- Read the note and the example statements.
- Ask a student, "How was the weather yesterday?" and elicit an answer with *it*. For example: *It was rainy.* Have students ask and answer similar questions in pairs.

⏱ **Identify the Grammar**: Have students identify the grammar in the opening conversation on page 68. For example:
  How was your vacation?
  Where were you?
  How long were you there?
  How was the weather?

Go to **www.myfocusongrammarlab.com** for grammar charts and notes.

Step 3: Focused Practice (pages 71–73)

See the general suggestions for Focused Practice on page 4.

Exercise 1: Discover the Grammar
- Have students complete the exercise. Then have them work in pairs to check their answers.
- Go over the answers as a class and clarify any questions.
- Have students ask and answer the questions in pairs.

Exercise 2: Word Order
- Have students complete the exercise individually. Then have them work in pairs to practice the conversations they created.
- For additional challenge, have students work in pairs to complete the exercise orally rather than in writing.

Exercise 3: Past *Wh-* Questions
- Go over the example with the class. Make sure students know to write questions about the underlined words.
- Have students complete the exercise. Go over the answers as a class.
- Have pairs practice asking and answering the questions two times. First, have them read the answers provided in the exercise. Then have them practice the questions with a variation of the answer provided. For example:
  S1: How was the weather?
  S2: Sunny.

  S2: Who was at the movies?
  S1: Mark.

Exercise 4: Past *Wh-* Questions
- Have students complete the exercise and work in pairs to practice the conversation. Have each pair practice two times so that each student can practice asking and answering the questions.
- Call on pairs to perform their conversations for the class.

Exercise 5: Editing
- Go over the example with the class. Make sure students understand that *was* is the correct word for the question.
- Have students complete the exercise individually. Call on students to write their corrected sentences on the board. Go over the answers as a class.
- Have students practice the conversations in pairs.

Go to **www.myfocusongrammarlab.com** for additional grammar practice.

Step 4: Communication Practice (pages 73–75)
See the general suggestions for Communication Practice on page 5.

Exercise 6: Listening
A
- Explain that Mark is asking Jason about his weekend. Pre-teach *weekend* and *beach*.
- Have students read the questions. Explain any unfamiliar vocabulary.
- Play the audio and have students complete the exercise. Go over the answers as a class.

B
- Play the audio again, pausing as needed, and have students complete the exercise. Go over the answers as a class.
- ⏱ Play the audio again as a dictation. Pause as needed so that students have time to write. Call on students to write their sentences on the board and ask the other students if they think each sentence is correct. Have anyone with a different answer write it on the board. Then play the audio again and have the class choose the correct version.

Exercise 7: Pronunciation
A
- Have students read the items and put a checkmark next to the question words they think will sound like /w/.
- Play the audio and have students complete the exercise. Have them check their predictions against their answers. Then have them work in pairs to check their answers.
- As a variation, you can do this as a whole group activity. Have the class decide which question words they think will begin with the /w/ sound. Have them complete the activity and check their answers against the class's predictions.

B
- Have students complete the exercise individually.
- Have them work in pairs to take turns asking and answering the questions.

Exercise 8: Clarification
- Model this exercise with a student. Then have students complete the exercise individually.
- Have students work in pairs to create five to eight new sentences. Have them practice their conversations, using the example as a model. Then have pairs exchange papers and practice another pair's conversation.
- Call on pairs to role-play their conversations for the class.

Exercise 9: Who Was Really There?

A

- Model the activity. Say: "I was in _____" and find two students who were not there. Have the two students come to the front of the class. Elicit questions from the class about the place. Answer the questions and have the other two students answer them. When the other two students can't answer a question, point out that we can now tell who really was at the place.
- Put students in groups of three and have them choose a place.

B

- Call a group to the front of the class. Have the students each say: "I was in _____."

C

- Have the class ask questions to discover who was really there. Repeat for the other groups.
- For variation, give each student a photo from a travel brochure or a magazine. Have each student come to the front of the class and display the photo. Have other students in the class ask five to six questions of the student at the front. Encourage students to come up with as many different questions as they can. For example:
  S1: Where were you?
  S2: In Belize.
  S3: Who were you with?
  S2: My family.
  S4: When were you there?
  S2: Last year.
  S5: How long were you there?
  S2: Nine days.
  S6: How was the food?
  S2: It was interesting.

Exercise 10: Writing

A

- Review the vocabulary words in the box on page 69.
- Have students complete the exercise. As students write, have them underline any words they used from the box.

B

- Have students correct their work using the Editing Checklist. Then have them exchange papers and check each other's work. Encourage students to make corrections as needed.

C

- Have students practice reading and asking questions in pairs. Then call on students to read their papers to the class.

- Encourage the other students to ask as many different questions as they can.

OUT OF THE BOX ACTIVITIES

Reading, Speaking, Listening, and Writing

- Write or photocopy information about the weather in major cities around the world. Include the weather for today and yesterday. You can find this information on the Internet. Make one card for each student in the class. If you have a large class, have students work in pairs or groups.
- Distribute the cards. Have students work in pairs or groups to describe the weather in the cities you gave them.
- Then have students take turns describing yesterday and today's weather to the class. If they are working in pairs or small groups, make sure each person speaks.
- As the rest of the students listen, have them take notes in the chart.
- Have each student pick a city to write about. Have them write five to six sentences about that city. For example:
  My city is Cairo. Today it is hot and windy. It is very sunny. Yesterday it was hot, but it was cloudy. It isn't rainy or very cold in Cairo.

Writing, Reading, Listening, and Speaking

- Have each student write a riddle about a place they have lived or visited.
- Have students work in groups to take turns reading their riddles and asking questions to guess the name of the place. For example:
  I was in this city in Canada last year. It was sunny in the daytime, but it wasn't hot. At night it was cold. I was with my parents. We were in a beautiful park. We were near the mountains and near the Pacific Ocean. The Chinese food was wonderful. The skiing was great. Where was I? (Vancouver)

Go to **www.myfocusongrammarlab.com** for additional listening, pronunciation, speaking, and writing practice.

Note:
- See the *Focus on Grammar Workbook* for additional in-class or homework grammar practice.

Unit 8 Review (page 76)

- Have students complete the Review and check their answers on Student Book page UR-1. Review or assign additional material as needed.

Go to **www.myfocusongrammarlab.com** for the Unit Achievement Test.

From Grammar to Writing (page FG-2)

See the general suggestions for From Grammar to Writing on page 9.

Go to **www.myfocusongrammarlab.com** for an additional From Grammar to Writing Assignment, Part Review, and Part Post-Test.

UNIT 9 OVERVIEW

Grammar: IMPERATIVES

Unit 9 focuses on the meanings and uses of affirmative and negative imperatives.

- To form imperatives, use the base form of the verb.
- For negative imperatives, use *do* + *not* + the base form of the verb.
- Imperatives are used to give directions and instructions or to make requests.

Theme: GIVING DIRECTIONS

Unit 9 focuses on language that is used for giving and following simple directions and instructions.

Step 1: Grammar in Context (pages 78–80)

See the general suggestions for Grammar in Context on page 1.

Before You Read

- Have students discuss their answers in pairs. Call on pairs to share the names of restaurants with the class.
- Make a simple map grid on the board with the names of streets nearby. Have each pair mark the location of the restaurant on the map.

Read

- To encourage students to read with a purpose, write on the board:
  1. Where are Mark and Steve? *(in the car on the way to a restaurant)*
  2. Who is hungry? *(Mark)*
  3. Is the restaurant Chinese? *(No, it's not. It's Italian.)*
  3. Where is the restaurant? *(on Third Avenue)*
  4. Is the restaurant full of people? *(No, it's not. It's empty because it's closed.)*
- Play the audio and have students follow along in their books.
- Have students discuss the questions in pairs or groups of three. Call on pairs or groups to share answers with the class.

After You Read

A. Practice

- Point out the two footnotes in the conversation. Explain that both expressions are common in spoken and informal written language but would not usually be used in formal written text. Since this text is a conversation, these expressions are quite natural.

- Read the conversation aloud and have students repeat. Have students practice the opening conversation in pairs. Call on pairs to read the conversation for the class.

B. Vocabulary
- Play the audio and have students repeat each word or phrase. Encourage them to use the pictures to figure out the meaning.
- Have students write new words and their meanings in their notebooks and compare with a partner.
- Ask students which word is the opposite of *packed (empty)*. Have students identify the verbs *(turn, walk, drive, park)*.

C. Vocabulary
- Write on the board:
  A: Is a _____ sign near our school?
  B: Yes, it's on _____ Street.
  Yes, it's on the corner of _____ and _____.
  Yes, it's near / across from / next to _____.
  No, I don't think so.
- Model the conversation on the board with a student. Use the signs in the exercise. Elicit other ways of answering the question and write them on the board.
- Have students read the words in the signs aloud. Explain any unfamiliar words. Then have students complete the exercise in pairs. Call on pairs to share their answers with the class.
- Establish a reasonable time limit and send students out of the building in pairs to look for the signs they discussed and any others they notice near the building. Have them keep track of what they find. When students return, have them share what they found. Talk about the meaning of other signs the students found.

D. Comprehension
- Read the instructions. Remind the students that the opening conversation is on page 78.
- Have pairs complete the exercise. Then have them compare their route with another pair.
- Have one pair of students draw their map on the board.

Go to **www.myfocusongrammarlab.com** for an additional reading, and for reading and vocabulary practice.

Step 2: Grammar Presentation (page 80)
See the general suggestions for Grammar Presentation on page 3.

Grammar Charts
- Have students read the examples in the chart. Ask them which words in the chart are imperatives *(turn, don't turn, park, don't park)*.
- Ask: "How are affirmative and negative imperatives different?" *(In the affirmative imperative the verb word is first. In the negative imperative* don't *comes before the verb word.)*
- Write the contractions *isn't, aren't, wasn't,* and *weren't* on the board. Ask students what two words each represents *(is not, are not, was not, were not)*. Ask students what two words the contraction *don't* represents *(do not)*.
- Point out that in imperatives, the understood subject is always *you*, and that it can be *you* singular or *you* plural.

Grammar Notes

Note 1
- Read the explanation aloud. Read the example sentences and have students repeat.
- Ask: "Which sentence is for directions?" *(Turn left.)* "Which is for instructions?" *(Answer the questions.)* "Which is for requests?" *(Please hand me my jacket.)* Elicit other examples of directions, instructions, and requests. Write them on the board.

Notes 2–3
- Read the explanations aloud. Read the example sentences aloud and have students repeat.
- Have students change the affirmative imperative to a negative. *(Do not open the door.)* Then have them use the contracted form. *(Don't open the door.)* Say other affirmative imperatives and have students make negative imperatives with and without contractions.
- Have students practice the same drill in pairs.

Note 4
- Point out that you can use *please* with any of the three types of imperatives to be more polite. Read the example sentences aloud and have students repeat. Encourage them to copy your intonation and tone of voice. Repeat with other affirmative and negative imperatives with *please*.

🕐 **Identify the Grammar**: Have students identify the grammar in the opening conversation on page 78. For example:
  Don't worry.
  Now **drive** to the corner and **turn** left at Jackson.

Go to **www.myfocusongrammarlab.com** for grammar charts and notes.

Step 3: Focused Practice (pages 81–83)

See the general suggestions for Focused Practice on page 4.

Exercise 1: Discover the Grammar

- Have students complete the exercise. Then have them compare their answers in small groups. Review the correct answers as a class.
- Have students work in pairs to sort the items into two groups: imperative forms (both affirmative and negative) and those that are not imperatives. Call on pairs to share their answers with the class.

Exercise 2: Directions

- Have students complete the exercise and work in pairs to check their answers.
- Have each pair think of other common signs and draw them. For example, a stop sign or a *No Smoking* sign. Have each show their signs to another pair. The other pair says what the sign means, using imperatives. Circulate and help with vocabulary as needed.

Exercise 3: Commands and Requests

- Have students complete the exercise individually. Then have them check their answers in pairs.
- Have each pair practice saying the sentences to each other.

Exercise 4: Responding to Imperatives

A
- Read the instructions aloud and have students repeat.
- Explain any unfamiliar vocabulary, such as *underline, circle, change,* or *line.* Have students complete the exercise.

B
- Read the instructions aloud and have students repeat.
- Have students complete the exercise. While students are working, copy the original sentences and lines for Parts A and B on the board.
- Call on students to show their answers on the board. Discuss the answers as a class.

Exercise 5: Editing

- Go over the example with the class. Ask: "How do we form a negative imperative?" (do + not + *base form of verb*) Make sure students understand why the original sentence is incorrect.

- Have students complete the exercise. Then call on students to write their corrected sentences on the board.

Go to **www.myfocusongrammarlab.com** for additional grammar practice.

Step 4: Communication Practice (pages 83–85)

See the general suggestions for Communication Practice on page 5.

Exercise 6: Listening

A
- Explain that students will hear a woman asking for directions to two places in a school. Have students suggest places the woman might be looking for, such as *library, office, computer lab, classroom.* Write their ideas on the board.
- Have students complete the exercise and discuss the answer as a class.

B
- As you play the audio, pause as needed so students have time to write.
- Call on students to write each sentence on the board. Discuss the answers as a class.
- Have students work in pairs and write simple directions to the locations listed on the board in Part A. Have them use the directions in the activity as a model and describe how you actually get from the classroom to these places in the school. Call on pairs to read their directions aloud and have the class guess the location.

Exercise 7: Pronunciation

A
- Have students read the statements silently. Then play the audio and have students repeat the words and statements.
- ⏱ Use the words and statements for a dictation. Randomly say the words and example sentences from each set. Have students write the word they hear and check their answers in pairs. As a variation, students can do a dictation in pairs.

B
- Read the instructions and the column headings aloud. Have students repeat.
- Play the audio and have students complete the exercise. Go over the answers as a class. If needed, play the audio again and have students repeat. Point out the differences in pronunciation.

Exercise 8: Make Requests

- Read the instructions. Have students repeat each of the verbs in the box on page 84 as you say them. Model the exercise with three students.
- Have students do the exercise. Circulate and help as needed.

Exercise 9: Directions

A

- Have students cover the directions below the map with a piece of paper. Have students look at the map. Have them point to the place marked *You Are Here*. Ask: "Where is this?" *(the corner of Union Street and Third Avenue)* Have them point to the three parks on the map. Ask: "Where are they?" *(Regrade Park: the corner of Blanchard Street and Third Avenue; Victor Steinbrueck Park: Western Avenue and Stewart Street; Westlake Park: Pike Street and Fourth Avenue)*
- Explain that students will work in pairs. One partner will read the directions below the map. The other will listen and say which park the directions lead to.
- Have students continue the exercise in pairs and give directions from *You Are Here* to other parks. Circulate and give help as needed.

B

- Have students change partners and continue to practice giving directions. Point out that the starting and ending places can be any intersection on the map.

Exercise 10: Writing

- As an alternative or for students who are not familiar with the area, draw a simple map of the area and mark the locations of several places in the area: restaurants, the library, the bus station, the theater, a grocery store, etc. Be sure to clearly mark the location of your class on the map.
- Have students work in pairs. One student chooses a place from the map but does not tell his or her partner. He or she writes directions and reads them to the other student. That person must find the building or place on the map.

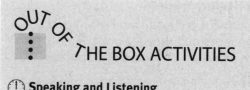

OUT OF THE BOX ACTIVITIES

Speaking and Listening

- Play a version of the popular game *Simon Says*. In this game, a speaker gives a command, sometimes preceded by the words *Simon Says*. For example, if the speaker says "Simon says sit down," the listeners must sit down. However, if the speaker just says "Sit down," the listeners should do nothing. Listeners are out if they perform an incorrect action or follow the command even though the speaker does not precede it with "Simon says."
- Brainstorm a list of commands that the students have learned in the unit or that the students already know. Write these on the board. Have students take turns giving two or three commands each.

Reading, Listening, and Speaking

- Choose a place in the area that would be fun for students to visit or see. You may want to choose a museum, restaurant, coffee shop, park, etc. Don't tell the students what it is.
- Have students work in pairs or small groups. Give each pair or group a different set of directions to the same location. Be sure to choose a place that they can walk to in a short amount of time. Make sure you have a cell phone number for at least one person in each group.
- Have students follow the directions. Each person should take a turn reading part of the directions to the others in the group. Give them a time limit to reach the location.
- Once all the groups have reached the destination, do something together. Take a tour of the museum or have a cup of coffee, a snack, or a picnic. Have groups exchange directions with another group, and use the new one to return to the location of the class.

Go to **www.myfocusongrammarlab.com** for additional listening, pronunciation, speaking, and writing practice.

Note:
- See the *Focus on Grammar Workbook* for additional in-class or homework grammar practice.

Unit 9 Review (page 86)

Have students complete the Review and check their answers on Student Book page UR-1. Review or assign additional material as needed.

Go to **www.myfocusongrammarlab.com** for the Unit Achievement Test.

Go to **www.myfocusongrammarlab.com** for the Unit Achievement Test.

UNIT 10 OVERVIEW

Grammar: SIMPLE PRESENT: STATEMENTS

Unit 10 focuses on the meanings and uses of affirmative and negative simple present statements.

- Use the simple present to talk about facts or things that happen again and again.
- In affirmative statements, use the base form of the verb with *I, you, we,* and *they*.
- With third-person singular subjects, add *-s* or *-es* to the base form of the verb.
- To form negative statements, use *do not or does not* + the base form of the verb.
- We often use the contractions *don't* and *doesn't* in speaking and informal writing.
- *Be* and *have* are irregular verbs. *Be* has three forms in the present: *am, is,* and *are. Have* has two forms: *have* and *has*.

Theme: LIKES AND DISLIKES

Unit 10 focuses on language that is used to to give personal information and talk about personal likes and dislikes.

Step 1: Grammar in Context (pages 87–88)

See the general suggestions for Grammar in Context on page 1.

Before You Read

- Read the words and phrases in the box aloud and have students repeat.
- Have students put a checkmark next to the things they like and an *x* next to things they don't like.
- Go over the example with the class. Have the students work in pairs to compare their likes and dislikes.

Read

- To encourage students to read with a purpose, write on the board:
  1. Who has more coffee? *(Judy and Mark)*

  2. Who has new photos? *(Mark)*
  3. Who lives in Kenya? *(Nick / Mark's brother)*
  4. Who speaks Chinese? *(Mark)*
  5. Who speaks Swahili? *(Nick)*
- Have students look at the three pictures and the names of the speakers in the conversation on page 87. Ask them who and where they think the people in the pictures are. Write their guesses on the board.
- Have students read silently as you play the audio. Then have the class discuss answers to the questions.

After You Read

A. Practice

- Have students practice both roles in the conversation in pairs. Circulate and help as needed.
- You may find that students are confused by the different pronunciations of the verb endings: *likes*, in which the *s* sounds like an *s; lives,* in which the *s* sounds like a *z; teaches,* in which the *-es* is pronounced as a separate syllable—*/iz/*; and *goes,* in which the *es* sounds like *z* and is not pronounced as a separate syllable.
- Have students practice the conversation as a choral reading. Divide the class into two groups. Have one group read Judy's part and the other Mark's.

B. Vocabulary

- Play the audio and have students repeat each word or phrase. Encourage them to use the pictures to figure out the meaning. Have students write new words and their meanings in their notebooks.
- You may want to point out the difference between *like* (enjoy something), *look like* (have a similar appearance), and *be like* (have similar personality or habits).

C. Vocabulary

- Have students repeat the names of the languages in the box on page 88 after you say them. Go over the example with the class.
- Have students complete the activity in pairs. Call on pairs to share answers with the class. Write their answers on the board.

D. Comprehension

- Have students complete the exercise individually and then compare answers in pairs or groups of three.
- For each question, have students point to the line in the conversation that gives the answer.

Go to **www.myfocusongrammarlab.com** for an additional reading, and for reading and vocabulary practice.

Step 2: Grammar Presentation (page 89)

See the general suggestions for Grammar Presentation on page 3.

Grammar Charts

- To explain affirmative simple present statements, write on the board:
  I need more coffee.
  He lives in Kenya.
  We both have brown hair and green eyes.
  Nick likes computers.
- Point to each sentence and ask: "What is the subject?" Elicit the answers and circle the subjects on the board. Ask: "Which verbs end in -s?" (lives, likes) "What subjects come before them?" (He, Nick)
- To explain negative simple present statements, write on the board:
  I don't (do not) like computers.
  Nick doesn't (does not) like parties.
- Ask: "How do we form negative statements in the simple present?" (Use do + not or does + not and the base form of the verb.) Ask: "When do we use don't or do not?" (with I, you, we, and they) "When do we use doesn't or does not?" (with he, she, it)

Grammar Notes

Notes 1–2

- Give additional examples from your life and write the verb words on the board. Include facts and things that happen habitually. For example:

Say:	Write:
I live with my husband.	live
I work ten hours every day.	work
I come from Illinois.	come
It's in the Midwest.	is
I drive an old car.	drive
I walk fifteen miles every week.	walk

- Point to one of the verbs and have students make true sentences about themselves.
- Say a verb and a pronoun. Have students respond with the correct form of the verb. For example:

T: work, you	S: you work
T: work, she	S: she works
T: read, we	S: we read
T: Nick, live	S: Nick lives

Note 3

- Read the example sentences aloud and have students repeat.

- Say a verb and a name or pronoun. Have students respond with the correct negative form of the verb.
- Have students work in groups to write three true negative sentences about themselves. Call on groups to write their sentences on the board. Correct any mistakes with the simple present.

Note 4

- Review with students what they learned in Units 3 and 5 about form and use of be in the present. Say: "Name the three forms of be." (am, is, are) Ask students how we make a simple present negative statement with be. (use am, is, or are + not)
- Point out that have is like be because it is an irregular verb. Its two forms in the present are has and have. Ask students how we make a simple present negative statement with have. (use does + not + have or do + not + have)

⏱ **Identify the Grammar**: Have students identify the grammar in the opening conversation on page 87. For example:
  I **need** more coffee.
  He **lives** in Kenya.
  He **teaches** English there.
  He **looks** like you.

Go to **www.myfocusongrammarlab.com** for grammar charts and notes.

Step 3: Focused Practice (pages 90–93)

See the general suggestions for Focused Practice on page 4.

Exercise 1: Discover the Grammar

A

- Go over the example with the class. Point out that the first sentence is an imperative, not simple present.
- Have students complete the exercise. Go over the answers as a class.
- Have students work in pairs to change the affirmative simple present statements to negative and the negatives ones to affirmative. Call on pairs to write their sentences on the board. Discuss the sentences and clarify any questions.

B

- Read the instructions. Have students give examples of pronouns or names that are third-person singular. For example: *Maria, she, Tom, it, my car*. Go over the examples with the class.

- Have students complete the exercise. Then have them work in pairs to check their answers.
- Have students work in pairs to change the sentences they didn't check to third-person singular subjects. For example, for the first sentence, *Annie and I don't like fish*, students can write: *Tom doesn't like fish.*
- Have students compare answers with another pair. Call on pairs to write their answers on the board.

Exercise 2: Third Person
- Have students complete the exercise individually. Go over the answers as a class.
- Brainstorm a list of verbs with the class and write them on the board. Have students use verbs from the list to write one more sentence about each of the people. Then have them share their new sentences in small groups. For example: *Heng lives in Beijing, China. He speaks Chinese. He drives a car to work.*

Exercise 3: *Want*
- Read the instructions. Point out that students should use a negative form when the word *not* is beneath the blank, as in item 3.
- Have students complete the exercise. Go over the answers as a class.
- Have students practice the conversation in groups of four. Students should repeat until everyone has practiced each character's lines.

Exercise 4: Affirmative and Negative
- Have students look at the pictures. Then have students complete the exercise. Go over the answers as a class.
- Divide the class into small groups. Have each group choose a picture and write three or four more sentences about the person. For example: *Jeremy has an old car. He doesn't have a new car. He wants a new car. Jeremy works in an ice cream store. He doesn't have money for a new car now.*
- Call on groups to share their sentences with the class.

Exercise 5: Editing
- Go over the example with the class. Have students complete the exercise individually.
- Call on students to write their corrected sentences on the board.

Go to **www.myfocusongrammarlab.com** for additional grammar practice.

Step 4: Communication Practice (pages 93–95)
See the general suggestions for Communication Practice on page 5.

Exercise 6: Listening
A
- Read the instructions aloud. Ask: "How many people are in the conversation?" *(two—Tim Olson and a man)* "Where are the people?" *(on a train)* Have students read the questions as a class.
- Have students close their books. Play the audio. Then have students open their books. Play the audio again and have students answer the questions.
- Have students work in pairs to check their answers. Call on pairs to share their answers with the class. Replay the audio to clarify, if needed.

B
- Have students look at the question in Part B. Then play the audio again and have students complete the exercise individually. Go over the answer as a class.
- Give students copies of the audioscript and have them practice the conversation in pairs.

Exercise 7: Pronunciation
A
- Play the Pronunciation Note and have students follow along in their books.
- You may want to take time here to go over Appendix 5 on page A-4.

B
- Read the instructions. Ask students what information they will be listening for. *(the pronunciation of the verb ending)*
- Play the audio and have students complete the exercise. You may need to play the audio again so that they can get all of the answers.
- Have students work in pairs to check their answers. Call on pairs to share their answers.

C
- Play the audio again and have students repeat. Pause as needed.
- For additional practice, create a chart on the board like the one in Part B. Elicit verbs from the students. Say each verb in third-person singular form and have students say where it goes in the chart. Then say the verbs again and have students repeat.

Exercise 8: True or False?
- Read the instructions and model the example with a student.

- Have students complete the exercise in pairs. Have them compare answers with another pair. Then have them look at page 153 for the correct answers.
- Have students write four more statements in small groups—two that are true and two that are false. Have groups exchange papers, mark each statement as true or false, and correct the false statements.
- Call on groups to share a few of their statements with the class. Then have the class decide whether the statements are true or false.

Exercise 9: Writing

A

- Read the instructions. Elicit some ways to complete the first few sentences and write them on the board. Then have students complete the exercise individually.

B

- Put students in pairs and read the instructions. Point out that students need to listen carefully to their partner's sentences and take notes about him or her.

C

- Have students complete the task individually. Then have them check their work in pairs.
- Call on pairs to read the sentences they wrote about their partners without saying the person's name. Have the class guess the person.

D

- Have students check their work in pairs.

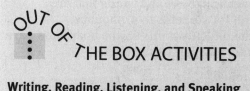

OUT OF THE BOX ACTIVITIES

Writing, Reading, Listening, and Speaking

- Explain the difference between wants and needs. Point out that sometimes it is difficult to decide between what they really need and what they want.
- Have each student complete this chart:

I really need	I really want
1.	1.
2.	2.
3.	3.
4.	4.

- Have students share their answers in small groups. Encourage them to challenge each other. Model this with a student. For example:
  S1: I really need a car.
  S2: You don't need a car. You can walk.
  S3: You don't need a car. You can take the bus.

Listening and Speaking

- Have students play a modified version of the card game *Go Fish*. The object of the game is for a player to get two cards of the same value—for example, two 2s, two aces, two queens, etc.
- Teach the names of the aces and face cards: king, queen, jack. Have students work in groups of three or four. The dealer shuffles the cards and gives each player five cards. The rest go face down in the center of the table.
- Students take turns asking each other for cards. For example:
  S1: Mai, I need queens.
  If the student asked has the card, he or she gives it to the student making the request. Each time students have two of the same kind, they put them face up on the table next to them. If the student asked doesn't have the card, he or she says, "I don't have queens. Go fish." The student asking takes a card from the facedown pile in the center of the table. If he or she gets the card asked for, the pair of cards is placed face up next to the student, and he or she gets another turn. If not, the next student gets a turn to ask.
- When all of the cards in the facedown pile are gone, students continue to ask each other for cards. The person with the most pairs when no one has cards left wins the game.

Go to **www.myfocusongrammarlab.com** for additional listening, pronunciation, speaking, and writing practice.

Note:
- See the *Focus on Grammar Workbook* for additional in-class or homework grammar practice.

Unit 10 Review (page 96)

Have students complete the Review and check their answers on Student Book page UR-1. Review or assign additional material as needed.

Go to **www.myfocusongrammarlab.com** for the Unit Achievement Test.

From Grammar to Writing (page FG-3)

See the general suggestions for From Grammar to Writing on page 9.

Go to **www.myfocusongrammarlab.com** for an additional From Grammar to Writing Assignment, Part Review, and Part Post-Test.

PART V OVERVIEW

SIMPLE PRESENT: QUESTIONS, *Be* AND *Have*; ADVERBS OF FREQUENCY

UNIT	GRAMMAR FOCUS	THEME
11	Simple Present: *Yes / No* Questions	Shopping for Electronics
12	Simple Present: *Wh-* Questions	Cross-Cultural Differences
13	Simple Present: *Be* and *Have*	Describing People
14	Simple Present with Adverbs of Frequency	Habits

Go to **www.myfocusongrammarlab.com** for the Part and Unit Tests.

Note: PowerPoint® grammar presentations, test-generating software, and reproducible Part and Unit Tests are on the *Teacher's Resource Disc*.

UNIT 11 OVERVIEW

Grammar: SIMPLE PRESENT: *Yes / No* QUESTIONS

Unit 11 focuses on the meanings and uses of *yes / no* questions in the simple present.

- Use *do* or *does* + a subject + the base form of the verb to ask *yes / no* questions.
- In speaking we often use short answers to *yes / no* questions.

Theme: SHOPPING FOR ELECTRONICS

Unit 11 focuses on language that is used when talking about, and shopping for, electronic devices.

Step 1: Grammar in Context (pages 98–99)

See the general suggestions for Grammar in Context on page 1.

Before You Read
- Have students complete the exercise in pairs. Then have them share their answers with the class.
- Have a student record students' responses on the board. For example:

Device	Has		Wants	
	Yes	No	Yes	No
TV	√√√	√		√
GPS	√	√√√	√√	√

Read
- To encourage students to read with a purpose, write on the board:
  1. Who doesn't have a flat screen TV? *(Steve)* Why? *(His old TV works very well. He doesn't need a flat screen.)*
  2. Who has a smart phone? *(Josh and Amanda)*
  3. Where is the sale? *(at Goodbuys)*
  4. Who has a broken radio? *(Steve)*
- Play the audio and have students follow along in their books.
- Have students discuss the questions in pairs or groups of three. Call on students to share answers with the class.

After You Read

A. Practice
- Circulate as students practice the conversation. Note any words that are difficult for students to pronounce.
- List the difficult words on the board and have students practice saying them.

B. Vocabulary
- Play the audio and have students repeat each word. Encourage them to use the pictures to figure out the meanings.
- Have students write new words and their meanings in their notebooks.
- Have students work in pairs and take turns asking and answering simple questions about the vocabulary. Model the practice with a student. For example:
  S1: (points to picture of a computer) What is this?
  S2: That's a computer.
  S2: (points to picture of GPS) Is this a smart phone?
  S1: No, it's not. It's a GPS.

- For variety, you can do this as a whole-group activity. Call on students to bring their books to the front of the class, point to a picture, and ask a student in the class a question about that picture. The person who answers is the next one to ask a question.

C. Vocabulary
- Read the example aloud and have students repeat. Have students brainstorm electronics stores they know, their locations, and the items they sell.
- Have students complete the exercise in pairs. Then have them form new pairs. Have students take turns talking about an electronics store in their home city or country.

D. Comprehension
- Have students complete the exercise individually and check their answers in pairs.
- Call on pairs to share answers with the class. Have students find the lines in the conversation that give the answer. Some of the answers, such as for Questions 3 and 6, require making an inference. You may want to point out that this is a higher level thinking skill that requires "reading between the lines"—figuring out answers based on a combination of what they already know and information in the text.

Go to **www.myfocusongrammarlab.com** for an additional reading, and for reading and vocabulary practice.

Step 2: Grammar Presentation (page 100)
See the general suggestions for Grammar Presentation on page 3.

Grammar Charts
- Write on the board:
  You want a flat screen TV.
  Ask students whether this is a question or a statement. (statement)
- Call on a student to make the statement into a yes / no question. (Do you want a flat screen TV?) Write the question on the board. Point out that this question was formed by putting do before the subject.
- Then write on the board:
  Steve wants a flat screen TV.
  Have students change the statement to a question. (Does Steve want a flat screen TV?) Point out that this question is formed differently, by using Does + Steve + the base form of want.

- Elicit from students the rules about placement and use of do and does in yes / no questions. Then have them look at the first column of the grammar charts on page 100 to see if their rule is correct. Read the questions and answers aloud and have students repeat.

Grammar Notes
Note 1
- Do an oral drill with the class to practice use of do / does in questions. For example:

T: I	S: Do I . . . ?
T: she	S: Does she . . . ?
T: you	S: Do you . . . ?

- Expand the drill by adding verbs and eliciting complete questions. For example:

T: I speak Spanish.	S: Do I speak Spanish?
T: He knows a good doctor.	S: Does he know a good doctor?

Note 2
- Create a chart like the following, either on the board or as a handout:

know	doctor	GPS
have	hair cutter	flat screen TV
need	appointment	DVD player
want	phone number	smart phone
like	dentist	service department
speak	another language	manager
_____ (your idea)	computer	_____ (your idea)

- Have students work in groups of three or four to take turns asking and answering yes / no questions using the cues in the chart. Have them use different subjects in the questions. For example:

S1: Do you know a good doctor?	S3: Does Marisol know a good doctor?
S2: No, I don't.	S4: No, she doesn't.

⏱ **Identify the Grammar**: Have students identify the grammar in the opening conversation on page 98. For example:
  Do you **need** a new one?
  Do you **want** a flat screen TV?
  Does she **need** anything?
  Do Tim, Jeremy, or Ben **want** anything?

Go to **www.myfocusongrammarlab.com** for grammar charts and notes.

Step 3: Focused Practice (pages 101–103)

See the general suggestions for Focused Practice on page 4.

Exercise 1: Discover the Grammar
- Read the instructions. Then go over the example with the class. Have students underline the *yes / no* questions individually and check their answers. Go over the answers as a class.
- Have students complete the rest of the exercise individually and work in pairs to check their answers.
- Have pairs practice the questions and answers. Call on pairs to read a question and answer for the class.

Exercise 2: *Do* or *Does*
- Have students read the words in the box. Explain any unfamiliar vocabulary, such as *cost* or *mean*. Have students complete the exercise individually and go over the answers as a class.
- Have students work in pairs to rewrite each conversation with the opposite answer followed by new information. For example:
  A: Do you know a good electronics store?
  B: No, I don't. I'm sorry. I get all my electronics on the Internet.

  A: Does that smart phone cost a lot?
  B: Yes, it does. It's very expensive. It costs $500.
- Have students practice the new conversations. Then have them exchange their conversations with another pair and practice the new conversations.

Exercise 3: *Yes / No* Questions
- Go over the example with the class. Have students complete the exercise individually. Then call on students to write their answers on the board. Go over the answers as a class and make corrections as needed.
- Have students ask the questions to various students in the class. Students should give true answers and use short answers.

Exercise 4: *Yes / No* Questions
- Read the note aloud as students listen and follow along. Explain any unfamiliar vocabulary.
- Have students complete the exercise individually and check their answers in pairs.

- For additional practice with questions and answers, have students form a circle. Have the first student read the first question and call on another student to answer it. The person who answers asks the next question to another student.

Exercise 5: Editing
- Go over the example with the class. Ask: "Do *yes / no* questions use the base form of the verb?" *(yes)* Make sure students understand that *know* is the correct word for the question.
- Have students complete the exercise individually. Call on students to write one sentence from the conversation on the board. Go over the sentences as a class.
- Have students practice the conversation two times in pairs, changing roles after the first time.

Go to **www.myfocusongrammarlab.com** for additional grammar practice.

Step 4: Communication Practice
(pages 104–105)

See the general suggestions for Communication Practice on page 5.

Exercise 6: Listening

A
- Read the instructions. Ask: "Who is talking on the audio?" *(Mark and Judy)* Have students read the question and the answer choices. Then play the audio. Have students complete the exercise. Then go over the answer as a class.

B
- Have students read the questions and answer choices. Explain any unfamiliar vocabulary. Then play the audio again and have students complete the exercise individually. Have students check answers in pairs. Go over the answers as a class.
- Play the audio again as a dictation. Pause as needed so that students have time to write. Call on students to write each of the sentences on the board. Discuss the sentences. Play the audio again to resolve any conflicting answers among students.
- Have students practice the conversation in pairs.

Exercise 7: Pronunciation

A
- Play the audio. Have students listen and repeat.

B

- Play the audio. Have students listen and complete the exercise. Then go over the answer as a class. Have students identify the words they underlined as verbs or nouns.

C

- Play the audio again and have students repeat.
- (!) Have students write six new questions in pairs, using the questions from the exercise as a model. Encourage them to use the vocabulary from this unit or preceding units. Then have pairs exchange questions. Student A reads the first question and Student B underlines the important words. Student B reads the second question and Student A underlines the important words. Circulate and make corrections as needed.

Exercise 8: Do You . . . ?

A

- Read the instructions. Model the example conversation with two students. Go over the chart and explain that students will write the questions they ask in the chart. Have students read the phrases in the box aloud. Explain any unfamiliar vocabulary.
- Put students in groups of five and have them complete the exercise. Circulate and help as needed.

B

- Go over the example with the class. Have students practice in pairs. Then have students report the information they heard to the class.
- Brainstorm a list of other items they would like to interview each other about. Write the items on the board. Brainstorm enough so that small groups can each have four different items. For example:

| rent DVDs | have a flat screen TV | watch podcasts |
| own DVDs | have an MP3 player | surf the Internet |

- Have students work in groups of four to create a new survey form. Each group should choose four items from the list on the board. Have each member of each group choose one of the questions on their survey, interview the rest of the students in the class, and record their results on their form. Then have two groups work together and compare answers.

Exercise 9: Writing

- Have students work in pairs to correct each other's work, using the Editing Checklist as a guide.

- Then have two pairs work together to do Part C. Make sure that students record the answers to their questions. Then call on groups to report their answers to the class.
- For additional practice, have groups continue to work together. Each person writes a *yes / no* question about each person in the group. Have them leave space below each question for a written answer.
- Have students pass their questions to the right. The person that gets the paper writes an answer to the first question in the space. Have students continue to pass their papers to the right and answer one of the questions until each student has his or her own questions. Call on groups to share some of their questions and answers with the class.

OUT OF THE BOX ACTIVITIES

Listening and Speaking

- Have students play "What's my job?" The purpose of this game is to guess someone's profession by asking *yes / no* questions.
- Have students brainstorm a list of occupations they know. Write these on the board. Have a student come to the front of the class and whisper to you one of the occupations from the board. Students in the class ask *yes / no* questions in order to guess the occupation. Encourage students to get as much information as they can before they make a guess.

Go to **www.myfocusongrammarlab.com** for additional listening, pronunciation, speaking, and writing practice.

Note:

- See the *Focus on Grammar Workbook* for additional in-class or homework grammar practice.

Unit 11 Review (page 106)

Have students complete the Review and check their answers on Student Book page UR-1. Review or assign additional material as needed.

Go to **www.myfocusongrammarlab.com** for the Unit Achievement Test.

Grammar: SIMPLE PRESENT: *Wh-* QUESTIONS

Unit 12 focuses on the meanings and uses of *Wh-* questions in the simple present.

- *Wh-* questions ask for information.
- Use *Why, Who, When, What, Where,* and *How* to begin *Wh-* questions in the simple present.
- To form these information questions, use a *Wh-* question word + *do* or *does* + subject + base form of the verb.

Theme: CROSS-CULTURAL DIFFERENCES

Unit 12 focuses on language that describes and compares ways of life in different cultures.

Step 1: Grammar in Context (pages 107–108)

See the general suggestions for Grammar in Context on page 1.

Before You Read

- Spend a few minutes talking about different things that students do in a typical day. Make a list of these things on the board.

Read

- To encourage students to read with a purpose, write these questions on the board:
  1. How does Yoshio like the United States? *(He likes it a lot.)*
  2. Where is Yoshio from? *(Japan)*
  3. What does Yoshio's father do? *(He's a businessman.)*
  4. Where do Jeremy and Yoshio need to go? *(a calculus class)*
  5. What time is the class? *(2:00)*
- Have students read the questions aloud. Have students think about them as they read and listen to the conversation.
- Play the audio and have students read along in their books. Have students discuss the questions in pairs or groups of three. Call on pairs or groups to share answers with the class.

After You Read

A. Practice

- Have students in each pair decide who will be Jeremy and who will be Yoshio. Circulate as students practice the conversation. Make corrections as needed.
- Have the students who read Jeremy's role find a partner who reads Yoshio's role. Have students switch roles and practice the conversation again.

B. Vocabulary

- Play the audio and have students repeat each word. Have students write any new words and their meanings in their notebooks.
- Point out that *get up, stay up,* and *take off* are special verbs because they are two words. Explain that they have different meanings from *get, stay,* and *take.*

C. Vocabulary

- Review the *Wh-* words that students learned in Unit 5 (*Who* and *What*), Unit 6 (*Where*), and Unit 8 (*How, How long, Who, When*) and talk about the meaning of each. Write the *Wh-* words on the board.
- Model the example with a student. Show students how to choose from the options separated by slashes.
- Have students complete the exercise in pairs. Have them use the example to ask about the activities in the vocabulary box. If students finish early, have them ask similar questions about the daily activities you listed on the board in Before You Read.

D. Comprehension

- Have students complete the exercise and work in pairs to check their answers. Have each pair write corrections for the false statements.
- Call on pairs to share their corrected statements either orally or by writing them on the board.

Go to www.myfocusongrammarlab.com for an additional reading, and for reading and vocabulary practice.

Step 2: Grammar Presentation (page 109)

See the general suggestions for Grammar Presentation on page 3.

Grammar Charts

- Call on students to read the sentences in the first chart.
- Ask students questions to help them notice the grammar:
  — When do we use *do*? (with *I, you, we, they,* and plural subjects)
  — When do we use *does*? (with *he, she, it,* and third-person singular subjects)
  — In the first sentence in the chart, what word is the subject? *(I)* The base verb? *(get)*
- Have a student read the sentences in the second chart.

- Help students recognize that *Wh-* questions about the subject do not use *do / does*. Ask:
  — What are the verbs in these sentences? (*wakes up* and *happens*)
  — Are these questions about the subject or another noun or pronoun in the sentence? (*about the subject*)
  — Why don't we use *do* in these sentences? (*because the question is about the subject*)

Grammar Notes

Note 1
- Read the explanation. Then read the example questions and have students repeat. Draw attention to the *Be Careful!* note.
- Have students work in pairs to change the questions with *do* into questions with *does*. For example, *What time do you start work?* becomes *What time does Tom start work?* Call on pairs to write their questions on the board.

Note 2
- Since students are likely to be confused about *Wh-* questions about the subject, you may need to repeatedly explain this idea. Have a student read Note 2.
- Emphasize that a question about the subject really means a question about the subject of **the answer** sentence. For example:
  Q: **Who** wakes you up in the morning?
  A: **My mother** (wakes me up).
  Q: **What** has eight legs?
  A: **A spider** (has eight legs).
- To elicit questions with *who has*, form a sentence with a feature of each student in the class. Have students make a question. For example:
  T: Regina has green eyes.
  S: Who has green eyes?
  T: Yano has a red backpack.
  S: Who has a red backpack?
- To elicit questions with *what* + a verb, form sentences about animals and elicit questions from the students. For example:
  T: A bat has wings, but it isn't a bird.
  S: What has wings but isn't a bird?
  T: A whale lives in the ocean, but it isn't a fish.
  S: What lives in the ocean but isn't a fish?

Note 3
- Have a student read Note 3. Point out that these two questions are very helpful for language learners.
- Have students work in pairs to practice asking and answering both questions. They can use the vocabulary from this unit or any words that they want to know.

Note 4
- Have students read the Pronunciation Note. Then write a statement, a *yes / no* question, and a *Wh-* question on the board. Tell students you are going to read each of the sentences. Have them listen for intonation— whether your voice goes up or down at the end of each one.
- Read the first statement two times. Then ask students if your voice went up or down (*down*). Read the *yes / no* question two times. Ask students if your voice went up or down (*up*). Read the *Wh-* question two times. Ask again whether your voice went up or down (*down*).

🕐 **Identify the Grammar**: Have students identify the grammar in the opening conversation on page 107. For example:
So **how do** you **like** the United States?
What do you **mean**?
What time do Japanese people **go** to bed?
Why does he stay up so late?

Go to **www.myfocusongrammarlab.com** for grammar charts and notes.

Step 3: Focused Practice (pages 110–111)
See the general suggestions for Focused Practice on page 4.

Exercise 1: Discover the Grammar
- Have students complete the exercise individually and work in groups of three to check their answers.
- Then have students in each group take turns reading the conversation. One person is Mark, the other is Josh, and the third is listening for intonation in the questions. Have them read the conversation three times so that each person has an opportunity to have each role.

Exercise 2: *Wh-* Questions
- Have students complete the exercise individually. Go over the answers to the exercise as a class.
- Have students work in pairs to practice asking and answering the questions. The person answering should give true information about himself or herself. Have them practice twice, changing roles after the first practice.

Exercise 3: *Wh-* Questions
- Go over the example with the class. Explain that the underlined words are clues about which *Wh-* word to use.

- Have students complete the exercise individually. Call on students to give their answers. You may want to point out that questions 2–5 and 7 begin with a person's name. Explain to students that questions like this almost always use *you*.
- Have students practice saying the questions and answers in pairs.

Exercise 4: Editing

- Go over the example with the class. Have students complete the exercise individually. Then have them work in pairs to correct their answers.
- Have pairs practice the conversation two times, switching roles after the first practice. Circulate and make corrections as needed.

Go to **www.myfocusongrammarlab.com** for additional grammar practice.

Step 4: Communication Practice
(pages 112–115)

See the general suggestions for Communication Practice on page 5.

Exercise 5: Listening

A

- To establish a purpose for listening, have students look at the picture and read the questions. Play the audio and have students complete the exercise. Go over the answers as a class.
- Have students correct the two false statements. Play the audio again if needed.
- Call on students to write their corrected sentences on the board and discuss them as a class. Point out that the information about Jason's and Margaret's jobs is explicit—it is stated directly. Some of the information about getting to work is implied rather than directly stated.

B

- Have students complete the exercise and then work in pairs to check their answers. Go over the answers as a class. Play the audio again if needed.
- Have students underline *do* or *does* and the main verb in each of the questions. Then ask them why questions 2 and 3 have both *do* and *does*. (*In both questions* do *is the main verb and* does *is the word used to help form the question.*) Ask students why question 1 does not have *do* or *does*. (*Question 1 is a question about the subject. In these types of questions, we do not use* do *or* does.)

Exercise 6: Pronunciation

- Read the examples aloud and emphasize the stressed words. Play the audio for the first item and go over the example with the class.
- Play the audio and have students complete the exercises. Go over the answers as a class.
- Play the audio again and have students repeat.

Exercise 7: Ask and Answer

- Read the instructions and model the conversation with a student. Point out the stress on the capitalized words. Have students read the words from the box. Explain any unfamiliar vocabulary.
- Have students complete the exercise. Call on pairs to ask and answer questions in front of the class. Write the questions they ask on the board.
- Have students find new partners and complete the exercise again, this time using new questions. They can use their own ideas or the questions on the board.

Exercise 8: Information Gap

- Divide the class into pairs and have Student B turn to page 115. Model the example with a student. Make sure the students understand how to do the exercise. Point out that each student has the definitions to their partner's words, but they do not know which word each definition goes with. This means that Student B's answers are definitions of Student A's words, and Student A's answers are definitions of Student B's words.
- Have students complete the exercise. Then have them check their answers on page P-1.
- Have students work in groups to write sentences with the words from the exercise. Call on groups to read their sentences to the class.

Exercise 9: Writing

A

- Have students complete the task individually.

B

- Have students work in pairs to correct each other's work using the Editing Checklist.
- ⏱ If students do not know one another well, have them interview each other in pairs. If the students know one another well, have them complete the interview with someone from outside the class. Then have each student tell the class about the person they interviewed.

OUT OF THE BOX ACTIVITIES

Reading and Writing

- Have students write a short paragraph about the person he or she interviewed in Exercise 9. Then have students work in pairs to edit each other's work, using the checklist on page 114. Have students rewrite their paragraphs.
- Put the paragraphs together in a book and make enough copies of the book to give one to each student.

Reading, Listening, and Speaking

- Have students play a variation of the game "Concentration." The object of the game is to get the most pairs of cards.
- Write each of the vocabulary words from this unit, and some from previous units if you like, on a plain white index card. Write a brief definition or synonym for each of these words on a separate plain white card. You will need one set of word and definition cards for each pair or group of students.
- Divide the class into groups and give each group a set of cards. Shuffle the word cards and place them face down on a table or the floor. Then shuffle the definition cards and place them face down on the table or floor next to the group of word cards. The first student turns a card over from the word group and asks the next student: *What does _____ mean?* The second student turns a card over from the definition group and reads it. If it matches the word, the second student keeps both cards. If the word and definition do not match, both cards are turned face down again in the same exact spot. Play continues with students taking turns asking the question and reading the definition until all of the cards are gone. The person with the most pairs wins.

Go to **www.myfocusongrammarlab.com** for additional listening, pronunciation, speaking, and writing practice.

Note:
- See the *Focus on Grammar Workbook* for additional in-class or homework grammar practice.

Unit 12 Review (page 116)

Have students complete the Review and check their answers on Student Book page UR-1. Review or assign additional material as needed.

Go to **www.myfocusongrammarlab.com** for the Unit Achievement Test.

UNIT 13 OVERVIEW

Grammar: SIMPLE PRESENT: *Be* AND *Have*

Unit 13 focuses on the meanings and uses of *be* and *have* in the simple present.

- *Be* and *have* are common irregular verbs.
- *Be* has three forms in the simple present: *am, is,* and *are.*
- *Have* has two forms in the simple present: *have* and *has.*
- To form negative statements with *be*, use *am, is,* or *are + not.* To form negative statements with *have*, use *do* or *does + not + have.*
- To form *yes / no* questions with *be*, put the verb before the subject. To form *yes / no* questions with *have*, use *do* or *does +* subject *+ have.*
- For *Wh-* questions with *be*, use the question word + verb + subject. To form most *Wh-* questions with *have*, use the question word *+ do* or *does +* a subject + the base form of the verb.
- For questions about the subject with *have*, use statement word order. Do not use *do* or *does.*
- Use *be*, not *have*, to talk about age.

Theme: DESCRIBING PEOPLE

Unit 13 focuses on language that describes people's physical appearance.

Step 1: Grammar in Context (pages 117–119)

See the general suggestions for Grammar in Context on page 1.

Before You Read

- Write on the board:
  How many students in the class have:
  brown eyes _____   blue eyes _____
  green eyes _____   another color _____
- Have students do a quick tally and report to the class.

- Have students complete the exercise in groups. Call on groups to report their answers to the class.

Read

- To encourage students to read with a purpose, write on the board.
  1. What does Rick want Judy to do? (*Give some tickets to Sonia Jones.*)
  2. What does Sonia Jones look like? (*She has dark hair and dark eyes and she's pregnant.*)
  3. How old is she? (*early 20s*)
- Go over the questions with the class. Have students read the conversation. Then have students work in pairs to discuss the answers to the questions.

After You Read

A. Practice

- To assure that each student practices both roles, have them practice the conversation two times, switching roles after the first time.
- For variation, you may want to have students practice reading the conversation chorally. Divide the class into two groups. Have one group read Rick's part and the other read Judy's part. Then have the groups switch roles.

B. Vocabulary

- Have students listen to and repeat the vocabulary words. Then have them work in pairs to practice them. Student A points to a picture, and Student B says the word. Then they switch.
- Circulate as students are practicing and note any difficulties they have with pronunciation. Choose some of the words that students found difficult. Have the class repeat them as you say them.
- You may also want to point out that *heavy* is a more polite way to talk about someone who is overweight. Students may know the word *fat*. Explain that saying someone is *fat* is often considered rude or impolite.
- Many of the words in this unit are antonyms, or opposites. Have students identify the antonym pairs. (*tall / short; thin / heavy; straight / wavy or curly*)

C. Vocabulary

- Read the instructions and model the exercise with a student.
- Have students complete the exercise in pairs. Call on a few students to describe another student to the class without saying that student's name. Have the class guess who the student is describing.

D. Comprehension

- Remind the students that the opening conversation is on page 117. Have students complete the exercise individually. Go over the answers as a class.
- Have students work in pairs to write true statements about the questions in the activity that have negative answers. For example: *Is Sonia in Music Appreciation 1? No, she isn't. She's in Music Appreciation 101.* Have partners take turns asking and answering those questions and adding the true statements.

Go to **www.myfocusongrammarlab.com** for an additional reading, and for reading and vocabulary practice.

Step 2: Grammar Presentation (pages 119–120)

See the general suggestions for Grammar Presentation on page 3.

Grammar Charts

- First have students look at the grammar chart for *be*.
- Set up a quick oral drill to review the use of *am, is, are*. You may also want to have students do this type of drill in pairs or small groups. For example:

  T: I   S: am
  T: we   S: are
  T: Jose and Marga   S: are

- Set up similar drills for the negative statements and *yes / no* questions sections of the chart. For example:

  T: Mara / tall   S: Mara isn't tall.
  T: Jairo / thin   S: Is Jairo thin?

- Next, have students look at the chart for *have*. Set up similar drills for the affirmative / negative statements and the *yes / no* questions sections of the chart.
- Have students look back at the conversation on page 117. Have them underline the forms of *be* and circle the forms of *have*.
- Have students work in pairs to see if they can come up with a rule for the use of *be* and *have* in descriptions. (*In general, we use* be *to talk about height, weight or size, age, and some states:* She's tall and thin. She's in her early twenties. She's pregnant. *We use* have *to talk about physical characteristics:* She has dark hair and dark eyes.)

Grammar Notes

Note 1
- Have students read the explanation. Answer any questions. Then read the example sentences aloud and have students repeat.

Note 2
- Read the example sentences aloud and have students repeat. Ask: "How are the negative forms different?" *(for* be, *the word* not *goes after the verb; for* have, *do / does +* not *goes before the verb)*
- Have students say the full forms and contracted forms of the negative sentences with *have*.
- You may want to review the various forms of contractions with *be* and *does* in negative statements and short answers to *yes / no* questions.

Note 3
- Read the example questions aloud and have students repeat after you. Ask: "How are the *yes / no* question forms different?" *(for* be, *the form is* be + *subject; for* have, *the form is* do / does + *subject +* have)

Note 4
- Write on the board:
  <u>Wh- Questions with Be</u>
  Question word + _____ + _____
  <u>Wh- Questions with Have</u>
  Question word + _____ + subject + _____
- Have students read the example questions aloud. Ask: "How do we form *Wh-* questions with *be*?" Call on a pair to come to the board and complete the blanks. Then do the same for *Wh-* questions with *have*. Discuss the answers as a class.

Note 5
- Read the explanation. Then model the example conversation with a student. Then call on a pair of students to practice the conversation. Have students practice asking and answering the question in groups.
- Ask a student, "How old is _____?" and have the student answer. If the student doesn't know, have him or her ask the person. Have the students practice asking and answering in groups.

🕐 **Identify the Grammar**: Have students identify the grammar in the opening conversation on page 117. For example:
  You**'re** in Music Appreciation 101.
  She**'s** in your music class.
  Well, she **has** dark hair and dark eyes.
  Half the women **have** dark hair and dark eyes.

Go to **www.myfocusongrammarlab.com** for grammar charts and notes.

Step 3: Focused Practice (pages 121–122)
See the general suggestions for Focused Practice on page 4.

Exercise 1: Discover the Grammar
- Have students complete the exercise. Then have them work in pairs to check their answers.
- Call on pairs to share their answers and explain why *be* or *have* is used in each question.
- Have students practice saying the questions and answers in pairs.

Exercise 2: *Be* and *Have*
- Have students quickly read through the paragraph. Explain any unfamiliar vocabulary, such as *Austria* (a country in Europe), *violin / violinist*, *harpsichord* (a musical instrument), *middle name*. Ask: "Who is this person?" *(Wolfgang Amadeus Mozart, a famous composer)*
- Read the instructions and have students complete the exercise individually. Have students check their answers in pairs. Then have pairs practice reading the paragraph aloud.

Exercise 3: *Be* and *Have*
- Go over the example with the class. Explain that Midori is a famous musician shown in the pictures in the exercise. Ask: "Where do you think she's from?" and similar questions. Elicit some guesses. Then have students complete the exercise individually.
- To check answers, call on students to write their questions on the board. Discuss them as a class.
- Have each student think of someone famous and write the person's name at the top of a piece of paper. Then have students write six to eight true statements about that person. Have them leave enough space above each statement to allow room for a written question. They can use B's statements from this exercise as a model. Have students work in pairs, exchange papers, and write questions for each statement.

Exercise 4: Editing
- Go over the example. Ask: "Do we use *be* or *have* to ask about age?" *(be)* Make sure students understand that the correct word for the question is the word *is*, not *has*.

- Have students complete the exercise individually and work in pairs to check their work. Have pairs practice the corrected conversation with each other. Assign one person in each pair to read Judy's role and the other to read Mark's role. Have them switch roles, then practice again with a new partner.

Go to **www.myfocusongrammarlab.com** for additional grammar practice.

Step 4: Communication Practice (pages 123–124)

See the general suggestions for Communication Practice on page 5.

Exercise 5: Listening

A

- Read the instructions and make sure students understand what they are going to hear. Have students read the questions.
- Play the audio and have students complete the exercise. Go over the answers as a class.

B

- Have students read the paragraph and complete it with the information they remember from the audio. Have them compare answers in pairs. Then play the audio and have students complete the exercise. Play the audio again, pausing as needed so students can write their answers.
- Give students the audioscript. Have them work in pairs to practice the conversation. Call on pairs to perform the conversation for the class.

Exercise 6: Pronunciation

A

- Play the audio. Answer any questions.

B

- Play the audio and have students repeat.

C

- Play the audio and have students repeat. Circulate as students practice with a partner. Then ask different pairs to perform the conversations for the class.

Exercise 7: Describe People

- Write the following headings on the board: This person is _____.   The person has _____.

- Call on pairs or groups of students to come to the board and write words or phrases that describe people. Have them write the words under the correct column. For example, *20 years old* would go under the left column. Discuss the words on the board as a class. Add, correct, change, or move items as needed.
- Have the students look at the pictures of people on page 123. Describe a person, using the language on the board, and have students guess whom you are describing. Then have students do the same activity in pairs.
- As an alternative, you could also do this activity with magazine photos or personal photos that you or students bring to class.

Exercise 8: Writing

A

- Go over the instructions and example with the class. Have students identify the verbs in the example and match them with the categories of personal information in the box on page 124. For example: *She's from the United States* goes in the *Country* category and uses *be*.
- Have students complete the exercise individually.

B

- Have students edit their work individually or in pairs. Circulate and help as needed. You may want to have them underline *be* and *have* to make sure they have made the correct choices.

C

- Have a few students read their descriptions to the class without saying who the person is.
- Call on students to ask two or three questions of the student at the front. Then have them guess the person's identity.

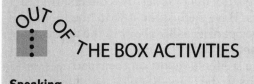

OUT OF THE BOX ACTIVITIES

Speaking

- Write the words *hair, eyes, age,* and *height* on the board.
- Have students mingle and find partners who are similar in one or two of the ways written on the board.
- When students have matched themselves in pairs or groups, have each person tell the class how they are alike. For example: *We are tall. We have brown hair. We have curly hair.*

Writing, Reading, and Speaking

- Have students write a "Who Am I?" paragraph similar to the one on page 121. Make sure students have not revealed the name of the person. Have them use the Editing Checklist to correct their paragraphs. Post the paragraphs around the classroom, and put a sheet of paper or index card under each one.
- Have students circulate, read each paragraph, and then write the name of the person they think it is about on the paper or card under the paragraph.
- Have each student read his or her paragraph to the class and reveal the identity of the person he or she wrote about.

Listening, Speaking, and Writing

- Have students play a version of "Spot the Differences." In this game, students look at two pictures that are different in a limited number of details. Students must find the differences and explain them to a partner. You can find pictures on the Internet. Use a search engine for "spot the differences" or "find the differences." Other sources are children's game books, magazines, and menus or placemats from restaurants that offer a children's menu.
- Make sure students focus on using *be* and *have* to describe the differences.
- For added challenge, give one picture to Student A and the other to Student B. Have them ask each other questions to find the differences. For example:
  S1: Does the girl in your picture have blond hair?
  S2: No, she doesn't. She has brown hair. That's a difference.

Go to **www.myfocusongrammarlab.com** for additional listening, pronunciation, speaking, and writing practice.

Note:
- See the *Focus on Grammar Workbook* for additional in-class or homework grammar practice.

Unit 13 Review (page 125)

Have students complete the Review and check their answers on Student Book page UR-2. Review or assign additional material as needed.

Go to **www.myfocusongrammarlab.com** for the Unit Achievement Test.

UNIT 14 OVERVIEW

Grammar: SIMPLE PRESENT WITH ADVERBS OF FREQUENCY

Unit 14 focuses on the meanings and uses of adverbs of frequency with the simple present.

- Adverbs of frequency tell how often something happens.
- Adverbs of frequency come after the verb *be*.
- Adverbs of frequency usually come before other verbs.
- Use *ever* in *yes / no* questions. *Ever* means "at any time." Do not use *ever* in affirmative statements.
- Use *How often* to ask about how frequently something happens.

Theme: HABITS

Unit 14 focuses on language that is used to talk about habitual activities.

Step 1: Grammar in Context (pages 126–127)

See the general suggestions for Grammar in Context on page 1.

Before You Read

- Read the instructions and the example. Explain *always* and *never*. Have pairs complete the exercise. Call on pairs to share their statements with the class.

- Tell the students that in this opening conversation, they will see these words and expressions: *kind of, fast food, skip,* and *enough*. Read each of the sentences that contain these words or expressions aloud and have students repeat. Ask students what the word or expression means. If needed, provide other examples of the words and expressions in context to assure that students understand them. For example, you can say:
  — What are some examples of *fast food*?
  — I eat breakfast every day. I never *skip* it. Do you ever *skip* breakfast?
  — A big hamburger costs $2.50. I have $2.00. It that *enough*?

Read
- To encourage students to read with a purpose, write these questions on the board.
  1. Why is Steve tired? *(He doesn't get enough sleep. He skips breakfast and eats junk food. He doesn't exercise.)*
  2. What time does Steve go to bed? *(around 12:30 or 1:00 A.M.)*
  3. Does Steve sleep late? *(sometimes on the weekends)*
- Go over the questions with the class. Have students think about these questions as they read and listen to the conversation.
- Have students work in pairs to answer the questions on the board. Discuss the answers as a class.

After You Read

A. Practice
- Have pairs practice the reading conversation two times, switching roles after the first practice.

B. Vocabulary
- Have students listen to and repeat the vocabulary words. Then say the words aloud as students repeat. Encourage them to use the pictures to figure out the meanings. Have students write new words and their meanings in their notebooks.
- Have students work in groups to sort these food items into two groups: healthy and unhealthy. Discuss their answers as a class.

C. Vocabulary
- Have students make three columns on a sheet of paper. Have them label one column *never*, one column *sometimes*, and the last column *often*. Model the example conversation with a student.

- Have students practice the conversation in pairs. Have each student write the foods his or her partner talks about in the appropriate column.
- Have students report on their partners' eating habits to the class. Keep a tally of answers on the board.

D. Comprehension
- Remind the students that the example conversation is on page 126. Have students complete the exercise individually. Then go over the answers as a class.
- Now have students work individually to complete each of the statements about themselves. Have them work in pairs or groups, exchange papers, and tell the class about their partner's habits.

Go to **www.myfocusongrammarlab.com** for an additional reading, and for reading and vocabulary practice.

Step 2: Grammar Presentation (page 128)
See the general suggestions for Grammar Presentation on page 3.

Grammar Charts
- Ask students questions to help them notice the position of the adverbs of frequency in the example sentences in the charts. First have them identify the verb in the sentence. Then have them identify the adverb and tell where it is in relation to the verb.
- Ask:
  — How do we use *ever*? *(in questions)*
  — Do adverbs of frequency come before or after *be*? *(after)*
  — Do adverbs of frequency come before or after other verbs? *(before)*
  — In short answers, where are the adverbs of frequency? *(before* do)*
- In the Adverbs of Frequency chart, read the adverbs aloud and have students repeat. Give an example sentence for each adverb. For example, "I always put milk in my coffee. I never put juice in my coffee. I rarely drink coffee at night."

Grammar Notes

Note 1
- Read the explanation. Have students read the example sentences aloud. Change the adverbs in the example sentences to make them true for you. For example: *I never skip breakfast. I often skip lunch.* Then call on students to do the same.

Note 2

- Read the explanation. Write the example sentences on the board and have students read them aloud. Call on students to come to the board and circle the adverbs. Then have them underline the *be* verb. Ask: "Does the adverb come before or after *be*?" *(after)*
- Leave these sentences on the board for Note 3.

Note 3

- Read the explanation and write the first two example sentences on the board. Have students underline the verb and circle the adverbs. Ask: "Is the verb *be*?" *(no)* "For these verbs, does the adverb come before or after?" *(before)* Point out that the rules for *be* verbs and other verbs are different.
- Read the remaining example sentences aloud and have students repeat. You may also want to point out that *often* can be used at the end of a sentence. For example, *I skip breakfast often.*

Note 4

- Read the explanation aloud. Emphasize that *ever* is only used in questions. Model the example conversation with a few students. Encourage them to use the frequency adverb that is true for them.

Note 5

- Read the explanation aloud. Model the example conversation with a few students. Encourage them to change the expression *three times a week* so the number is true for them. For example, *two times a week, five times a week.*

🕐 **Identify the Grammar**: Have students identify the grammar in the opening conversation on page 126. For example:
I **usually** stay up till 12:30 or 1:00.
Do you **ever** sleep late?
Sometimes—on the weekend.
And I hear you **always** have fast food for lunch.

Go to **www.myfocusongrammarlab.com** for grammar charts and notes.

Step 3: Focused Practice (pages 129–131)

See the general suggestions for Focused Practice on page 4.

Exercise 1: Discover the Grammar

- Have students complete the exercise. Go over the answers with the class. Then have students work in pairs or groups to practice reading the paragraph aloud.

Exercise 2: Adverbs of Frequency

- Have students complete the exercise. Go over the answers as a class.
- Have students work in pairs to take turns asking and answering the questions.
- Then have pairs work together to write four more questions. They can use the questions in the exercise as a model. Make sure each student writes the questions on a piece of paper. Have students form new pairs to ask and answer the questions they wrote.

Exercise 3: Adverbs of Frequency

- Have students look at the pictures and describe them. Elicit the vocabulary *take a shower, drive to work, arrive at work on time,* and *cook dinner.* Then have them look at the days and checkmarks. Ask: "Does she always _____?" Elicit some adverbs of frequency.
- Have students complete the exercise individually, then have them work in pairs to check their answers.
- Ask students which one of the four sentences could be written another way using the same adverb of frequency. *(In sentences 3 and 4, the adverbs of frequency could be placed at the end of the sentence. In sentence 4, the adverb of frequency can go at the beginning, before the verb, or at the end of the sentence.)*

Exercise 4: Editing

- Go over the example. Make sure students understand that *often* is needed to make the question correct.
- Have students complete the exercise individually. Then go over the answers with the class.

Go to **www.myfocusongrammarlab.com** for additional grammar practice.

Step 4: Communication Practice

(pages 132–133)

See the general suggestions for Communication Practice on page 5.

Exercise 5: Listening

A

- Read the instructions and have students look at the pictures. Ask: "Who is Ken? Who is his grandmother?"
- Have students read the statements. Then play the audio and have students complete the task.

B

- Play the audio, pausing and replaying as needed. Have students complete the exercises individually. Then go over the answers as a class.

Exercise 6: Pronunciation

A

- Play the audio. Answer any questions.

B

- Play the audio, pausing as needed, and have students complete the exercise individually.
- Go over the answers as a class. Play the audio again and have students repeat.

C

- Have students practice the words in pairs. Circulate and help as needed.

Exercise 7: About You

- Circulate as students are writing to provide assistance as needed.
- Have students work in groups of three or four to read their statements to each other. Then have students exchange papers and form new groups. Have students tell the new group about the student whose paper they have.

Exercise 8: Writing

- For added challenge, you may want to ask students to write two or three *Wh-* questions.
- Have them look over each other's work in pairs, using the Editing Checklist as a guide. Then have partners interview each other and report to the class.

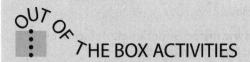

OUT OF THE BOX ACTIVITIES

Speaking, Listening, Writing, and Reading

- Have students use the questions they wrote in Exercise 8 to interview a different classmate or someone from another class or context. They can also use the questions from Exercise 2 on page 129 as a model. Make sure that students have at least three *Wh-* questions in addition to the *yes / no* questions. You may want to suggest that students include some questions about likes and dislikes as well.
- When the interview is complete, have students write a complete paragraph about the person they interviewed. Have each student use the same opening sentence: *(Classmate's/Interviewee's name) has an active life.*

- Have students write their paragraphs individually, then have them work in pairs to correct each other's work. They can use the Editing Checklist on page 133. Have students make any corrections needed and write a final copy of the paragraph. Display them on the walls or a bulletin board in the classroom.

Listening and Speaking

- Write a set of interesting verb phrases on the board and have students add to the list. For example, *eat popcorn, fly first class, go to an art museum, buy jewelry, babysit, lie about your age,* etc. Then write these question stems on the board:
  Do you ever . . . ?
  When do you usually . . . ?
  Where do you usually . . . ?
- Put the students in groups. Have students use the question stems and verbs to practice asking and answering the questions. To add interest, give each group a ball or crumpled sheet of paper. The student asking a question tosses the ball to another student, who answers the question, then asks another question and tosses the ball to another student. Continue until everyone has asked and answered at least three questions.

Reading, Listening, and Speaking

- Use the information about frequency of foods that you wrote on the board in the Before You Read section on page 63 of this book. Have students work in pairs or small groups to ask and answer questions about the information. For example:
  S1: How many people never eat broccoli?
  S2: Five people never eat broccoli.
- For variation, you can conduct a class survey about another topic, post it on the board, and have students practice asking and answering questions about it.

Go to **www.myfocusongrammarlab.com** for additional listening, pronunciation, speaking, and writing practice.

Note:
- See the *Focus on Grammar Workbook* for additional in-class or homework grammar practice.

Unit 14 Review (page 134)

Have students complete the Review and check their answers on Student Book page UR-2. Review or assign additional material as needed.

Go to **www.myfocusongrammarlab.com** for the Unit Achievement Test.

From Grammar to Writing (page FG-4)

See the general suggestions for From Grammar to Writing on page 9.

Go to **www.myfocusongrammarlab.com** for an additional From Grammar to Writing Assignment, Part Review, and Part Post-Test.

Step 1: Grammar in Context (pages 136–139)

See the general suggestions for Grammar in Context on page 1.

Before You Read
- Have students complete the exercise individually. Then have a few students share their answers with the class.
- You may want to write some more action verbs on the board and have students make sentences with them, using the sentences in this section as a model.

Read
- To encourage students to read with a purpose, write these questions on the board:
  1. Who is writing the email? *(Jessica)*
  2. Who is Lauren? *(Lauren is Jessica's friend from high school.)*
  3. Who are Steve and Tim? *(Tim is Jessica's husband and Steve is her brother.)*
  4. Who are Annie, Jeremy, and Ben? *(They are Jessica's children.)*
- Establish a purpose for reading. Call on students to read the questions for the class. Have students keep these questions in mind as they read and listen to the conversation.

- Play the audio and have students follow along in their books. Have students discuss the questions in pairs or groups of three. Call on pairs or groups to share answers with the class.

After You Read

A. Practice

- Point out the expressions *believe it or not* and *your long lost friend*. Ask students what they think each expression means. Explain that these expression are idioms: words or phrases that have a meaning other than the literal meaning of the words. The expression *believe it or not* actually has a figurative meaning close to the literal meaning: *it's surprising but it's true*. *Your long lost friend* simply means someone with whom a person has lost contact over a period of time. It does not mean that the friend is literally lost.
- You may also want to point out the sentence *Mom is happy, but Dad misses work.* Students may be confused by the meaning of *misses*. Explain that in this sentence *miss* means that Jessica's dad is not happy that he is no longer working.
- Circulate as students practice the conversation. Note any words that are difficult for students to pronounce. List the difficult words on the board and have students practice saying them.

B. Vocabulary

- Play the audio and have students repeat each word. Have students write new words and their meanings in their notebook.
- Write the vocabulary words *sit, watch, smile, text, play,* and *stand* on the board. Ask: "How are these verbs different?" *(The first set are non-action or stative verbs. They express states of being. The second set are action verbs. They express actions that people do.)* Point out that we usually do not use stative verbs in the present progressive.

C. Vocabulary

- Read the instructions. Model the example conversation with a student. Then repeat with another student, this time changing the words so they describe a student in the class. Have students guess who you are describing.
- Have students complete the exercise. Then call on students to share their descriptions with the class. Have the class guess which student is being described.

D. Comprehension

- Go over the example with the students. Make sure students understand that the phrases on the left go with the phrases on the right to make sentences.
- Remind students that the opening email is on page 137. Have students complete the exercise individually. Then call on students to write the complete sentences on the board.
- Have students chorally practice saying each of the complete sentences.

Go to **www.myfocusongrammarlab.com** for an additional reading, and for reading and vocabulary practice.

Step 2: Grammar Presentation (pages 139–140)

See the general suggestions for Grammar Presentation on page 3.

Grammar Charts

- Write these questions on the board or prepare them as a handout:
  What is the ending of the verb in all forms of the present progressive? *(-ing)*
  Which form of *be* do we use with *I, he, it, we,* and *they*? *(am, is, are, are)*
  How do we make a negative present progressive statement? *(subject + be + not + verb + ing.)*
  What is the position of *not*? *(after be and before verb + -ing)*
  How many contractions of *I am not* do you see? *(one)*
  How many contractions of *is not* do you see? *(two)*
  How many contractions of *are not* do you see? *(two)*
- Have students work in pairs to look over the example sentences in the grammar charts and answer the questions. Go over the answers as a class. For contractions that have more than one form, have students provide both forms of the contraction. For example, *He's not standing / He isn't standing.*

Grammar Notes

Note 1

- Walk around the room and perform a variety of actions. As you perform each one, say what you are doing using the present progressive. For example, *I'm opening the window. I'm erasing the board. I'm turning off the lights.*

- Choose a student to repeat the actions with you. Say what you are doing using *we*. Then call on a student to perform the actions. Have the class say what the student is doing using *he* or *she*.
- You may want to continue the activity using two students and having the class say what they are doing using *they* or the students' names.

Note 2
- Create a chart like the following, either on the board or as a handout:

listen	read
talk	answer
write	underline
run	jog
grow	snow
fix	tax
play	pay
_____ (your idea)	_____ (your idea)

- Use the verbs in the left column as a model. Have students look at Note 2 and tell you how to write the present progressive form of each verb. Then have students write the present progressive form of each verb in the right column.
- Call on students to write their answers on the board. Discuss the answers. Have each student tell you the rule about the verb that he or she writes on the board.

Note 3
- Read the explanation and the example sentences aloud. Say a sentence with full forms (*He is watching TV*) and have students say it with contractions (*He's watching TV*). Have students continue the drill in pairs.

Note 4
- Do a quick transformation drill. Make an affirmative present progressive statement and have the class make it negative.
- You can do this as a simple drill or a bean bag toss. Have students stand in a circle. The first person makes a present progressive affirmative statement and tosses the bean bag (or a crumpled sheet of paper) to another student. That student makes the statement negative, makes a new affirmative statement, and tosses the bean bag to someone else. Continue the activity until each student has made at least one affirmative and one negative statement.

Note 5
- Call on a student to read the note. Then write these sentences on the board:

Jessica is writing an email.
Jessica and Tim are living in Redmond.
Steve isn't being an artist.
Jeremy is texting a friend.
Ben isn't having a cell phone.
Jessica's dad is needing a job.
Jessica's mom isn't wanting a job.

- Have students work in groups or pairs to identify the incorrect sentences and write corrections for them. Call on groups or pairs to write their answers on the board. Discuss the answers as a class.

Note 6
- Call on a student to read the note. Then divide the class into two teams. Write a subject and two *-ing* verbs on the board. For example: *Tom, sitting, playing cards*. Have one person from each team write a sentence that connects the subject with both verbs and does not repeat *be*. For example, *Tom is sitting and playing cards*.

⏱ **Identify the Grammar**: Have students identify the grammar in the opening reading on page 137. For example:

I'm living in Redmond with my husband and children.
He's wearing the gray sweatshirt.
They're watching a ball game.
They're not smiling because **their team is losing**.

Go to **www.myfocusongrammarlab.com** for grammar charts and notes.

Step 3: Focused Practice (pages 141–143)

See the general suggestions for Focused Practice on page 4.

Exercise 1: Discover the Grammar
- Have students complete the exercise. Then go over the answers as a class.
- Students may be confused by the expression *I'm just kidding*. Ask them what they think it means. (*I'm joking*, or *I'm not serious*.)
- Have students work in pairs to take turns reading the email to each other. Circulate as students are reading. Make corrections in pronunciation as needed.

Exercise 2: Present Progressive
- Have students complete the exercise individually and work in pairs to check their answers.
- Have pairs practice reading the conversation two times, changing roles after the first practice.

Exercise 3: Affirmative and Negative

- Have students complete the exercise. Then have students write their answers on the board. Go over the answers as a class and make corrections as needed.
- Call on students to create a sentence that adds more information to each statement. For example: *Lauren isn't wearing black boots. She's wearing brown boots.*

Exercise 4: Editing

- Have students complete the exercise individually. Then have them work in pairs to check their answers. Call on pairs to write the correct sentences on the board.
- Have each pair change each of the affirmative statements to negative statements. Then have them write a second version of the negative statements. For example, for the first item:
  She's wearing her new boots.
  She's not wearing her new boots.
  She isn't wearing her new boots.
- Circulate as students complete the task. Give help as needed.

Go to **www.myfocusongrammarlab.com** for additional grammar practice.

Step 4: Communication Practice (pages 143–145)

See the general suggestions for Communication Practice on page 5.

Exercise 5: Listening

A
- Have students complete the exercise. Then go over the answers as a class.

B
- Have students complete the exercise in pairs. Then have them correct the false statements.

Exercise 6: Pronunciation

A
- Play the audio. Answer any questions.

B
- Play the audio and have students repeat. Repeat as needed, calling on individual students.

C
- Play the audio and have students repeat.
- Have students take turns saying the sentences in pairs. Circulate and monitor pronunciation as needed.

D
- Play the audio and have students complete the task. Go over the answers as a class.

- ⏱ Use the sentences in the answer choices of this part as a dictation, but do not say them in order. Pause as needed so that students have time to write. Have students write their answers on the board and read them to the class. Make corrections as needed.

Exercise 7: True Statements

A
- Read the instructions. Have students complete the exercise individually.

B
- Have students compare their statements in pairs. Then call on students to read their statements aloud.
- ⏱ Have students write four true statements of their own using information about things happening in the classroom or outside. Call on students to write their sentences on the board and read them to the class.

Exercise 8: Picture Differences

- Have students look at the picture. Read the example and have students circle the differences in the picture. Have students work in small groups to complete this exercise.
- Read the instructions. Explain that there are more than five differences in the picture. Students should find at least five. Then have pairs continue to work together to find as many differences as they can. Have them write sentences about the differences.
- Have the pair that found the most differences read them to the class.

Exercise 9: Writing

- Have students complete the exercise. Then have students work in small groups to share their photos and talk about the differences.

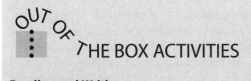

OUT OF THE BOX ACTIVITIES

Reading and Writing

- Bring in pictures that show a lot of things going on—street scenes, a busy office, sporting events, etc. Divide the class into small groups and give a different picture to each group. Place it face down so that no one in the group can see it.
- At your signal, students turn the picture over and have one minute to look at it. Then have them turn the picture over (or take it away), and have students write everything they can remember about the picture using the present progressive. If you want to make this a competition, give them a time limit for writing.
- When time is up, have students read their sentences. The person or group who has the most details is the winner.

Speaking and Listening (and Reading as a Variation)

- Have students play "Concentration." For this game, you will need sets of cards made of identical pictures. Each pair should show someone or something doing an easily recognizable activity. You will need at least twenty pairs. You can make these by drawing stick figures or downloading pictures or clip art from the Internet.
- Have students work in small groups. Each group needs a set of cards. These are randomly placed face down on a table or the floor. The first person turns two cards over and says what is happening in each. For example: *He is running. She is brushing her teeth.* If the cards do not match, the student turns them face down again, but they must be put in the same place on the table or floor. Then the next student gets a turn. If the cards match, the student keeps them and gets another turn. The object of the game is to remember where matching cards are. The person with the most pairs at the end of the game wins.
- As a reading variation, you can make the card sets with one picture and one sentence that describes what's happening in the picture.

Go to **www.myfocusongrammarlab.com** for additional listening, pronunciation, speaking, and writing practice.

Note:
- See the *Focus on Grammar Workbook* for additional in-class or homework grammar practice.

Unit 15 Review (page 146)

Have students complete the Review and check their answers on Student Book page UR-2. Review or assign additional material as needed.

Go to **www.myfocusongrammarlab.com** for the Unit Achievement Test.

UNIT 16 OVERVIEW

Grammar: PRESENT PROGRESSIVE: *Yes / No* QUESTIONS

Unit 16 focuses on the meanings and uses of *yes / no* questions in the present progressive.

- In a *yes / no* question in the present progressive, put *am*, *is*, or *are* before the subject.
- You can use short answers in speaking and informal writing.
- Do not use contractions in affirmative short answers.

Theme: BABYSITTING

Unit 16 focuses on language used to ask about what is happening at home while the children are home with a babysitter.

Step 1: Grammar in Context (pages 147–149)

See the general suggestions for Grammar in Context on page 1.

Before You Read
- Have students look at the vocabulary on page 148 for the pictures of *babysit* and *celebrate an anniversary*.
- You may want to point out that *watching* (as in *Is Jeremy watching Annie and Ben?*) is similar to *babysitting* in this context. It does not have the same meaning as *watching* as in *He's watching the game.*

Read
- To encourage students to read with a purpose, write the following questions on the board:
  1. What special day is it for Tim and Jessica? *(It's their wedding anniversary.)*
  2. Where do they go to celebrate? *(a restaurant)*
  3. Who's babysitting? *(Kelly Brown)*
  4. What is Ben doing? *(baking cookies)*
  5. What does Kelly think Annie and Gail are doing? *(studying)*
- Establish a purpose for reading. Call on students to read the questions. Have students think about the questions as they read and listen to the conversation. Play the audio and have students read along in their books.
- Have students discuss the questions as a class. Ask students how the information about Annie in the conversation is different from the information about her in the picture. *(The babysitter says she is probably studying. The picture shows that she is cutting Gail's hair.)*

After You Read

A. Practice
- Write these two sentences on the board: Jeremy is watching Ben and Annie. Is Jeremy watching Ben and Annie?
- Ask: "How are the two sentences different?" *(The first is a statement and the second is a question.)*
- Read the questions aloud and have students listen carefully for intonation. Then read the sentences. Ask students what they noticed. *(The voice goes lower at the end of a statement and goes up at the end of a yes / no question.)*
- Point out that the conversations have *yes / no* questions. Have students focus on intonation as they read those questions in the conversations. Circulate as students practice. Make corrections as needed. You might want to have students practice the conversations three times, changing roles after each practice.

B. Vocabulary
- Play the audio and have students repeat each word. Say the vocabulary words and have students point to the picture. Have students continue practicing the words in pairs.
- Write on the board:
  help <u>someone</u> with homework
  cut <u>someone's</u> hair

- Explain that you can replace *someone* with a name, a person, or a pronoun. You can replace *someone's* with a name + *'s* or a possessive adjective. Give some examples, e.g., *help Tom with homework, help my classmates with homework, cut Joe's hair, cut her hair*. Call on a few students to give more examples.
- Make sure students understand the difference between *get a haircut* and *cut someone's hair*.

C. Vocabulary
- Read the instructions. Explain that students will complete the blanks with the new vocabulary words in *-ing* form. Say a few of the new phrases and have students say the *-ing* form. Make sure students know which words change to *-ing* form. For example, *getting a haircut*, not *get a haircutting*.
- Tell students that some blanks take more than one word, and that sometimes part of a phrase is on one blank and another part is on another blank. *(Items 4 and 5: She's <u>helping</u> Ben <u>with homework</u>.)*
- Have students complete the exercise individually and check answers in pairs. Then call on pairs to read their paragraphs aloud. Have students practice saying the completed paragraph.

D. Comprehension
- Remind students that the opening conversation is on page 147. Have students complete the exercise. Then have them work in pairs to check their answers.
- Have pairs take turns asking and answering the questions.

Go to **www.myfocusongrammarlab.com** for an additional reading, and for reading and vocabulary practice.

Step 2: Grammar Presentation (page 149)
See the general suggestions for Grammar Presentation on page 3.

Grammar Charts
- Have students look over the grammar chart. Ask what the word order is for *yes / no* questions in the present progressive. *(a present form of* be + *subject* + *verb* + -ing)
- Write these examples based on the reading on the board:
  Is Jeremy watching Annie and Ben?
  Is Mrs. Brown babysitting?
  Is Ben doing his homework?

- Ask students to answer the questions based on information in the reading. As they provide the answers, ask them if there's another way to answer the question with a negative response. Elicit from students that there are two ways to answer these questions: *No, he / she isn't* and *No, he's / she's not.*
- Ask students contrasting questions to help them notice that short answers in the present progressive are the same as short answers in the simple present. For example:

T: Is it cold?   S: Yes, it is./ No, it isn't./ No, it's not.

T: Is it raining?   S: Yes, it is./ No, it isn't./ No, it's not.

Grammar Notes

Notes 1–3

- Ask students how the present progressive is similar to the simple present. (*Word order of the subject and verb in statements and yes / no questions is the same. Short answers are also the same—their use is the same. We don't use contractions in affirmative responses to yes / no questions in the simple present or the present progressive.*)
- Have students read over the grammar notes to confirm their answers.

🕐 **Identify the Grammar**: Have students identify the grammar in the opening conversation on page 147. For example:

Is Jeremy watching Ben and Annie?
Is Mrs. Brown babysitting?
Are the children listening to you?
So **are you helping** Ben with his math?

Go to **www.myfocusongrammarlab.com** for grammar charts and notes.

Step 3: Focused Practice (pages 150–152)

See the general suggestions for Focused Practice on page 4.

Exercise 1: Discover the Grammar

A

- Read the instructions. Have students check the questions in the present progressive. Then elicit the answers.
- Have students match the questions and answers. Then have them check their answers in pairs.
- 🕐 Have pairs take turns asking and answering the questions. Remind them to use correct intonation for the questions.

B

- Have students look at the title of the cartoon. Ask them what they think it means. (*Dennis is a very smart little boy. They call him "the menace" because he is always doing things that get him in trouble.*) Then call on students to describe what they see in the cartoon, using present progressive. For example, *The boy is eating a sandwich. The babysitter is sleeping. The parents are wearing nice clothes.*
- Have students discuss the question in groups. Then call on students from each group to tell the class their group's answer to the question. Make sure students understand why this is funny.

Exercise 2: Present Progressive

- Read the instructions and go over the examples. Explain that students will complete some of the blanks with questions and some of the blanks with statements.
- Have students complete the exercise and compare their answers in pairs.
- Have pairs practice the completed conversation twice, changing roles after the first practice.

Exercise 3: Questions and Answers

- Have students complete the exercise. Then call on students to give their answers. If the answer is a negative response, make sure students give both ways to say it.
- Divide the class into two groups. Have one group ask the questions chorally and the other respond. Then have the groups switch roles and practice again.

Exercise 4: Editing

- Have students complete the exercise individually. Then call on students to write their answers on the board. Have each person read his or her sentence to the class.
- Have students practice the corrected questions and answers in pairs.

Go to **www.myfocusongrammarlab.com** for additional grammar practice.

Step 4: Communication Practice

(pages 152–154)

See the general suggestions for Communication Practice on page 5.

Exercise 5: Pronunciation

A

• Have students look at the pictures. Read the words *watch* and *wash* aloud and have students repeat. Then play the audio and have students repeat.

B

• Play the audio, pausing as needed, and have students complete the task. Replay the audio so that student can check their answers.

C

• Play the audio and have students repeat.

D

• Have students take turns saying all of the possible sentences in Part B in random order. The speaker says a sentence and the listener says the word he or she thinks the partner said. Circulate as students are working. Make corrections as needed.

Exercise 6: Listening

A

• Read the instructions. Have students read the question and answer choices. Then play the audio and have students complete the exercise. Go over the answer as a class.

B

• Have students read the questions. Then play the audio, pausing as needed, and have students complete the exercise. Then have pairs exchange papers. Play the audio again and have students check each other's papers.

Exercise 7: Act Out Sentences

A

• Have students complete the task individually.

B

• Have students complete the task in pairs.

C

• Model the example conversations. Call on students to act out one sentence for the class. Help students think of questions to guess what the person is doing.
• Have students continue the exercise as a class or in large groups. Make sure that the students are acting out sentences that use different verbs.

Exercise 8: Writing

A

• Have students look at the cartoon. Remind students that they saw the same cartoon earlier on page 150. Elicit some descriptions of the cartoon using the present progressive and the items in the list. For example: *The woman is wearing a coat. The boy is drinking a glass of milk.*

B

• Read the instructions. If needed, give the students an example question. For example: *Is the boy sleeping?*
• Have students complete the task. You may want lower-level students to work in pairs to complete these parts of the exercise. For mixed-level classes, pair lower- and higher-level students with each other.

C

• Have students check their work using the Editing Checklist. Call on pairs to write one of their questions on the board. Correct any mistakes as a class.

D

• Have students ask and answer their questions in large groups or as a class.

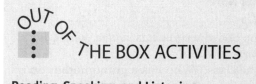

OUT OF THE BOX ACTIVITIES

Reading, Speaking, and Listening

- On the board, write a list of actions that can be mimed. For example: *putting in contact lenses, climbing a ladder, looking up a word in a dictionary, playing with a cat.* You can have students help you brainstorm the list. Try to elicit unusual or interesting actions and teach any unfamiliar words.
- Have each student choose an action from the list on the board and mime it for the class. The other students ask *yes / no* questions in the present progressive and try to guess what the action is.

Writing, Reading (for Variation Listening and Speaking)

- Bring in (or have students bring in) pictures of people doing various activities.
- Give each student (or pair of students) a picture. Have students write six to eight questions about the picture. Four of them must be *yes / no* questions in the present progressive. Have students exchange pictures and questions and answer each other's questions.
- For variation, have students work in small groups. Give each group a picture. Groups must write six to eight questions (four must be *yes / no* questions in the present progressive). Have groups exchange pictures and questions and answer each other's questions.

Go to **www.myfocusongrammarlab.com** for additional listening, pronunciation, speaking, and writing practice.

Note:
- See the *Focus on Grammar Workbook* for additional in-class or homework grammar practice.

Unit 16 Review (page 155)

Have students complete the Review and check their answers on Student Book page UR-2. Review or assign additional material as needed.

Go to **www.myfocusongrammarlab.com** for the Unit Achievement Test.

Grammar: PRESENT PROGRESSIVE: *Wh-* QUESTIONS

Unit 17 focuses on the meanings and uses of *Wh-* questions in the present progressive.

- We can use *Wh-* words and the present progressive to ask questions about the object of a sentence.
- We can also use *Wh-* words and the present progressive to ask questions about the subject of a sentence.

Theme: WAYS OF TRAVELING

Unit 17 focuses on language that describes different ways to travel.

Step 1: Grammar in Context (pages 156–158)

See the general suggestions for Grammar in Context on page 1.

Before You Read

- Have students complete the activity and compare answers in groups. You may want to have them brainstorm other ways of travel and talk about whether they like traveling in those ways and why.

Read

- To encourage students to read with a purpose, write on the board:
  1. Who is Nick? *(Mark's brother)*
  2. Why is he calling Mark? *(He's calling to say that he's back in the United States.)*
  3. Where is Nick going? *(He's going to Denver.)*
  4. How is he getting there? *(by car)*
- Call on students to read each of the questions. Have students read the conversation. Then have them work in pairs to discuss the questions. Have a few students share their answers with the class.

After You Read

A. Practice
- Have students practice the conversation in pairs. Call on pairs to read the conversation for the class.

B. Vocabulary
- Play the audio and have students repeat. Encourage them to figure out the meaning from the pictures. Have students write new words and their meanings in their notebooks.

C. Vocabulary

- Read the instructions. Model the example conversation with a student. Then call on a pair to read the conversation. Encourage them to change B's line so it is true for them.
- Have students complete the exercise in pairs. Circulate and help as needed. Make sure they ask about how they get to school, work, their friends' homes, and the supermarket.
- Have students find new partners and talk about how their previous partners get to places.

D. Comprehension

- Remind the students that the opening conversation is on page 156. Have students complete the exercise. Then have students work in pairs to check their answers.
- Divide the class into two groups. Have groups take turns asking and answering the questions chorally.

Go to **www.myfocusongrammarlab.com** for an additional reading, and for reading and vocabulary practice.

Step 2: Grammar Presentation (pages 158–159)

See the general suggestions for Grammar Presentation on page 3.

Grammar Charts

- Have students look over the grammar charts. Have them practice reading the questions and answers in pairs.
- Have students compare the word order of *Wh-* questions and *yes / no* questions. Ask: "Is the word order of *Wh-* questions and *yes / no* questions the same or different?" (*the same*) "Where is the *Wh-* word?" (*at the beginning of the sentence*) "Where is the subject?" (*after* am, is, *or* are)
- Ask students what they remember from previous units about *Wh-* questions about the subject.
- Ask them if the word order in questions about the subject is the same or different from word order in other *Wh-* questions. (*It's different. The* Wh- *word is actually the subject of these questions.*)
- Remind students that questions about the subjects are really questions about the subject of **the answer**. For example:
  Q: What's happening? (*What* is the subject.)
  A: Nothing is happening. (*Nothing* is the subject.)

Grammar Notes

Notes 1–2

- On the board write *what, where, why, who,* and *how.*
- Ask the class: "Who has a grandmother or grandfather who is still living?" Choose one student and ask present progressive questions about the grandparent. For example:

T: Where is your grandfather living?	S: He's living in Beijing.
T: Who is he living with?	S: My mother and father.
T: Why is he living there?	S: Because in my culture parents live with their oldest son.
T: How is your grandfather doing?	S: Well. His health is good.
T: What is he probably doing right now?	S: It's 3 A.M. in Beijing. He's probably sleeping.

- Have the class ask you similar questions about a relative of yours.
- To practice the pattern of question with *who,* ask about students' relatives and friends who are in different time zones. For example:

T: Who is sleeping now?	S: My parents. They're in Paris.
T: Who is eating dinner?	S: My brother. He's living in New York City.
T: Who is getting up?	S: My cousin in Hawaii. It's early morning there.

- Ask students to write three to four questions with *Who* as the subject. Then have them work in pairs to ask and answer their questions.

Note 3

- Have students read the explanation. Call on a pair of students to read the example conversation.
- Explain that the answers to many *why* questions begin with *Because.* For example, the answer to the example question could be *Because you don't check your email.*
- Ask a student, "Why are you studying English?" and elicit an answer with *because.* For example, *Because I want a good job.* Have students ask and answer the same question in pairs. Call on a few pairs to share their answers with the class.

Note 4

- Have students read the note and practice the example conversations in pairs.

- Make sure students understand not to use contractions in affirmative short answers. Ask a student, "Who is sitting next to you?" and elicit a short affirmative answer that does not use contractions. Have pairs practice answering the same question in pairs.

⏱ **Identify the Grammar**: Have students identify the grammar in the opening conversation on page 156. For example:
  Hey, little brother . . . **what's happening**?
  I can't believe it. **Why are you calling** me?
  What are you doing?
  How are you traveling?

Go to **www.myfocusongrammarlab.com** for grammar charts and notes.

Step 3: Focused Practice (pages 159–160)

See the general suggestions for Focused Practice on page 4.

Exercise 1: Discover the Grammar
- Have students complete the exercise. Then go over the answers as a class.
- Have students work in pairs to practice asking and answering the questions twice. Have them change roles after the first practice.

Exercise 2: *Wh-* Questions
- Have students complete the exercise. Then have them work in pairs to check their answers. Call on students to share their answers with the class.
- Have pairs write three more *Wh-* questions about the opening conversation. Have pairs exchange their questions with another pair and answer them. Circulate as students are working and provide assistance as needed.

Exercise 3: *Wh-* Questions
- Have students complete the exercise. Then call on students to write their questions on the board. Discuss them as a class.
- Have pairs work together to practice asking and answering the questions.

Exercise 4: Editing
- Go over the example with the class. If students have trouble understanding the mistake, go over the grammar charts again.
- Have students complete the activity individually. Then have them work in pairs to check their answers. Have pairs practice the corrected conversations with each other. Make sure students practice both roles in each conversation.

Go to **www.myfocusongrammarlab.com** for additional grammar practice.

Step 4: Communication Practice
(pages 161–163)

See the general suggestions for Communication Practice on page 5.

Exercise 5: Pronunciation
A
- Play the audio to the Pronunciation Note and have students listen. Then have them repeat the questions after you say them. Exaggerate the intonation as you say the questions.

B
- Read the instructions and go over the example with the class. Play the audio, pausing as needed, and have students complete the exercise.

C
- As students are reading the questions in Part C to each other, circulate and give assistance as needed.
- Have students change partners. Have them practice reading the questions and answering them twice, changing roles after the first practice.

Exercise 6: Listening
A
- Have students complete the exercise individually. Go over the answers as a class.
- Call on students to add information for the sentences that are not true. For example: *Mark is not alone. He is with his friend Kathy.*

B
- Go over the example with the class. Read the instructions. Make sure students know to write complete sentences with the present progressive.
- Play the audio, pausing and replaying as needed, and have students complete the exercise. Call on students to write their answers on the board. Discuss the answers as a class.
- Ask students about the intonation in these questions. Is it rising or falling? (*It rises in the middle and falls at the end because these are all* Wh- *questions.*)
- Have students work in pairs to practice asking and answering the questions twice, changing roles after the first practice. Circulate as students are practicing. Make corrections as needed.

Exercise 7: Picture Discussion

• Have students look at the pictures. Elicit basic information about each place, such as which country the places are in, the language people speak there, things to see or do, things to eat. Then read the instructions. Read the example questions aloud and have students repeat. Model the exercise with the class. Have them ask you questions to guess which place you are visiting.

• Have students complete the activity in pairs. Circulate and help with questions as needed. To provide additional support, you might want to write the *Wh-* question words on the board.

Exercise 8: Writing

A

• Read the instructions and go over the example. Have students write their email messages and edit their work individually.

B

• Divide the class into small groups. Have group members exchange papers and correct each other's work using the Editing Checklist. Have students underline the present progressive words in each sentence of their partner's paper. If elements are missing, have them suggest corrections.

• ⏱ Call on pairs to read their email messages to the class.

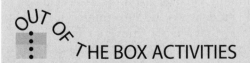
OUT OF THE BOX ACTIVITIES

Speaking and Listening

• Have students work in pairs. Have them imagine that they are best friends. One friend is in his or her home country, and the other is traveling. They have not seen each other for several months, but they often talk on the telephone.

• Have them role-play a conversation and talk about what they are doing, where they are doing it, who they are doing it with, etc. Have each pair start the conversation in this way:
S1: Hello?
S2: Hi _____! Guess what I'm doing?
S1: I have no idea! What are you doing?

Go to **www.myfocusongrammarlab.com** for additional listening, pronunciation, speaking, and writing practice.

Note:

• See the *Focus on Grammar Workbook* for additional in-class or homework grammar practice.

Unit 17 Review (page 164)

Have students complete the Review and check their answers on Student Book page UR-2. Review or assign additional material as needed.

Go to **www.myfocusongrammarlab.com** for the Unit Achievement Test.

From Grammar to Writing (page FG-5)

See the general suggestions for From Grammar to Writing on page 9.

Go to **www.myfocusongrammarlab.com** for an additional From Grammar to Writing Assignment, Part Review, and Part Post-Test.

PART VII OVERVIEW

NOUNS; *This / That / These / Those*; *Some* and *Any*; ARTICLES; *Can / Can't*

UNIT	GRAMMAR FOCUS	THEME
18	Possessive Nouns; *This / That / These / Those*	Clothing
19	Count and Non-count Nouns; *Some* and *Any*	Food
20	*A / An* and *The*; *One / Ones*	Shopping for Clothes
21	*Can / Can't*	Abilities

Go to **www.myfocusongrammarlab.com** for the Part and Unit Tests.

Note: PowerPoint® grammar presentations, test-generating software, and reproducible Part and Unit Tests are on the *Teacher's Resource Disc*.

Grammar: POSSESSIVE NOUNS; *This /That / These /Those*

Unit 18 focuses on the meanings and uses of singular and plural possessive nouns. It also reviews meanings and use of *this, that, these,* and *those* as pronouns and introduces them as possessive adjectives. In addition, the use of *that's* as a way to refer to an idea that has just been stated is presented.

- Possessive nouns show belonging. To show belonging, add an apostrophe (') + *-s* to singular nouns and irregular plural nouns. Add an apostrophe to plural nouns that end in *-s*.

- *This, that, these,* and *those* can be pronouns or adjectives. *This* and *that* are singular, and *these* and *those* are plural. *This* and *these* refers to people or things near you; *that* and *those* refer to people or things that are away from you.

- We often use *that's* in speaking and informal writing to refer to an idea that someone has just stated.

Theme: CLOTHING

Unit 18 focuses on language that describes clothing, whom it belongs to, and the way it looks on someone.

Step 1: Grammar in Context (pages 166–168)

See the general suggestions for Grammar in Context on page 1.

Before You Read

- Go over the example and have students complete the exercise in groups. Write the students' birthdays on the board. (You may want to make a chart and hang it in the classroom or establish a special way to celebrate students' birthdays as they occur throughout the year.)

Read

- To encourage students to read with a purpose, write these questions on the board:
  1. Who is Mark having dinner with? *(Kathy and her parents)*
  2. Where are they having dinner? *(at the Water Grill)*
  3. Is Mark nervous about the dinner? *(He probably is. He is worried about how he looks. He also wants Kathy's parents to like him.)*
  4. Does Judy think Mark looks nice? *(Yes, she does. She says he looks really sharp.)*

- Ask students what the expressions *look sharp, a good fit,* and *be yourself* mean. Point out the footnoted definitions of these expressions on page 166.
- Play the audio and have students follow along in their books. Then have students discuss the questions in pairs or groups of three. Call on students to share answers with the class.

After You Read

A. Practice

- Circulate as students practice the conversation.
- Call on students from different groups to read each person's part in the conversation and perform it for the class.

B. Vocabulary

- Play the audio and have students repeat each word.
- Have students look at the conversation on page 166 in pairs and find other words related to clothing and appearance. *(sharp, suspenders, goatee)* Ask: "What does _____ mean?" and elicit a definition. Have students write new words and their meanings in their notebooks.
- Write this question stem on the board: What do you think looks good with _____? Have students work in groups of three to ask each other the question, filling in the blank with each of the vocabulary items. Have students answer the questions with complete sentences. For example,
  S1: What do you think looks good with a tie?
  S2: I think a tie looks good with a white shirt and jeans.

C. Vocabulary

- Have students look at the conversations. Pre-teach *a pair of* _____ . Explain that *a pair of* is always followed by a plural noun. Ask: "Which of the vocabulary words are plural?" *(slacks, dress shoes)* You may also want to pre-teach other words from the exercise such as *navy, tan,* and *casual.*
- Have students complete the exercise individually. Then have them work in pairs to check their answers. Have students practice the conversations in pairs. Make sure students practice each role for each conversation.

D. Comprehension

- Go over the example with the class. You may also want to pre-teach key words such as *borrow* and *belongs to.* Explain that the sentence *Judy asks if anything belongs to Mark* means that Judy asks, "Is anything yours?"

- Remind students that the opening conversation is on page 166. Then have students complete the exercise individually and work in pairs to check their answers. Go over the answers as a class. Have students read the lines in the conversation that give the answers.
- For additional comprehension practice with the opening conversation, have pairs work together to write four or five *Wh-* questions based on the sentences in the exercise. Have pairs exchange papers with another pair and answer the questions. Call on pairs to share some of their questions by asking them of the other students.

Go to **www.myfocusongrammarlab.com** for an additional reading, and for reading and vocabulary practice.

Step 2: Grammar Presentation (pages 168–169)

See the general suggestions for Grammar Presentation on page 3.

Grammar Charts

- Have students look at the first chart. Call on students to paraphrase each sentence to show its meaning. For example, the first sentence *My sister's car is red* can be paraphrased as *My sister has a red car.*
- Ask students where the apostrophe goes if the noun is singular and if the noun is plural. You may want to point out the example using *actress's*. Explain that a singular noun or name ending in *-s* still receives *'s* at the end. Give more examples with names ending in *-s*, such as *Luis's* or *Chris's*. Point out that the *'s* is pronounced as an extra syllable, /ɪz/.
- The second chart builds on information presented in Unit 1. Students will probably know these structures already. The new information involves the use of *this, that, these,* and *those* with nouns as demonstrative adjectives.
- Ask: "What is the subject of each sentence on the left side of the chart?" (*this, that, these, and those*) Then ask: "What is the subject of the sentences on the right side?" (*cell phone, tie, keys*)
- Point out that when *this, that, these,* or *those* precedes a noun, it functions as an adjective and answers the question *Which one?* about the noun. For example:
  A: That tie is Steve's.
  B: Which tie?
  A: **That** tie.

- Have students look at the third chart. Ask: "What is the long form of *that's*?" (*that is*) Then ask what *that* refers to. (*It refers to the previous idea or statement:* It's their thirtieth anniversary.)
- Have students look at the third and fourth sentences in this chart. Then ask them what *that's* refers to in the fourth sentence. (*the previous statement:* He's in the hospital.) Ask the same questions about the last sentence. (That *refers to the fact that the speaker is studying tonight.*)

Grammar Notes

Note 1

- Collect objects from students and put them in a bag or basket. Have a student draw an object from the bag and say whom it belongs to. For example: *It's Chin's pencil. It's Dalia's.* Continue the activity with different students until all of the objects have been discussed. Leave the objects at the front of the room for the next activity.

Note 2

- Have students look over Note 2. For singular nouns, repeat the activity above as a dictation. A student picks up an object from the table and says whom the object belongs to, then gives the object back to the student it belongs to. Then all of the students write the name of that student in its possessive form. When all of the objects have been returned, go over the answers as a class by having individual students write their answers on the board.
- For plural possessives and irregular plural nouns, dictate some phrases that have each of the forms and have the students write their answers. Then go over the answers by having individual students write them on the board. For example: *her parents' house, his roommates' families, the men's locker room, the Smiths' anniversary, the students' papers, the sisters' car.*

Note 3

- Write on the board:
  1. This / That is _____ .
  2. These / Those are _____ .
  3. This / That _____ is _____ .
  4. These / Those _____ are _____ .
- Ask: "In sentences 1 and 2, is *this / that / these / those* a pronoun or an adjective?" (*pronoun*) "In sentences 3 and 4, is *this / that / these / those* a pronoun or an adjective?" (*adjective*).

- Give some example sentences using each sentence structure and have students say *pronoun* or *adjective*. For example: *That is delicious!* (pronoun) *This jacket is cool.* (adjective) Have students continue the activity in pairs.
- Call on pairs to write some of their sentences on the board. Point to *this / that / these / those* and have students say *near* or *away*.

Note 4
- Write these expressions on the board:
  That's nice.
  That's terrible.
  That's terrific.
  That's awesome.
  That's awful.
  That's bad news.
  That's good news.
  That's too bad.
- Have students take turns making statements and responding to them with one of the expressions on the board. For example:
  S1: My sister is   S2: That's awesome.
      expecting a baby.
  S1: She's very sick.   S2: That's too bad.

🕐 **Identify the Grammar**: Have students identify the grammar in the opening conversation on page 166. For example:
  It's her **parents'** anniversary.
  That's nice. Is **that** a new sports jacket?
  It's my **brother's** jacket.
  Are **these** suspenders OK?

Go to **www.myfocusongrammarlab.com** for grammar charts and notes.

Step 3: Focused Practice (pages 169–172)
See the general suggestions for Focused Practice on page 4.

Exercise 1: Discover the Grammar
- Have students complete the exercise. Then have them work in pairs to check their answers.
- Call on pairs to read each numbered statement and the accompanying response.

Exercise 2: *This / That / These / Those*
A
- Have students complete the exercise individually and then work in groups of four to check their answers.
- Have groups practice the conversation four times, switching roles after each practice.

B
- Have students stay in their groups of four to complete this part. Go over the answers as a class. Call on a group to perform the conversations for the class.

Exercise 3: Possessives
- Have students look at the opening conversation on page 166. Read the following line aloud: *Kathy's mom is Bea Harlow, and her dad is Lee White.* Point out that the husband and wife have different last names because the wife did not change her name after marriage. Explain that this is common in the United States and other countries.
- Have students quickly skim the paragraph and circle any unfamiliar words. Explain any circled words. You may need to pre-teach *family name, marry, change their name, match,* and verbs in the past tense.
- Have students complete the exercise individually. Then have them work in pairs to check their answers and practice reading the paragraph to each other.
- Write on the board:
  In your country, do women usually change their names?
- Have pairs join another pair to talk about the custom of names in their own country or family. Have them answer the question and give two examples. Circulate and help as needed.

Exercise 4: *That's . . .*
- Read the phrases from the box. For each phrase, ask: "Does this come after good news, bad news, a good idea, or something true?" Have students complete the exercise individually. Then go over the correct answers as a group.
- Have students work in pairs or small groups to brainstorm for more expressions with *That's* (or brainstorm these as a class and write them on the board). Then have each pair or group write four more statements similar to the ones in this exercise. They should make sure that each of the *That's* expressions match one of the statements they wrote.
- Have pairs or groups exchange papers to match the statements and the *That's* expressions and practice reading them aloud. Circulate as students practice. Give assistance as needed.

Exercise 5: Editing

• Have students check their answers in pairs. Go over the answers as a class by having students write individual corrected sentences on the board. Have pairs practice reading the corrected versions to each other.

Go to **www.myfocusongrammarlab.com** for additional grammar practice.

Step 4: Communication Practice
(pages 172–174)

See the general suggestions for Communication Practice on page 5.

Exercise 6: Pronunciation

A

• Play the audio and have students read the Pronunciation Note as they listen. Have students repeat the sentences in the Pronunciation Note as you say them.
• Call on a student to read all three of the sentences. Have the rest of the students provide feedback by raising their hands if the pronunciation is correct. This will also give you feedback about students' listening.

B

• Play the audio, pausing as needed, and have students write the possessive noun they hear. Then have students listen again and check the sound they hear. Go over the answers as a class.
• Play the audio again as a dictation. Pause as needed to give students enough time to write. Have students write their sentences on the board and discuss them as a class.

C

• Have students complete the exercise individually. Call on students to write the sentences on the board. Have each student read his or her sentence aloud.

Exercise 7: Listening

A

• Go over the instructions and answer choices. Then play the audio and elicit the answer.

B

• Have students read the instructions and questions. Explain any unfamiliar vocabulary. Then play the audio, pausing and replaying as needed, while students complete both exercises. Have them work in small groups to check their answers. Then go over the answers as a class.

• Play the audio again and have students write down the possessive nouns they hear. Then give students a copy of the audioscript and have them check their answers in groups. You may want to point out that some words in the script end in 's but are not possessive nouns (e.g., Her *dad's* a really nice guy; *That's* good).
• Have groups identify the final sound for each of the possessive nouns. Call on groups to share their answers with the class. Then have students practice the conversation in pairs.

Exercise 8: Picture Differences

A

• Have students look at the picture. Read the example aloud.
• Have students work in pairs or groups to complete the exercise. Have each student in the pair or group write the differences on a sheet of paper. They should write complete sentences like the one in the example.
• Have pairs or groups exchange papers and compare their list of differences. Then have them take turns reading each of the sentences.

B

• Read the instructions. Write on the board:
  S1: What's different?
  S2: _____ is wearing _____'s glasses / backpack / watch / shoes / etc. _____ isn't wearing his / her _____ .
• Have two students exchange glasses, backpacks, watches, or similar items. Model the exercise with the class, using the language on the board. Then call on students to describe the same changes using the language on the board.
• Have students complete the activity as a class or in large groups. For variation, you may want to try this exercise with teams. Have one team leave the room (or put their heads down on the desk to cover their eyes). The other team or groups exchange personal items. The group or team that was outside tells the rest of the class about the changes.

Exercise 9: Writing

A

• Read the instructions and go over the example. Have students complete the exercise individually.

B

• Have students correct each other's work in pairs, using the Editing Checklist as a guide. Then have them take turns reading their paragraphs to each other.

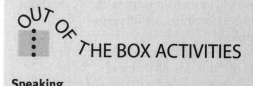

OUT OF THE BOX ACTIVITIES

Speaking

- Divide the class into two groups. Have one group put several of their personal items on a table or on their desks. Then send that group out of the room. Have the students in the room "borrow" the left items. Have them put on the wearable items and hold the others.
- Call the first group back in the room. Each person must find and collect his or her items by saying a sentence to claim the item. For example: *That's my backpack. Those are my keys. This is my hat.*

Speaking and Listening

- Write two column headings on the board: Clothes and Accessories. Brainstorm items that can go in each column and write them on the board. For example: *shirt, jeans, sweater* (clothes); *earrings, ring, belt* (accessories). For each item, ask: "Is it singular or plural?"
- Write the following conversation on the board and model it with a student:
  A: Maria, those earrings are beautiful!
  B: Thanks. They were a present from my grandmother. That's a very nice sweater, Pat.
  A: Thank you. Yes, it is.
- Point out the use of *those* and *that* before plural and singular nouns. Model the conversation with another student, this time substituting clothing and accessories that the student is actually wearing. Divide the students into pairs and have them practice the conversation. Then have them mingle as a class and continue practicing.
- You may want to point out that complimenting someone's clothes or accessories is an important part of small talk in North American culture. You may also want to point out that it is acceptable in North America to respond to a compliment by saying, "Thank you." Ask students if this is different in their cultures.

Writing, Reading, Speaking, and Listening

- Have students write a paragraph about one of the following topics (or one of their own). They can use the paragraph from Exercise 3 on page 171 or Exercise 5 on page 172 as a model.
  — Women's last names in their cultures
  — Their family members' favorite foods
  — Their family members' favorite things to do
  — Celebrations of their family members' birthdays
- Have students edit each other's paragraph in pairs, using the Editing Checklist on page 174 as a guide. Call on pairs to read their paragraphs to the class. Encourage students in the class to ask questions of the reader after he or she has read.

Go to **www.myfocusongrammarlab.com** for additional listening, pronunciation, speaking, and writing practice.

Note:
- See the *Focus on Grammar Workbook* for additional in-class or homework grammar practice.

Unit 18 Review (page 175)

Have students complete the Review and check their answers on Student Book page UR-2. Review or assign additional material as needed.

Go to **www.myfocusongrammarlab.com** for the Unit Achievement Test.

Grammar: COUNT AND NON-COUNT NOUNS;
Some AND *Any*

Unit 19 focuses on the meanings and uses of
count and non-count nouns.

- Count nouns refer to separate things.
- To form the plural of most count nouns, add
  -s or *-es*.
- Non-count nouns refer to things that are
  difficult to count. We use quantifiers to help
  us talk about non-count nouns.
- Use singular verbs with non-count nouns.
- Use *a* or *an* before singular count nouns.
- Use plural count nouns or non-count nouns
  to talk about things you like or dislike in
  general. Do not use *a, an, some,* or *any.*

The unit also introduces meanings and uses
of *some* and *any* with plural count nouns and
non-count nouns in affirmative and negative
statements and questions.

- *Some* and *any* are quantifiers. Use *some* (or
  no word) in affirmative statements with
  plural count nouns and non-count nouns.
- Use *any* (or no word) in negative statements
  and questions with plural count nouns or
  non-count nouns.

Theme: FOOD

Unit 19 focuses on language that is used to
talk about food.

Step 1: Grammar in Context (pages 176–178)

See the general suggestions for Grammar in
Context on page 1.

Before You Read

- Read the instructions and go over the
  example with the class. Explain the meaning
  of *healthy* and have students give examples of
  foods that are healthy and foods that are not
  healthy.
- Have students complete the exercise in groups
  of five. Then have them compare answers
  with another group. Have each student in the
  group fill in his or her information on a chart
  like the following:

Name	Foods	Healthy? Yes or No
Jair	coffee and donuts	no
Esperanza	fruit and yogurt	yes
Dania	cookies and milk	no

- Have each student report to the class about
  someone else in his or her group. For
  example:
  S1: Jair eats coffee and donuts for breakfast.
  That's not a healthy meal.
  S2: Esperanza eats fruit and yogurt. That's a
  healthy meal.
  S3: Dania's breakfast is cookies and milk.
  That's not a healthy meal.

Read

- To encourage students to read with a purpose,
  write these questions on the board:
  1. What is Jessica doing? (*She's interviewing
     people.*)
  2. What is she asking them about? (*their
     eating habits*)
  3. Does the man drink juice with his
     breakfast? (*not usually*)
  4. What does the first woman have for
     breakfast? Why? (*nothing, because she is
     always on a diet*)
- Establish a purpose for reading. Have
  students read each of the questions on the
  board. Have students keep these questions in
  mind as they read and listen to the interviews.
- Play the audio and have students read along
  in their books. Have students discuss the
  questions in pairs or groups of three. Call
  on pairs or groups to share answers with the
  class.

After You Read

A. Practice

- Circulate as students practice the interviews.
  Call on students from different groups to read
  each person's part in the conversation and
  perform it for the class.

B. Vocabulary

- Play the audio and have students repeat each
  word. Have students look at the interviews
  on pages 176–177 and find other food words.
  For example: *a cup of tea, a bowl of cereal, a
  banana, a peach, an orange, some strawberries,
  eggs, a glass of juice.* Have students write new
  words and their meanings in their notebooks.
- Write these questions and response stems on
  the board:
  What do you usually have for lunch?
  I _____ have _____ .
  I never have _____ .

  Do you ever have _____ at lunch?
  Yes, I do. / No, I don't.
  I _____ have _____ .

- Have students work in small groups to ask and answer the questions using the vocabulary items. They should use an adverb of frequency in the response sentences.

C. Vocabulary

- Write on the board:
  I like _____ , _____ , and _____ .
  I don't like _____ , _____ , or _____ .
  I like _____ , but I don't like _____ .
  How about you?
  Do you like _____ ?

- Model the exercise with a student, using the language on the board. Have students repeat the words in the box on page 177 as you say them. Then have students complete the exercise in pairs.

- Have students complete the exercise, then have pairs report their answers to the class. Keep a tally on the board. Have students work in pairs or groups to make questions or statements about the information on the board. For example:
  S1: Ian, how many students in our class don't like bagels?
  S2: Twelve students in our class don't like bagels.
  S3: Janica, do students in our class like candy?
  S4: Yes. Twenty students in our class like candy.

D. Comprehension

- Have students read the questions and complete the exercise individually. Remind them that the opening interviews are on pages 176–177.

- Call on students to write their answers on the board in sentence form. For example: *It is morning.* Have each student who wrote a sentence read it to the class. Discuss the statements and have students make corrections as needed.

Go to **www.myfocusongrammarlab.com** for an additional reading, and for reading and vocabulary practice.

Step 2: Grammar Presentation (pages 178–179)

See the general suggestions for Grammar Presentation on page 3.

Grammar Charts

- To show the differences between things we can count and things we cannot count, write on the board:
  I want a banana, two peaches, and an orange.
  Then ask students these questions:
  — How many bananas do I want? (*one*)
  — How many peaches do I want? (*two*)
  — How many oranges do I want? (*one*)
  — Can we count bananas, peaches, and oranges? (*yes*)

- Now write this sentence on the board:
  I like cereal with milk for breakfast. I also have milk in my coffee.
  Then ask students: "Can we count cereal or milk?" (*no*) "Can we count coffee?" (*no*)

- Remind students that *a* and *an* are for singular count nouns only. Point out that *a* comes before words that start with consonants and *an* before words that begin with vowels. If more review is needed, you may want to review the material on *a / an* in Unit 2.

- To teach the meaning and use of *some* and *any*, write on the board:
  I want some peaches, some cereal, and some milk.
  I don't want any bananas or coffee.

- Have students work in small groups to come up with a rule for the use of *some* and *any* with count and non-count nouns. (*Use* some *in affirmative statements with either count or non-count nouns. Use* any *in negative statements with both count and non-count nouns.*) If students have trouble coming up with a rule, have them look at the second chart. If they come up with a rule, have them look at the second chart to confirm their ideas.

- Have students look at the pictures in the last chart and read the captions aloud. For each caption, have students brainstorm other words that can go in the parentheses. For example, *a cup of* can go with *tea, water, juice, milk,* etc.
- Point out that these phrases—*a cup of, a slice of, a bowl of, a bottle of, a glass of*—are quantifiers and can go with non-count nouns. Brainstorm other quantifiers students may know. For example, *a bag of, a box of.*

Grammar Notes

Note 1
- Have a student read Note 1 aloud to the class. Have students look back at the words in the box for (C) Vocabulary on page 177. Have students identify the count nouns *(bagels, eggs, sandwiches)* and tell you their singular forms *(bagel, egg, sandwich).*
- Have students work in pairs or groups to brainstorm a list of singular countable food words. Have pairs or groups exchange lists and write the plural form next to each of the words. Call on pairs to share singular and plural items from their lists with the class. If students are having trouble deciding when to add *-s* or *-es* to form plurals, you may want to review or refer them to Unit 2, page 13 or Appendix 3, page A-3.

Note 2
- Have another student read Note 2 aloud. Write these quantifiers on the board:
  a bag of   a cup of
  a bottle of   a glass of
  a bowl of   a slice of
- Have students work in groups to come up with as many different food items as they can that are appropriate for each of the quantifiers. The group that has the most correct items wins.

Note 3
- Read the explanation and have students look at the example sentence.
- Write on the board:
  _____ is / isn't good for you.
  Say a non-count food noun and have students use it in a sentence like the one on the board. For example: *milk—Milk is good for you; candy—Candy isn't good for you.*

Note 4
- Write on the board:
  a _____ an _____ some _____
- Have students give examples of words that can go in each blank. For example, *a banana, an orange, some oranges, some juice.* Write their examples on the board. Ask:

  — What word goes with singular count nouns that begin with a consonant sound? *(a)*
  — What word goes with singular count nouns that begin with a vowel sound? *(an)*
  — What word goes with plural count nouns and non-count nouns? *(some)*
- Have students read Note 4 aloud to confirm their answers. Point out that you can often omit *some.*

Note 5
- Have a student read Note 5. Write on the board:
  some   any
  — affirmative   — negative
  statements   statements
  — questions
- Read the example sentences aloud and have students repeat. Then say a non-count food word and have students substitute it in the example sentences. For example, for *coffee: I have some coffee. I don't have any coffee. Do you have any coffee? Do you want some coffee?*

Note 6
- Have students look over Note 6. Then model this sentence: *I like oranges, but I don't like grapefruit.*
- Have a student make a similar statement. Then have that student pick someone else to make another statement, using the last half of your statement to start and then adding a new food. Students can only add new foods that have not been mentioned previously. For example:
  T: I like oranges, but I don't like grapefruit.
  S1: I don't like grapefruit, but I like apples.
  S2: I like apples, but I don't like cheese.
  S3: I like cheese, but I don't like meat.

⏱ **Identify the Grammar**: Have students identify the grammar in the opening conversation on pages 176–177. For example:
  I generally have **a bagel** and **a cup of tea**.
  That's all? Do you have **any juice** or anything else to drink?
  Once in a while I have **coffee** instead of **tea**.
  Oh, I usually have **a bowl of cereal** and **some yogurt** with **fruit—a banana, a peach,** or **an orange,** or **some strawberries.**

Go to **www.myfocusongrammarlab.com** for grammar charts and notes.

Step 3: Focused Practice (pages 180–182)
See the general suggestions for Focused Practice on page 4.

Exercise 1: Discover the Grammar

- Have students read the paragraph aloud. Answer any questions and explain unfamiliar vocabulary. Then have students complete the exercise individually and work in groups to check their answers.
- To provide more practice, you might want to have partners ask each other about their likes and dislikes of the foods in the exercise. For example:
  S1: Munh, do you like crackers?
  S2: No, I don't.

Exercise 2: Count and Non-count Nouns

- Read the instructions. Point out the Ø in item 6. Ask students what they think it means. (*It means that one of the answer choices is* salad *without a quantifier.*)
- Have students complete the exercise individually. Go over the answers to the exercise as a class. Then have students work in groups of four to practice the conversation four times. Have them change roles after each practice.

Exercise 3: *Some* or *Any*

- Have students complete the exercise. Then call on students to share their answers.
- Have students work in pairs to practice the conversation two times. Have them change roles after the first practice.

Exercise 4: Editing

- Have students complete the exercise individually. Call on students to write their corrected sentences on the board. Discuss the answers as a class.
- Have students practice reading the corrected conversations in pairs.

Go to **www.myfocusongrammarlab.com** for additional grammar practice.

Step 4: Communication Practice (pages 183–185)

See the general suggestions for Communication Practice on page 5.

Exercise 5: Listening

A

- Have students read the instructions and statements. Then play the audio and have students complete the task. Elicit the correct answers from the class.

B

- Have students read the instructions and statements aloud. Pre-teach any unfamiliar vocabulary from the audioscript such as *be out of (something)*. Make sure students understand when to check *NI* (no information).

- Play the audio and have students complete the exercise. Then have them check their answers in groups.
- Give students a copy of the audioscript and have them read it in pairs. Have students explain the meanings of the expressions *No kidding!* and *I don't believe this place.* ("No kidding!" is the equivalent of saying "Really?" to express surprise. "I can't believe this place!" means that the speaker is not happy with the place or the situation.)

Exercise 6: Pronunciation

A

- Play the audio. Have students practice the sounds.

B

- Play the audio and have students complete the exercise. Then go over the answers as a class.

C

- Play the audio and have students complete the exercise. Then have them check their answers in pairs. Play the audio again as needed.

D

- Have pairs practice saying the sentences to each other. Circulate and note any difficulties the students are having. Review as a class the pronunciation of any problem words you noted.

Exercise 7: Discuss Foods

A

- Explain the task. Have students discuss the questions in groups.

B

- Have one student in each group make a list. Then ask that person to read the list to the class.
- For variation, students can complete this exercise as an interview and record their partner's answers in a chart like the following:

Partner's Name	Likes	Dislikes

Exercise 8: Writing

A
- Have students read the composition and guess the answer in pairs.

B
- Go over the instructions. Have students write their compositions individually.

C
- Have students correct each other's papers in pairs using the Editing Checklist. Then have students make revisions as needed.
- ⏱ Have students read their paragraphs to the class. The class guesses the food.

OUT OF THE BOX ACTIVITIES

Speaking and Listening
- Have students sit in a circle. Begin this memory game by saying: "I'm very hungry. I want a piece of chicken." The student to your right repeats what you said and adds something new. Continue around the circle with each speaker repeating what previous speakers have said and adding something new. For example:

  T: I'm very hungry. I want a piece of chicken.
  S1: I'm very hungry. I want a piece of chicken and a big salad.
  S2: I'm very hungry. I want a piece of chicken, a big salad, and some ice cream.

- If a student misses an item, he or she is out of the game. The last person to remember all of the items, in order, wins.

Writing, Reading, Listening, and Speaking
- Bring in magazine photos (or have students bring them) of different foods or prepared food dishes. Give a photo to each student. Have each person write a riddle similar to the paragraph they wrote in Exercise 8 on page 185. Have them write the riddle from the first-person point of view, as if they were the food they are describing. For example:
  I can be many different colors. Sometimes I'm sweet, and sometimes I'm not. You can use me to make a salad or a delicious dessert. I grow on a tree. What am I?

- Collect all of the pictures and place them on one side of the classroom. Be sure to label the pictures with the name of the food or the dish. Then collect the riddles, label them with a number or a letter, and place them in another part of the room. If you have a large class you can put groups of pictures and riddles in different places around the room.
- Have students circulate with a piece of paper and pencil, looking at the riddles and the labeled pictures. Have them match each riddle with a picture. Have each student read his or her riddle aloud and have the class say which picture matches it.

Go to **www.myfocusongrammarlab.com** for additional listening, pronunciation, speaking, and writing practice.

Note:
- See the *Focus on Grammar Workbook* for additional in-class or homework grammar practice.

Unit 19 Review (page 186)
Have students complete the Review and check their answers on Student Book page UR-3. Review or assign additional material as needed.

Go to **www.myfocusongrammarlab.com** for the Unit Achievement Test.

Grammar: *A /An* AND *The*; *One /Ones*

Unit 20 focuses on the meanings and uses of the indefinite articles *a / an* and the definite article *the*. It also introduces the pronouns *one* and *ones*.

- Use the indefinite articles *a* or *an* before singular count nouns to talk about things in general. Use *a* before nouns that begin with a consonant sound and *an* before nouns that begin with a vowel sound. Do not use *a* or *an* before non-count or plural count nouns.

- Use the definite article *the* for specific things that the speaker and the listener know about. You can use *the* with singular and plural count nouns and with non-count nouns.

- Use *the* when there is only one of something or when you talk about something for the second time and afterwards.

- Use *one* to replace a singular noun and *ones* to replace a plural noun.

Theme: SHOPPING FOR CLOTHES

Unit 20 focuses on language that is used to talk about clothes and shopping for clothes.

Step 1: Grammar in Context (pages 187–189)

See the general suggestions for Grammar in Context on page 1.

Before You Read

A

- Go over the example with the class. Explain the difference between *want* and *need*. For example, *I need a coat in the winter. I have a good coat, but I want a cool new coat.* Brainstorm other examples with the class and write them on the board.
- Have students write their sentences individually.

B

- Have students compare their answers in groups of four. Then have them share their answers with another group or the class.

Read

- Have students look at the pictures. Ask: "What are the people doing?" *(They're shopping for clothes.)* Then write these questions on the board:
  1. Where are the speakers? *(in a clothing store)*
  2. What is Ken looking for? *(a sports jacket)*
  3. What color does Ken like? *(blue)*
  4. What color does Laura like? *(black)*

- Establish a purpose for reading. Have students think about these questions as they read and listen to the conversation. Then have students work in pairs to answer the questions on the board.

After You Read

A. Practice

- Divide the class into three groups and have them practice the conversation chorally. Read each role to lead each group. Then have groups of three practice the conversation three times so that each person has an opportunity to read each role.

B. Vocabulary

- Play the audio and have students repeat the words. Ask students what the antonyms are in this vocabulary set. *(bright / dull; formal / casual)* Ask students to give some other examples of clothing that would be *bright* or *dull* and *formal* or *casual*.

- Have students work in pairs to practice the vocabulary words. Student A points to a picture and Student B says the word. Have them switch roles.

C. Vocabulary

- Have students complete the exercise individually and compare answers in pairs. Have students circle their partners' answers in their own books.

- Have each pair join another pair. Students share their partners' answers with the other pair.

D. Comprehension

- Remind students that the opening conversation is on pages 187–188. Have students complete the exercise. Then go over the answers as a class.

- To provide more comprehension practice, you may want to have students work in pairs to write three more questions about the conversation. Have them use the questions in this exercise as a model. Have two pairs work together. Have them exchange their questions, answer them, and discuss them as a group.

Go to **www.myfocusongrammarlab.com** for an additional reading, and for reading and vocabulary practice.

Step 2: Grammar Presentation
(pages 189–190)

See the general suggestions for Grammar Presentation on page 3.

Grammar Charts

- Have students look at the example sentences in the first chart. Have them work in pairs to come up with a rule for the use of *a* and *an*. (*Use* a *before singular count nouns that begin with a consonant sound. Use* an *before a singular count noun that begins with a vowel sound.*)
- Call on pairs to share their rule with the class. Then have students look at Note 1 to confirm their ideas.
- To explain the definite article (*the*), write on the board:
  1. I like blue suits.
  2. I like the blue suit.
  3. I don't like the black suits.
- Ask: "How are sentences 1 and 2 different?" (*Sentence 1 talks about blue suits in general, and sentence 2 is about one specific blue suit.*) Have students look at the bottom picture on page 187. Ask: "Which sentence is right for this picture?" (*I like the blue suit.*) Explain that Ken is talking about a specific suit—the suit the clerk is holding—that the speaker and listener already know about.
- Now have students read sentence 3 aloud. Explain that the sentence is about two or more specific black suits that the speaker and listener know about, not about black suits in general.
- Have students read the example sentences for *one* and *ones* aloud. Remind students that pronouns are words that take the place of nouns. Ask students what the two pronouns are in the example sentences. (*one* and *ones*) Ask students what words *one* and *ones* replace. (*suit* and *suits*)

Grammar Notes

Note 1

- This note repeats information from the previous unit. Draw attention to the *Be Careful!* note. To review, write a few sentences with errors on the board. Then have students find the errors and state the rule. For example:
  I'm eating a bread.
  I want a apple.
  He's a student at an university.
  He's a honest person.
  I want to buy an necklace.

Note 2

- Read the explanation aloud. Point out that this note addresses both meaning and use of *the*. It may take a lot of practice before students understand the idea of "things that the speaker and listener know about." It is useful to continue to have students ask the question *Which one(s)?* If both speaker and listener know *which one* and are aware that each other knows, then they use *the*.
- Have two students read the example sentences. Then ask students why each speaker uses *the*. (*Both of them know which suits they're talking about because they can see them.*)
- Provide a few more examples. Have a student get up and open (or close) the door. Then ask the class why you said *the door*. (*Because everyone in the class knows which door. We can see it. It may also be that the room has only one door.*)
- Pick up a marker or other object, put it down somewhere, and then pretend you forgot where it is. Look around and say: "Where's the marker?" Then ask the class why you said *the marker*. (*We can see it and we all know about it.*)

Note 3

- Go over Note 3 with the class. Elicit examples of other nouns that are preceded by *the* because there is only one of them. Write these examples on the board (or prepare as a handout):

nature/the universe	your home	your school or classroom
the moon the stars the equator	the dog the kitchen the garage the bathroom the sofa	the teacher the office the elevator the board the parking lot

- Have students work in groups to brainstorm other examples and then share them with the class. (**Note:** If students give incorrect examples such as *the Mars* or *the Africa*, explain that we usually don't use articles with names in English. Exceptions are *the North Pole, the United States, the Czech Republic, the Philippines, the United Kingdom*, and others that have the structure *the* + adjective + noun.)

Note 4

- Model a few examples like the one in the book. For example: *I bought some bread and fish. The bread was on sale, but the fish wasn't.*

- Make statements with *a* or *an*. Have students make a follow-up comment. For example:
  T: The school has   S: The elevator is slow.
     an elevator.

Note 5
- A fun way to practice this point is to bring in candies of different colors such as M&Ms. Put the different colors on a plate or a tray. Walk around the room and offer them. Students must ask for them by saying, *I want a (color) one or I want some / two / three (color) ones.*

⏱ **Identify the Grammar**: Have students identify the grammar in the opening conversation on pages 187–188. For example:
  I have **an** interview tomorrow.
  We're having **a** sale on sports jackets.
  Yes! I really like **the** blue **one**.
  All **the** black **ones** are dull—really boring.

Go to **www.myfocusongrammarlab.com** for grammar charts and notes.

Step 3: Focused Practice (pages 190–192)

See the general suggestions for Focused Practice on page 4.

Exercise 1: Discover the Grammar
- Have students complete the exercise individually. Then go over the answers as a class.
- Have students practice each conversation chorally. Divide them into two groups and have one group read Speaker A's lines and the other Speaker B's. Then have them change roles and repeat.

Exercise 2: Articles
- Read the instructions. Make sure students know that Ø means no article is required.
- Have students complete the exercise individually. Then have students work in groups of three to check their answers. Have groups practice the conversation three times, changing roles after each practice.

Exercise 3: *One* and *Ones*
- Have students complete the exercise individually. Go over the answers as a class.
- To practice the questions and answers, divide the class into two teams. A student from the first team asks one of the questions from the exercise, and a student from the other team must answer with the correct response. Continue the activity until everyone has had a chance to ask or answer a question. Then switch and have the other team ask the questions.

Exercise 4: Editing
- Go over the example with the class. Have students complete the exercise individually. Discuss the answers as a class. Explain why each mistake is wrong. You may also have to explain why other sentences may sound wrong to students but are actually correct. Try to explain each mistake by referring back to the grammar charts or grammar notes.
- Have pairs practice reading the corrected letter to each other.

Go to **www.myfocusongrammarlab.com** for additional grammar practice.

Step 4: Communication Practice
(pages 192–194)

See the general suggestions for Communication Practice on page 5.

Exercise 5: Listening
A
- Have students look at the picture. Elicit that the people are talking about things to do for fun tonight.
- Have students read the statements. Explain any unfamiliar words. You may want to pre-teach terms such as *concert, downtown, rock, classical, Latin, umbrella*, and *there is / are*.
- Play the audio, pausing and repeating as needed, and have students complete the exercise. Have them work in pairs to check their answers. Then have pairs correct the false statements. Go over their corrections as a class.

B
- Have students read the questions. Explain the meaning of *There is* in the first item, as well as the term *more than one*.
- Play the audio again and have students complete the exercise. Go over answers with the class. Play the audio again as needed for clarification.

Exercise 6: Pronunciation
A
- Play the audio. Have students read and listen to the Pronunciation Note. Give additional examples if needed.

B
- Have students complete the exercise. Then have them exchange books in pairs and listen again. Have the students correct each other's work.
- Go over the answers as a class.

C
- Play the audio again as needed. Then have students practice the conversations in pairs.

Exercise 7: Picture Discussion

- As an extension for this activity, bring in pictures of different pieces of clothing, shoes, boots, etc., that are in different colors. You can find these in newspaper ads or clothing catalogs.
- Have students work in groups to discuss the pictures using *one / ones*. For example (about boots or shoes):

S1: I like the ones with high heels. They're sharp.
S2: I like the brown ones. They look comfortable.

Exercise 8: Writing

A

- Have students look at the picture. Brainstorm some strange and unusual things in the picture. Go over the example and make sure students understand why *a* and *the* are used.
- Have students write sentences individually.

B

- Have students check each other's work in pairs and discuss any errors.

C

- Have each pair work together with another pair and compare their sentences. Then have them look for other things that are wrong. Give the students a few extra minutes and have them try to write more correct sentences about the picture.
- Have each group compare lists with another group. Call on groups to read their sentences aloud. The group with the most sentences is the winner.

OUT OF THE BOX ACTIVITIES

Listening and Speaking

- Have students role-play a conversation similar to the one in the opening reading.
- Have them work in groups of three. Two students are friends and the third is a salesperson. The friends should decide who is shopping and what that person is looking for. They need to pick a style, size, and color. The salesperson should offer to help them and bring the friends several of the desired items to choose from. At the end of the conversation, one of the friends should choose an item to buy. Have students use indefinite and definite articles and the pronouns *one / ones* in their conversations. Circulate as students are practicing. Offer assistance as needed.

- Have each group perform the role play for the class or, if time is limited, have two groups perform for each other. You may also want to make a video recording of each group performing and replay it for the class.

Speaking and Listening

- Bring in clothing catalogs. You will need one for each pair of students. Have students work in pairs. Pretend each one is going somewhere and needs to find clothes for that event—it could be a party, a formal dance, a camping trip, a vacation, etc.—but they don't have the clothes they need for the event.
- Have partners look through the catalogs with each other and talk about the items they need and want to order for the event. You may want to model the discussion with a student. For example:

T: I'm going on a camping trip, and I need some things for it.
S: Well, you need a tent. Are you going alone?
T: No, I'm going with three friends.
S: Look at this tent. It's a good one.
T: Hmmm. That tent is too small. I like the one on this page.
S: Yes, it's a big one. Do you need a sleeping bag?
T: No, I have one, but I need a warm jacket. And I need boots.

- As students select items for their events, have them take notes. You may also want to have them cut and glue the pictures they select to a poster board. At the top of the board, have them write the name of the event and then label each item. Have each pair tell the class about the items they selected.

Go to **www.myfocusongrammarlab.com** for additional listening, pronunciation, speaking, and writing practice.

Note:
- See the *Focus on Grammar Workbook* for additional in-class or homework grammar practice.

Unit 20 Review (page 195)

Have students complete the Review and check their answers on Student Book page UR-3. Review or assign additional material as needed.

Go to **www.myfocusongrammarlab.com** for the Unit Achievement Test.

UNIT 21 OVERVIEW

Grammar: *Can / Can't*

Unit 21 focuses on the meanings and uses of *can* and *can't* to express ability and possibility and to make requests.

- *Can* is a modal. It changes the meaning of the verb that follows.
- *Can* has many different meanings. These include expressing ability (or inability), possibility (or impossibility), and making requests.
- *Cannot* is the negative form of *can*, and the contraction is *can't*.
- Use the base form of the verb after *can* or *can't*.
- For questions, put *can* or *can't* before the subject of the sentence.

Theme: ABILITIES

Unit 21 focuses on language that expresses the ability or inability to do something.

Step 1: Grammar in Context (pages 196–198)

See the general suggestions for Grammar in Context on page 1.

Before You Read

A
- Have students rate themselves.

B
- Have students compare answers in groups.
- Ask each group: "How many people are pretty good at _____ ? How many people are not so good at _____ ?" Tally the information on the board.

Read

- To encourage students to read with a purpose, write these questions on the board.
  1. What are Jeremy and Jessica talking about? *(Jeremy's Spanish class)*
  2. How well does Jeremy know the other students in the class? *(not well)*
  3. Who has a plan about how to solve Jeremy's problem? *(Jeremy)*

4. Is this a good plan? Why or why not? *(Answers may vary, but students will probably say it's a good plan because Jorge and Jeremy can help each other.)*
- Go over the questions with the class. Have them think about these questions as they read and listen to the conversation.
- Point out the first line of the conversation. Ask students what Jessica means when she says, "You look down." *(You look sad [or upset].)* Then have students read the conversation and discuss the questions in groups. Go over the answers as a class.

After You Read

A. Practice
- Have students practice reading the email conversation in pairs. Call on pairs to perform the conversation for the class or have two pairs perform the conversation for each other.

B. Vocabulary
- Have students listen to and repeat the vocabulary words. Then have them repeat them as you say them aloud.
- Have students look at the last four vocabulary items: *idea, pass, fluent, sounds like a plan.* Have students find the sentences in the conversation where each of these items appears. Call on students to read each of the sentences aloud, substituting the definition for the vocabulary item as they read. For example: *But that gives me a thought; The coach says he has to succeed in math; But he speaks Spanish well.*
- Point out to students that this kind of substitution is a good strategy to use to figure out what new or unknown words mean.

C. Vocabulary
- Have students complete the exercise individually. Then have them check their answers in pairs by reading each conversation, putting in the answers as they read. Go over the answers as a class.

D. Comprehension
- Have students read the questions. Remind them that the opening conversation is on page 196. Have students complete the exercise individually.
- Go over the answers as a class. Have a student read the first question. Then have another student read the complete answer and then say the letter of that answer. Continue in this way until each of the questions has been answered.

Go to **www.myfocusongrammarlab.com** for an additional reading, and for reading and vocabulary practice.

Step 2: Grammar Presentation
(pages 198–199)

See the general suggestions for Grammar Presentation on page 3.

Grammar Charts

- Have students look over both grammar charts. Then ask these questions to help students notice the grammar:
  — Which form of the verb do we use after *can* and *can't*? *(the base form)*
  — Do we use *to* with *can* and *can't*? *(no)*
  — What is the word order of *yes / no* questions with *can*? *(can + subject + verb)*
  — What are the short answers for *yes / no* questions with *can*? *(Yes, I can. / No, I can't.)*
- Point out the word order of *Wh-* questions with *can*. For questions about the object, the order is *Wh-* word + *can* + subject + verb. (For example, *What can I do?*) For questions about the subject, the order is *Wh-* word + *can* + verb. (*Who can help?*)

Grammar Notes

Note 1

- Read the explanation and have students read the example sentences aloud. Then have students reread the opening conversation on page 196 and underline sentences with *can* and *can't*. Have them work in groups to identify the meaning of each use of *can* and *can't*. (*The main use of* can *and* can't *in this conversation is to express ability or inability. There are two instances of* can *to express possibility: "**Can** someone in the class **help**?" and "Maybe he **can help** me with Spanish, and I **can teach** him math." There are no instances where* can *is used to make a request.)*

Note 2

- Have students close their books. Write the incorrect example sentences on the board but do not cross out the errors. Ask students, "What is wrong with these sentences?" Call on students to come to the board and correct the sentences. Discuss the answers as a class.
- Ask: "Do we use *to* after *can*?" *(no)* "Do we add *-s* or *-ing* to verbs after *can*?" *(no)* Then have students open their books and read the note to confirm their answers.

Note 3

- Have students read the example sentences aloud. Say a sentence with *cannot* and have students repeat it using *can't* instead of *cannot*. Then have students change a *can't* sentence into one that uses *cannot*. Have students continue in pairs.

Note 4

- Have students read the example questions aloud. Point out that the word order of *yes / no* questions with *can* is the same as simple present *yes / no* questions for verbs other than *be*. Write some examples on the board. For example: Does she speak English? Can she speak English?
- Have students look at the example *Wh-* questions. Ask: "How are they different?" (*In the second question,* who *is the subject.*)

⏱ **Identify the Grammar**: Have students identify the grammar in the opening conversation on page 196. For example:

  I **can't understand** my Spanish teacher.
  And no one **can understand** my Spanish.
  I **can read**. I just **can't speak**.
  Can someone in the class **help**?

Go to **www.myfocusongrammarlab.com** for grammar charts and notes.

Step 3: Focused Practice (pages 199–201)

See the general suggestions for Focused Practice on page 4.

Exercise 1: Discover the Grammar

- Have students complete the exercise individually. Then have them work in pairs to check their answers.
- Have pairs take turns reading and responding to the correctly matched items.

Exercise 2: *Can or Can't*

- Read the instructions and go over the example with the class. Explain that sometimes one word goes in a blank but sometimes a blank needs more than one word.
- Have students complete the exercise individually. Go over the answers with the class. Explain any unfamiliar words, such as *prepare a talk, technical stuff, pronunciation, review,* and *empty.*
- Have pairs practice the conversations two times, changing roles after each conversation.

Exercise 3: *Can or Can't*

- Have students complete the exercise individually. Then go over the answers as a class.
- Have students work in groups to identify the meaning of *can* or *can't* in each sentence. Have them use these descriptions: ability, possibility, and request. Discuss the answers as a class. *(1. (in)ability/request; 2.(in)ability/ request; 3. (in)ability/request; 4. (in)ability; 5. (in)ability)*

Exercise 4: Editing

- Have students complete the exercise individually. Have students compare answers in pairs. Then call on pairs to write the corrected sentences on the board. Have each pair explain the error and the correction.

Go to **www.myfocusongrammarlab.com** for additional grammar practice.

Step 4: Communication Practice

(pages 202–205)

See the general suggestions for Communication Practice on page 5.

Exercise 5: Pronunciation

A

- Play the audio and have students listen to the Pronunciation Note. Then read the example sentences aloud (*I can speak Spanish; I can't speak French*) and have students repeat.

B

- Play the audio and have students complete the exercise individually. Then have them work in pairs to check their answers. Play the audio as needed for clarification.
- Give students the audioscript and have pairs practice each conversation two times. Have them change roles after the first time.

C

- Read the instructions and go over the example with the class. Have students complete the exercise individually. Call on students to give their answers. Have them spell the word they wrote on the line.

D

- Have students change partners two or three times so that they are practicing the various conversations with different people. Circulate as students practice. Make corrections as needed.

Exercise 6: Listening

A

- Go over the answer choices. Then play the audio and have students complete the exercise. Elicit the answer.

B

- Play the audio and have students complete the exercise. Pause and replay the audio as needed. Then go over the answers as a class.
- Have students read each sentence aloud, saying the correct choice as they read.

Exercise 7: Find Someone Who . . .

- To prepare for this activity, make a handout like the following:

Who can . . .	
stand on his or her head?	
do a martial art well?	
fix a computer?	
lift fifty-pound weights?	
write poetry?	
cook well?	
say "yes" in five languages?	

- Tell students that when they find a person who can do that thing, they should have that person sign his or her name next to the thing that he or she can do. You may also want to model a question and answer with a student.

Exercise 8: Find Someone Who . . .

- Go over the instructions and the pictures on page 204. Have two students model the example conversation.
- Have students complete the task as a class. Circulate and give help as needed.
- **Note:** For a variation, you can set this up as an individual or team competition. For an individual competition, print the tasks in nine boxes on paper. Tell students that when they have three names in any direction to shout "Bingo!" Confirm the information by having them read it to you. For example: *Mari can water ski, Song Hee can speak Italian, and Marco can play chess.* For a team competition, divide the class into teams. Set a time limit for the competition. The team with the most names on their sheet wins.

Exercise 9: Writing

A

- Go over the instructions and the example. Give students a suggested range for the number of sentences to write based on your class's ability level.

B

- Have students correct their work using the Editing Checklist. Then call on students to read their paragraphs to the class.

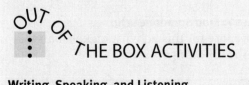

OUT OF THE BOX ACTIVITIES

Writing, Speaking, and Listening

- Bring in simple items or pictures of items. Divide the class into groups of three or four. Display all of the items or pictures so that all of the groups can see them. Have each group make a list of as many different (and unusual) things they can do with each item. Have each group share their ideas with the class or another group.
- For variation, give a different item or picture to each group and have them tell the class about things that the one item can be used for.

Writing, Reading, Speaking, and Listening

- Divide the class into two groups. Have each student fold a piece of paper lengthwise to make two columns. Then have each group brainstorm a list of things people can do that are unusual or interesting. Have students write the list of things they brainstorm in the left column. Give groups a few minutes to brainstorm their lists. Circulate and offer assistance as needed.
- Have students in each group interview each other to find out who in the class can do each thing on the list. Students should write the name of the person who can do it in the right column. For example:
  S1: Can you tie a cherry stem in a knot with your tongue?
  S2: No, I can't. Can you pat your head and rub your stomach at the same time?
- Have each group meet again to discuss the results of their interviews. Call on a student from each group to share some of their information with the class using *can* and *can't*.

Go to **www.myfocusongrammarlab.com** for additional listening, pronunciation, speaking, and writing practice.

Note:

- See the *Focus on Grammar Workbook* for additional in-class or homework grammar practice.

Unit 21 Review (page 206)

Have students complete the Review and check their answers on Student Book page UR-3. Review or assign additional material as needed.

Go to **www.myfocusongrammarlab.com** for the Unit Achievement Test.

From Grammar to Writing (page FG-6)

See the general suggestions for From Grammar to Writing on page 9.

Go to **www.myfocusongrammarlab.com** for an additional From Grammar to Writing Assignment, Part Review, and Part Post-Test.

PART VIII OVERVIEW

SIMPLE PAST

UNIT	GRAMMAR FOCUS	THEME
22	Simple Past: Regular Verbs (Statements)	Business Trips
23	Simple Past: Regular and Irregular Verbs; *Yes / No* Questions	A Biography
24	Simple Past: *Wh-* Questions	A Car Accident

Go to **www.myfocusongrammarlab.com** for the Part and Unit Tests.

Note: PowerPoint® grammar presentations, test-generating software, and reproducible Part and Unit Tests are on the *Teacher's Resource Disc.*

Grammar: SIMPLE PAST: REGULAR VERBS (STATEMENTS)

Unit 22 focuses on the meanings and uses of regular verbs in simple past statements.

• Use the simple past to talk about an event that happened in the past.

• Regular verbs in the simple past end in -ed. If the base form of the verb ends in -e just add -d. If the base form ends in -y that follows a consonant, change the y to i and add -ed.

• Use did + not + the base form of the verb for a simple past negative statement. You can use didn't in speaking and informal writing.

• Past time expressions such as last night, last year, last week, etc., can come at the beginning or end of the sentence.

Theme: BUSINESS TRIPS

Unit 22 focuses on language that is used to talk about an out-of-town trip.

Step 1: Grammar in Context (pages 208–210)

See the general suggestions for Grammar in Context on page 1.

Before You Read

• Have students read the sentences aloud. Explain any unfamiliar vocabulary. Have students say the past time expression in each sentence (Yesterday, last Sunday, last night, etc.) and give the day and month for each.

• Have students complete the exercise and compare answers in groups.

• Have groups brainstorm a list of other past time expressions they know. Have each group share their list with the class. Write their answers on the board.

Read

• To encourage students to read with a purpose, write these questions on the board:
  1. Who is writing the emails? (Kathy and Judy)
  2. Where is Kathy? (She was at a convention in Boston. Now she's staying in Boston with her cousin Ted)
  3. Does Kathy like Boston? (Yes, she does.)
  4. Who does Kathy want Judy to meet? (Kathy's cousin Ted.)

• Call on students to read the questions for the class. Have students keep these questions in mind as they read and listen to the conversation.

• Play the audio and have students follow along in their books. Have students discuss the questions in pairs or groups of three. Call on pairs or groups to share answers with the class.

After You Read

A. Practice

• Have students practice reading the messages in pairs. Have them switch roles.

B. Vocabulary

• Play the audio and have students repeat each word. Have students write any new vocabulary in their notebooks. Have students work in pairs to compare the new words that they wrote.

• Have students look at the pictures for convention and presentation. Call on students to explain in their own words what each of the words means.

• Write these questions on the board and then have students underline the new vocabulary words in the questions. Have students work in groups to ask and answer them. Have them answer in complete sentences.
  1. When do you usually <u>arrive</u> at school?
  2. Where is your favorite place to <u>stay</u> on a vacation?
  3. How long do you <u>stay</u> at school?
  4. Who is someone you <u>miss</u>?
  5. What is one family event you don't like to <u>miss</u>?

C. Vocabulary

• Have students repeat each of the words in the box as you say them. Emphasize that the pronunciation of stayed and enjoyed is different from the pronunciation of checked in, even though the endings of the words are the same.

• Have students complete the activity individually. Then have them work in pairs to check their answers and take turns reading the paragraph to each other.

D. Comprehension

• Have students read the questions and answer choices. Remind students that the opening email messages are on page 208.

• Have students complete the exercise. Then go over the answers as a class by calling on one student to read the question and another student to read the correct answer.

Go to **www.myfocusongrammarlab.com** for an additional reading, and for reading and vocabulary practice.

Step 2: Grammar Presentation
(pages 210–211)

See the general suggestions for Grammar Presentation on page 3.

Grammar Charts
- Have students look at the opening emails on page 208. Have them underline the simple past verb forms in the affirmative statements in Judy's email. (*enjoyed, missed*) Then have them look over the first chart on page 210.
- Ask: "How do we form a simple past affirmative statement?" (*add -ed or -d to the regular base verb*) "How do we form a negative statement?" (*use did + not + the base form of the verb*)
- Have students read the chart on page 211 aloud. Have students tell you some of the time expressions that are used with the simple past. Point out the lists that they generated in the Before You Read activity on page 97 of this book.
- Have a student say today's date. Then ask what the date was yesterday, two days ago, and last Monday. (*Answers will vary.*)

Grammar Notes

Notes 1–2
- Write each of the subject pronouns and some names of students in a column on the board. Write the base form of some regular verbs, including those from the opening emails, in another column on the board. Be sure to include verbs that end with -e and -y after a consonant. Write some past time expressions in a third column.
- Call on students to make affirmative sentences using the words from each column. Write the sentences on the board and correct any mistakes. Make sure students follow the spelling rules correctly.
- Have students read the sentences aloud. Ask: "Is the verb form the same or different for each subject?" (*The same. Regular simple past verbs have the same form for all subjects and do not change.*) Leave all of the sentences on the board.

Note 3
- Read the note aloud and have students repeat the example sentences. Draw attention to the *Be Careful!* note.
- Have students work in pairs to write negative statements based on the affirmative statements they wrote on the board.

- Have pairs share their negative statements with each other. Circulate as students are sharing, offering assistance as needed.

Note 4
- Have students read the explanation. Read the example sentences aloud and have students repeat.
- Have groups work together to reverse the position of the time expressions in each of the sentences on the board. They can do this orally or in writing.
- If students need additional help, you may want to review the grammar charts and notes for the past of *be* (Unit 7) or refer them to Appendix 6 on page A-4 for more information on the spelling of regular simple past verbs.

🕐 **Identify the Grammar**: Have students identify the grammar in the opening email messages on page 208. For example:
> Everyone at the party **enjoyed** them.
> The party was a blast, but we all **missed** you, especially Mark.
> I **arrived** here late Monday night.
> Tuesday I **worked** from 7:00 in the morning until 10:00 at night.

Go to **www.myfocusongrammarlab.com** for grammar charts and notes.

Step 3: Focused Practice (pages 212–214)

See the general suggestions for Focused Practice on page 4.

Exercise 1: Discover the Grammar

A
- Have students complete the task individually. Then have them compare answers in pairs.

B
- Have students complete the task in pairs. Circulate as students are working and give help as needed. Then go over the answers as a class.

Exercise 2: Simple Past
- Have students complete the exercise. Then go over the answers as a class.
- Read each of the sentences aloud and have students repeat them after you.
- Write these phonetic symbols on the board: /d/, /t/, and /id/. Say the simple past form of each of the verbs in the box. After each one, have students identify the final sound of each one. (*graduated /id/; helped /t/; learned /d/; opened /d/; stayed /d/; worked /t/*)

Exercise 3: Affirmative or Negative

- Have students look at the pictures and describe what they see. Make sure they notice the difference in weather and the woman's activities. Then have them complete the exercise. Call on students to write their answers on the board.
- Go over the answers as a class and make corrections as needed. Then call on students to create a sentence that adds more information to each statement. For example:
  Saturday it rained all day long. The weather wasn't nice.
  Judy stayed home. She didn't go outside.
  She cleaned her apartment. She didn't call her friends.

Exercise 4: Editing

- Have students complete the exercise individually and compare answers in pairs.
- Have pairs write the correct sentences on the board. Have each pair explain the error and the correction.

Go to **www.myfocusongrammarlab.com** for additional grammar practice.

Step 4: Communication Practice

(pages 214–216)

See the general suggestions for Communication Practice on page 5.

Exercise 5: Listening

A

- Read the directions aloud. Play the audio and have students complete the exercise.
- Go over the examples as a class. Play the audio again for clarification, if needed.

B

- Play the audio again. After each message, pause the audio and ask: "What pronouns did they use?" Make sure students understand that all of the messages are in the first-person.
- Have students read the sentences and blanks. Point out that the first item uses the speaker's exact words, but items 2–3 are in third-person, not first-person, and students will have to summarize what they hear.
- Have students complete the exercise. Then go over the answers as a class.

Exercise 6: Pronunciation

A

- Have students listen to and read the Pronunciation Note. Then have them look at the examples again. Have them work in groups or pairs to try to come up with a pronunciation rule. This may be a challenge, so don't worry if they can't do it.
- Explain again that the pronunciation of *-ed* depends on the final sound of the base verb. Generally, if the final sound is a soft, or voiceless, sound, the *-ed* is pronounced as /t/. If the final sound is a hard, or voiced, sound, the *-ed* is pronounced as /d/. If the final sound is /t/ or /d/, the *-ed* is pronounced as a separate syllable.
- Explain that there is a simple way to tell voiceless from voiced sounds. Have students put their hands on their throats over the larynx and say the word *miss*. Ask if they can feel a vibration when they say the /s/ sound. *(no)* Have them keep their hands on their throats and say the word *arrive*. If they prolong the final /v/ sound, they should be able to feel a vibration. Explain that for a voiceless sound, they will not feel a vibration. With a voiced sound, they will.
- Remind students that if the final sound of the base verb is /t/ or /d/, the *-ed* sounds like an extra syllable, /id/.

B

- Have students complete the exercise individually and check answers in pairs. Go over the answers as a class.

C

- Have students look at the first sentence. Demonstrate the technique explained above with the first base verb: *graduate*. Ask students if the final sound is /t/ or /d/. *(/t/)* Have them tell you the rule for verbs that end with either a /t/ or /d/ sound. (The *-ed* is pronounced as a separate syllable—/id/.)
- Have students look at number 3 and write the base form of the verb in the correct column. *(work)* Have them put their hands on their throats and say the base form aloud. Ask them if they feel a vibration when they say the base form and then write the base form in the correct column. *(It goes in the /t/ column on the chart).*
- Have students complete the exercise. Then play the audio so students can check their answers.

Exercise 7: True or False?

- Read the directions and have students read the words in the box aloud. Give an example of a true and false sentence about yourself.

- Have students write four false statements and one true statement about themselves using regular simple past verb forms. Then have them work in groups and exchange papers. Each student reads the sentences on the paper he or she has, replacing the subject *I* with the student's name. The rest of the group guesses the true statement, and the person who wrote the sentences reveals the true statement at the end of the discussion.

Exercise 8: Writing

A

- Give examples of something you did as a child, using the words in the box. Then have students complete the task individually.

B

- Have students use the Editing Checklist to correct their work. Circulate and give help as needed.

C

- Collect the papers and read the sentences. Have students guess who wrote it.
- For variation, collect the papers and redistribute them, making sure that no student has his or her own paper. Have each student read the paper to the class. The class guesses who wrote the paper. The reader then returns the paper to the writer.

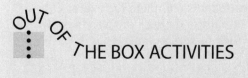 OUT OF THE BOX ACTIVITIES

Listening, Speaking, Reading, and Writing

- Play "Past Pronunciation Bingo." To prepare for the activity, make Bingo cards with nine boxes. In each box write /t/, /d/, or /id/. Vary the order from card to card. Be sure that there are more /t/ and /d/ endings than /id/ endings on the cards. For example:

/id/	/t/	/d/
/d/	/t/	/t/
/t/	/d/	/id/

- Write the base form of a variety of verbs on individual slips of paper. Here are some from this unit that you can use: *enjoy, look, miss, arrive, work, start, finish, end, check out, rain, clean.* Also choose verbs from previous units that have regular past forms such as: *like, call, belong, want, stop, worry, turn, park, hand, close, open, watch, surf, sound.*

- Put all of the slips into a bag or basket. To play, give each student a Bingo card. If you have a lower-level class, you may want students to play in pairs. If you have a multilevel class, put higher- and lower-level students together.
- Take a slip of paper from the bag and say the base form of the verb. Students must figure out how to pronounce the past form and write that verb in one of the appropriate boxes on the card. Remind them that they can only write a verb in ONE of the boxes with that sound. When students have filled three boxes in a row in any direction, they call "Bingo!" To check, have the student say the verbs in the past form.

Speaking, Listening, Reading, and Writing

- Bring in (or have students bring) photos that lend themselves to imaginative story-telling. Magazine ads, funny personal photos, or cartoons will work well. Bring enough photos for each student or pair of students.
- Explain that students are to write a story about what happened just before the photo was taken. Encourage them to be creative and imaginative. Circulate as students are writing and help as needed.
- Have each student (or pair) show the photo and read the story to the class. For large classes, have students work in groups. Encourage students to ask questions after they hear the story to get more details.
- For variation, give all students the same picture.

Go to **www.myfocusongrammarlab.com** for additional listening, pronunciation, speaking, and writing practice.

Note:
- See the *Focus on Grammar Workbook* for additional in-class or homework grammar practice.

Unit 22 Review (page 217)

Have students complete the Review and check their answers on Student Book page UR-3. Review or assign additional material as needed.

Go to **www.myfocusongrammarlab.com** for the Unit Achievement Test.

Grammar: SIMPLE PAST: REGULAR AND IRREGULAR VERBS; *Yes / No* QUESTIONS

Unit 23 focuses on the meanings and uses of irregular simple past verbs in statements and *yes / no* questions in the simple past with regular and irregular verbs.

- Regular verbs in the simple past end with *-ed*, but irregular verbs have different forms.

- To form a negative statement in the simple past, use *did not* + the base form of the verb. Use the contraction *didn't* + the base form in conversation and informal writing.

- To form a *yes / no* question in the simple past, use *Did* + subject + base form of the verb.

- In simple past short answers, you can use *did* or *didn't*.

Theme: A BIOGRAPHY

Unit 23 focuses on language that tells the story of someone's life.

Step 1: Grammar in Context (pages 218–220)

See the general suggestions for Grammar in Context on page 1.

Before You Read

- Ask students, "What does the word *admire* mean?" *(to have a very high opinion of someone)*
- You may want to write a few questions on the board to guide them in their discussions. For example:
  What is this person's name?
  Is this person still living? Where does (or did) this person live?
  What are some of the reasons that you admire this person?
  How do (or did) the things this person says or does change your life?
  What is one question you want to ask this person?

Read

- To encourage students to read with a purpose, write these questions on the board:
  1. What class is Jeremy's paper for? *(his drama class)*
  2. What is Jeremy's assignment? *(to write about an actor he admires)*
  3. Who does Jeremy write about? *(Christopher Reeve)*
  4. Why was he famous? *(He was the star of the* Superman *movies.)*
  5. Is he still living? *(No, he isn't.)*

- Call on students to read the questions. Have students think about them as they read and listen to the conversation.
- Play the audio and have students read along in their books. Have students discuss the questions as a class.

After You Read

A. Practice

- Have students work in pairs to practice the opening conversation. Have students decide who will be Tim and who will be Jeremy. Have students form new pairs with someone who read the opposite role. Have them change roles and practice again.
- Read the opening reading aloud and have students repeat. Then have students practice the reading in pairs.

B. Vocabulary

- Play the audio and have students repeat each word. Have students write any new vocabulary words in their notebooks.
- Point out that for the phrase *be born*, the simple past is formed by changing *be*, not *born*. We do not say "I was borned," but rather "I was born." (If necessary, you can explain that *born* is really the participle form of the verb *bear*.)
- Ask students whether these words are nouns, adjectives, or verbs. (*They are all verbs except for* be born, *which is a verb phrase*.) Ask students if the past of these verbs is formed by adding *-d* or *-ed*. They may recognize and/or know some of the past forms of these verbs. Point out that all of them except for *give up* are regular verbs. *Give up* is an irregular verb because we do not add *-d* to form the simple past form.

C. Vocabulary

- Have students complete the exercise individually. Then go over the answers as a class.

D. Comprehension

- Remind students that the opening conversation and reading are on pages 218–219. Have students complete the exercise. Then have them work in pairs to check their answers.
- You may want to review the use of *a* and *an*. Call on students to explain why each *a* or *an* is used in each answer choice.

Go to **www.myfocusongrammarlab.com** for an additional reading, and for reading and vocabulary practice.

Step 2: Grammar Presentation

(pages 221–222)

See the general suggestions for Grammar Presentation on page 3.

Grammar Charts

- Read the example sentences in the first chart aloud and have students repeat.
- Say the base form of the verb in each of the example sentences and have students say the irregular simple past form. (*eat—ate; have—had; drink—drank; go—went*) Have students write these verbs and their irregular forms in their notebooks.
- Have students work in pairs to come up with a rule about how to form simple past negative statements for irregular verbs. (*We form simple past negative statements with irregular verbs the same way that we form them with regular verbs: Use* did + not + *the base form of the verb*.)
- Have students read the example questions and answers in the second chart aloud. Ask what the word order is for *yes / no* questions in the simple past. (*Did* +*subject* + *base form of the verb*)
- Ask students these questions:
  — When making *yes / no* questions in the simple past, does it matter if the verb is regular or irregular? *(No, it doesn't.)*
  — Does the verb form change with different subjects? *(No, it doesn't.)*
  — In short answers, does the verb form change for singular or plural subjects? *(No, it doesn't.)*

Grammar Notes

Notes 1–2

- Have students look over Notes 1 and 2. Draw attention to the *Be Careful!* note.
- Review the affirmative and negative simple past forms of regular verbs. Do a quick transformation drill in which you say an affirmative or negative sentence in the simple past and the students provide the opposite. For example:

T: I watched TV last night.	S: I didn't watch TV last night.
T: The mail didn't arrive.	S: The mail arrived.

- You can use any or all of these verbs: *study, look, arrive, work, finish, talk, rain, travel, help, learn.*

- Tell students you'll talk more about irregular past forms when you look at Note 5.

Notes 3–4

- Call on students to read Notes 3 and 4.
- Do an oral drill with *yes / no* questions and short answers. First drill affirmative short answers. Provide a cue and have students form the questions and answers. You can divide the class into two groups to do this drill. For example:

T: sleep well last night
Ss1: Did you sleep well last night?
Ss2: Yes, I did.

T: eat a hamburger for lunch
Ss2: Did you eat a hamburger for lunch?
Ss1: Yes, I did.

- Next, drill negative answers using the same method. Finally, have students give true answers for the next set of cues. Ask the questions to individuals rather than the groups. For example:

T: go to bed early last night
S1: Did you go to bed early last night?
S2: No, I didn't. Did you go to bed early last night?
S3: Yes, I did.

Note 5

- Say the base verbs and irregular simple past forms aloud and have students repeat. Have students work in pairs to drill each other on the past forms in this chart. One student gives the base form, and the other says the simple past form. Have them take turns during this drill.
- You may want to give additional information by going over Appendix 7 on page A-5.

⏱ **Identify the Grammar**: Have students identify the grammar in the opening reading on page 218. For example:

I **wrote** this paper for my drama class.
Christopher Reeve **was born** on September 25, 1952, in New York City.
He **began** to act at the age of nine when he **got** a part in his first play.
He **acted** in a lot of plays during his teenage years and many more when he **went** to Cornell University.

Go to **www.myfocusongrammarlab.com** for grammar charts and notes.

Step 3: Focused Practice (pages 222–224)

See the general suggestions for Focused Practice on page 4.

Exercise 1: Discover the Grammar
- Have students complete the exercise. Have them work in pairs to check their answers.
- Ask students whether the intonation is rising or falling at the end of a *yes / no* question. *(rising)*
- Have pairs practice the conversation twice, changing roles after the first practice. Remind them to focus on correct intonation. Circulate and make corrections as needed.
- ⏱ Call on pairs to perform the conversation for the class.

Exercise 2: Simple Past
- Have students complete the exercise and work in groups of three to check their answers. Go over the answers with the class. For each simple past verb, ask: "Is it regular or irregular?" and elicit the correct answer.
- Have each group practice reading the paragraph aloud three times so that each student in the group has a chance to read.

Exercise 3: *Yes / No* Questions
- Have students complete the exercise. Go over the answers with the class.
- Divide the class into two groups. Have one group ask the questions chorally and the other respond. Then have the groups switch roles and practice again. If you prefer, have students work in pairs to practice twice, changing roles after the first practice.

Exercise 4: Editing
- Have students complete the exercise individually, then call on students to write their answers on the board. Have each person read his or her sentence to the class and explain the error and the correction.
- Have students work in pairs to practice the conversations twice, changing roles after the first practice.

Go to **www.myfocusongrammarlab.com** for additional grammar practice.

Step 4: Communication Practice (pages 224–226)

See the general suggestions for Communication Practice on page 5.

Exercise 5: Listening

A
- Read the instructions and play the audio. Elicit the answer from the class. Ask students to give reasons for their choice.

B
- Have students complete the exercise. Then have pairs exchange books. Play the audio again and have students check each other's answers. Replay the audio if students have different answers.
- Have students work in pairs to add more information to the false statements. For example: *Yoshio was not born in Hamamatsu. He was born in Tokyo.* You may need to play the audio again as students complete this activity.

Exercise 6: Pronunciation

A
- Play the audio and have students follow along in their books.

B
- Have students complete the exercises. Go over the answers as a class. Then play the audio again so students can check their answers.

C
- Have students practice in pairs. Circulate and correct their pronunciation as needed.

Exercise 7: Did You . . . ?
- If you have lower-level students, you may want to have them write out their questions first. Then have them complete the exercise.
- Have students interview each other. Then call on pairs to share their most interesting answers with the class.
- For large classes, have students work in groups or pairs to report their interesting answers.

Exercise 8: Writing

A
- Write the suggested questions from the Before You Read activity on page 218 on the board. Brainstorm a few more questions with the class and add them to the board.
- Have students complete the exercise. Encourage them to use the questions on the board to guide their writing.

B
- Have students check their own work. Then have them exchange papers and use the Editing Checklist to correct each other's work.

C
- For large classes or if you have time constraints, have students work in groups to read their biographies to each other and guess who the person is.

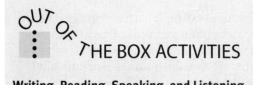

OUT OF THE BOX ACTIVITIES

Writing, Reading, Speaking, and Listening

- Have students play a variation of "Find Someone Who . . ." Brainstorm a list of verbs that students learned in this unit and others that they remember from other units. Brainstorm a second list of past time expressions. Have students write seven to nine *yes / no* questions using the verbs and past time expressions on the board. Have them leave a blank line between each of the questions.
- Have students mingle and ask different people their questions. If someone answers *yes*, that student should sign his or her name on the blank line under the question. The first person to get a signature for each question wins.
- Have students work in groups to report on the answers they got. For example: *Angel was born in 1979. Giovanni slept eight hours last night. Gladys ate chicken for dinner last night.*

Writing, Reading, Listening, and Speaking

- Have students write (or tell) real stories about unusual, dangerous, exciting, funny, or surprising experiences in the past. If they are telling the story rather than reading and writing it, have them use notes if needed. Remind them to use regular and irregular simple past verbs.
- Show students how to interrupt politely by saying "Excuse me" and asking a *yes / no* question for clarification. Tell them a story of your own, and have them interrupt and ask clarifying *yes / no* questions.
- Have students work in small groups to tell their stories. Have listeners politely interrupt and ask clarifying *yes / no* questions. Circulate as students are telling stories. Interrupt and ask clarifying *yes / no* questions.

Go to **www.myfocusongrammarlab.com** for additional listening, pronunciation, speaking, and writing practice.

Note:
- See the *Focus on Grammar Workbook* for additional in-class or homework grammar practice.

Unit 23 Review (page 227)

Have students complete the Review and check their answers on Student Book page UR-3. Review or assign additional material as needed.

Go to **www.myfocusongrammarlab.com** for the Unit Achievement Test.

UNIT 24 OVERVIEW

Grammar: SIMPLE PAST: *Wh-* QUESTIONS

Unit 24 focuses on the meanings and uses of *Wh-* questions in the simple past.

- Most *Wh-* questions in the simple past use a *Wh-* word + *did* + the subject + the base form of the verb.
- *Wh-* questions about the subject use a *Wh-* word + the simple past form of the verb.

Theme: A CAR ACCIDENT

Unit 24 focuses on language that is used to talk about a traffic accident.

Step 1: Grammar in Context (pages 228–230)

See the general suggestions for Grammar in Context on page 1.

Before You Read

- You may want to write these questions on the board to guide students in their conversations:
  Where was the accident?
  When was the accident?
  How was the weather that day (or night)?
  Who was in the car? Who was the driver?
  Was there another car? Who was in it?
  Was the driver hurt? Was anyone else hurt?
  Did the driver or anyone else go to the hospital?
  Give details about the accident.

Read

- To encourage students to read with a purpose, write these questions on the board:
  1. Who called Amanda? *(her brother, Rob)*
  2. What happened to Rob? *(He had a car accident.)*
  3. How did it happen? *(He tried to park and hit a sign.)*
  4. How is Rob? *(fine)*

5. What did Rob do to the car? *(He broke the headlights and dented the bumper.)*
6. Where is Rob now? *(at a body shop)*

- Call on students to read each of the questions. Have students think about the questions as they read and listen to the conversation.
- Have students read the conversation in pairs and discuss the questions. Call on pairs to share their answers with the class.

After You Read

A. Practice

- Have pairs practice the conversation twice, changing roles after the first practice.
- Call on pairs to perform the conversation for the class.

B. Vocabulary

- Model the pronunciation of the words and have students repeat. If possible, bring in a toy car or a picture of a car and point out the bumper and headlights. If students are interested, teach the names of other car parts as well. Have students write any new vocabulary in their notebooks.
- Explain to students that an *auto repair shop* is often called a *shop* or *body shop*. When someone's car is being repaired, the person may say that the car is *in the shop* or *at the garage*.

C. Vocabulary

- Have students complete the exercise and work in pairs to check their answers.
- Have pairs work together to practice the conversations. Have students choose to be Speaker A or Speaker B. Have them practice the conversations, then have them form new pairs with students who read the opposite role. Have them change roles and practice again.

D. Comprehension

- Remind the students that the opening conversation is on page 228. Have students complete the exercise. Then have students work in pairs to check their answers.
- Divide the class into two groups. Have groups take turns asking and answering the questions chorally.

Go to **www.myfocusongrammarlab.com** for an additional reading, and for reading and vocabulary practice.

Step 2: Grammar Presentation

(pages 230–231)

See the general suggestions for Grammar Presentation on page 3.

Grammar Charts

- Have students look over the first grammar chart. Write the example questions from the first chart on the board.
- Have students look at the questions on the board and in the book. Ask:
  — What is the word order for these *Wh-* questions? (Wh- *word* + did + *subject* + *verb*)
  — What form of the verb do we use? *(the base form)*
- Have students look at the questions in the next chart. Ask:
  — What is the word order? (Wh- *word* + *verb*)
  — How are these questions different from the first set of questions? *(The word and verb forms are different. The word order is* Wh- *word* + *the simple past form of the verb,* Did *is not used.)*
  — How do we answer questions with *who*? For example, how do we answer the question "Who drove?" *(with the person's name or the name* + did)
- Have students repeat the irregular verbs in the second chart after you say them. Have students close their books. Say the base form and have them say the past form.

Grammar Notes

Note 1

- Drill the form of most *Wh-* questions. Say answers and have students ask questions that match your cues. Do a dozen or more answer-and-question sets so that students can get in the habit. For example:

T: I went to a movie with Richard. / Who
S1: Who did you go to a movie with?

T: The movie started at 8:30 P.M. / When
S2: When did the movie start?

T: We ate dinner at home. / Where
S3: Where did you eat dinner?

T: I stayed home last night. / Why
S4: Why did you stay home?

- To enable students to ask genuine questions, say a simple sentence about something unusual you did or something that happened to you, for example: "I bought flowers yesterday." Have students ask questions with *who, where, when, why* and answer them truthfully. For example:

S1: Why did you buy flowers?
T: It was my mother's birthday.
S2: Where did you buy them?
T: At the supermarket.

Note 2

- Pick a student and tell the class that it was recently this person's birthday (wedding, anniversary, graduation, etc.), and he or she got a lot of wonderful gifts. The student wants to write thank-you notes to the people who gave the gifts, but unfortunately all the gift cards got mixed up. The student needs the class's help to figure out who gave which gift.
- With the class, brainstorm a list of gifts and write each one on a slip of paper. Give one or two slips to each student.
- Draw attention to the *Be Careful!* note. Using the gift list you prepared, model a few questions. For example:
  Who gave John a baseball bat?
  Who bought John a poster?
  Who got him a bag of coffee?
- The classmate who "bought" each gift should respond with "I did." Give the list to the student you picked and have him or her continue asking questions. For example: "Who bought me a wallet?"
- You may want to go over Appendix 7 on page A-5 to provide more practice with irregular past forms.

🕐 **Identify the Grammar**: Have students identify the grammar in the opening conversation on page 228. For example:
  When did it happen?
  Where did it happen?
  Why did you drive?
  What happened?

Go to **www.myfocusongrammarlab.com** for grammar charts and notes.

Step 3: Focused Practice (pages 231–233)

See the general suggestions for Focused Practice on page 4.

Exercise 1: Discover the Grammar
- Have students complete the exercise. Go over the answers as a class.
- Have students work in pairs to practice asking and answering the questions twice. Have them change roles after the first practice.

Exercise 2: *Wh-* Questions
- Have students complete the exercise. Then call on students to write their questions on the board. Discuss them as a class.
- Have students work in pairs to practice the conversation twice, changing roles after the first practice.

- Have pairs write three or four *Wh-* questions about the opening conversation. Have pairs exchange their questions with another pair and answer them. Circulate as students are working and provide assistance as needed.

Exercise 3: Questions with *Who*
- Have students complete the exercise, then call on students to write their questions on the board and read them aloud. Discuss them as a class.
- Have students work in pairs to ask and answer the questions. Call on pairs to share their answers with the class.

Exercise 4: Editing
- Have students check their work in pairs. Call on pairs to write their corrected sentences on the board and explain the error and correction.
- Have groups practice the corrected conversations with each other. Have them switch roles so that each person practices each role at least once.

Go to **www.myfocusongrammarlab.com** for additional grammar practice.

Step 4: Communication Practice
(pages 233–235)

See the general suggestions for Communication Practice on page 5.

Exercise 5: Pronunciation

A
- Play the audio and have students follow in their books.

B
- Play the audio and have students complete the exercise.
- Play the audio again and have students repeat. Pause as needed after each line.

C
- Play the audio again and have students complete the exercise individually. Pause as needed to give students enough time to write. Then call on students to write their questions on the board.
- Have students practice in pairs, taking turns reading the questions in full form and saying them with the contracted form.

Exercise 6: Listening

- Play the audio and have students complete the exercises. Go over the answers as a class. If necessary, replay the audio for confirmation.
- Give students the audioscript and have them work in pairs to underline the *Wh-* questions in the simple past. Ask: "Is the intonation rising or falling?" (*It rises in the middle and falls at the end because these are all* Wh-*questions*.) Ask: "Can you say these questions with contracted form?" (*yes*) Have students say the questions using the contracted form.
- Have students work in pairs to practice the conversation twice, changing roles after the first practice. Have them focus on correct intonation as they ask the questions. Circulate as students are practicing. Make corrections as needed.

Exercise 7: Interview

- Read the directions and go over the examples with the class. Brainstorm some questions students can ask each other. Write them on the board.
- Have students complete the exercise in pairs. Have two pairs work together and report to each other about their similarities and differences. Call on pairs to share answers with the class.

Exercise 8: Discuss Childhood

- Read the directions and go over the examples with the class. Brainstorm some questions students can ask each other. Write them on the board.
- Have students mingle as they do this activity. You may want to let lower-level students write their questions first. Have students take notes as they talk to people.
- Have students complete the exercise. Call on students to ask and give information about each other. For example:
  S1: Who can tell us something about Marisa?
  S2: I can. Her father taught her to ride a bike.

Exercise 9: Writing

A

- Have students complete the sentence individually. If needed, brainstorm ideas and write them on the board.

B

- Have students compare sentences in groups. Make sure that they take notes on the questions and answers.

C

- Have students complete the conversation individually. Circulate and give help as needed.

D

- Have students exchange papers in pairs and use the Editing Checklist to correct each others' work.
- ⏱ Have students practice each other's conversations in pairs. Then call on pairs to role-play their conversations for the class.

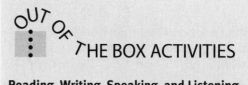

OUT OF THE BOX ACTIVITIES

Reading, Writing, Speaking, and Listening

- Have students read and summarize a news story and answer a partner's questions about it. Make a handout like the following and give one to each student:

Title: _____

Who	What	When	Where	Why

- Bring in (or have students bring) short news stories. Give one to each student. Have students read their stories and summarize the important information by filling in the chart.
- Have students work in pairs. Have them ask questions about their partner's story until they understand everything that happened. They must ask a minimum of five questions. They may not look at their partner's notes.

Listening and Speaking

- Have students bring in (or you can bring in) pictures from magazines or newspapers that show an interesting event. You will need one for each student.
- Brainstorm the various *Wh-* question words and write them on the board: Who, Where, When, What, Why, How long, How much, How many, etc. Have each student make up a story about what happened in the picture. Have them think about questions that begin with the words on the board as they are making up their stories.

(continued)

- Have students work in small groups. Each person shows the picture, and the other students in the group ask simple past *Wh-* questions about the picture. Circulate as students are working and give help as needed.

Go to **www.myfocusongrammarlab.com** for additional listening, pronunciation, speaking, and writing practice.

Note:
- See the *Focus on Grammar Workbook* for additional in-class or homework grammar practice.

Unit 24 Review (page 236)

Have students complete the Review and check their answers on Student Book page UR-3. Review or assign additional material as needed.

Go to **www.myfocusongrammarlab.com** for the Unit Achievement Test.

From Grammar to Writing (page FG-7)

See the general suggestions for From Grammar to Writing on page 9.

Go to **www.myfocusongrammarlab.com** for an additional From Grammar to Writing Assignment, Part Review, and Part Post-Test.

PART IX OVERVIEW

PRONOUNS; QUANTITY EXPRESSIONS; *There is / There are*

UNIT	GRAMMAR FOCUS	THEME
25	Subject and Object Pronouns	Gifts and Favors
26	*How much / How many*; Quantity Expressions	A Trip to the Galápagos Islands
27	*There is / There are*	Describing Places

Go to **www.myfocusongrammarlab.com** for the Part and Unit Tests.

Note: PowerPoint® grammar presentations, test-generating software, and reproducible Part and Unit Tests are on the *Teacher's Resource Disc*.

UNIT 25 OVERVIEW

Grammar: SUBJECT AND OBJECT PRONOUNS

Unit 25 focuses on a review of the meanings and uses of subject pronouns and introduces object pronouns.

- *I, you, he, she, it, we,* and *they* are subject pronouns. They replace noun subjects.
- *Me, you, him, her, it, us,* and *them* are object pronouns. They replace noun objects. Object pronouns often come after prepositions such as *to* or *for*.
- Notice that *you* and *it* are both subject and object pronouns. *You* is the same for singular or plural. To clarify when *you* is plural, we sometimes add the word *both*.

Theme: GIFTS AND FAVORS

Unit 25 focuses on language that is used to talk about giving a gift to someone.

Step 1: Grammar in Context (pages 238–240)

See the general suggestions for Grammar in Context on page 1.

Before You Read
- Have students complete the exercise in small groups. Survey the groups to find out the most popular gift in the class.

Read
- To encourage students to read with a purpose, write these questions on the board:
  1. Who is an American? *(Kathy)*
  2. What does Carlos want to get? *(a gift for Bill)*
  3. Who is Bill? *(Carlos's boss)*
  4. What gift does Kathy suggest? *(chocolates)*
  5. What is Kathy's "price" for driving Carlos and Tomiko to the party? *(a box of chocolates)*
  6. Is Kathy serious? *(No, she's joking.)*
- Call on students to read the questions. Have students keep these questions in mind as they read and listen to the conversation.
- Play the audio and have students follow along in their books. Have students discuss the questions in pairs or groups of three. Call on pairs or groups to share answers with the class.

After You Read

A. Practice
- Circulate as students practice the conversation. Provide help as needed.

- Call on students from different groups to read each person's part in the conversation and perform it for the class.

B. Vocabulary
- Play the audio and have students repeat each word. Have students write any new vocabulary in their notebooks.
- Have students use the vocabulary items to rate the gifts on a scale from 1 to 5 with 1 being the most favorite and 5 the least favorite. For example: 1. a gift certificate, 2. flowers, 3. chocolates, 4. tickets, 5. a DVD.
- Have students work in groups to share how they rated each gift and why. For example:
  S1: My favorite gift is a gift certificate. I can buy what I want. I like flowers, too. They're pretty. I like chocolates, but I always eat a lot. I don't want tickets or a DVD. People usually don't know what I like.

C. Vocabulary
- Have students complete the exercise. Then have them work in pairs to check their answers.
- Have those pairs take turns reading the sentences to each other.

D. Comprehension
- Remind students that the opening conversation is on pages 238–239. Have students complete the exercise individually and work in pairs to check their answers.
- Have pairs work together to correct the false statements. Call on pairs to write their corrected statements on the board and discuss them as a class.

Go to **www.myfocusongrammarlab.com** for an additional reading, and for reading and vocabulary practice.

Step 2: Grammar Presentation (pages 240–241)
See the general suggestions for Grammar Presentation on page 3.

Grammar Charts
- Have students look at the left side of the chart. Write this sentence stem on the board:
  _____ gave them chocolates.
- Do a quick transformation drill with all the singular and plural subject pronouns. Use one of the sentences as a model. Point to yourself and the sentence stem and say: "I gave them chocolates." Then point to a female student and the sentence stem and say: "She gave them chocolates." Then point to a male student and have another student make the correct sentence: "He gave them chocolates."

- For sentences with object pronouns, write on the board:
  They gave _____ chocolates.
- Drill the object pronouns in the same manner as the subject pronouns above. Point to yourself and elicit the sentence: "They gave me chocolates." Then point to other students or groups of students and have students say the sentences.
- Have students work in pairs. Have them look back at the opening conversation and find three sentences that have both subject and object pronouns. Call on pairs to write the sentences they chose on the board. Have them identify the subject and object pronouns for the class.
- To reinforce the word order in sentences with object pronouns, take sentences from the opening conversation and write them on the board with the words out of order. Call on students to put them in the correct order.

Grammar Notes

Note 1
- Since the subject pronouns are essentially a review, you may not want to spend too much time practicing them.
- Make up a list of sentences with noun subjects. Have students change the nouns to pronouns. For example:
  T: Tina likes flowers.
  S: She likes flowers.

Note 2
- Have students look over Note 2.
- Say sentences about people's likes and dislikes, and have students replace the object pronouns. For example:
  S1: Tina loves chocolates.
  S2: That's not true. She doesn't like them.
  S2: Sergei likes motorcycles.
  S3: No, he doesn't like them.

Note 3
- Read the explanation aloud. Have students read the examples aloud. Point out the labels over the subject and object pronouns.

Note 4
- Tell the students that, as with *both*, some Americans sometimes use *all* to indicate that *you* is plural, e.g., "Where are you all going tonight?" or "Where are all of you going tonight?" Note that in the southern United States, *you all* is often contracted in spoken language to *y'all*.
- Point out that *both* can be used in two ways: *you both* or *both of you*. It is also correct to say *the two (three,* etc.) *of you*.

⏱ **Identify the Grammar**: Have students identify the grammar in the opening conversation on pages 238–239. For example:

I want to get **him** a gift.

Let **me** think.

He has a wife. Can I give **them** to **her**?

Go to **www.myfocusongrammarlab.com** for grammar charts and notes.

Step 3: Focused Practice (pages 241–243)

See the general suggestions for Focused Practice on page 4.

Exercise 1: Discover the Grammar

- Have students complete the exercise and work in pairs to check their answers.
- Have pairs work together to practice the conversation twice, changing roles after the first practice.

Exercise 2: Subject and Object Pronouns

- Have students complete the exercise individually and go over the answers as a class.
- Have students work in pairs to practice the conversation. Circulate as students practice and offer help as needed.
- Have two pairs work together to perform the conversation for each other. Then have students switch partners and roles and have the new pairs practice one more time.

Exercise 3: Object Pronouns

- Read the instructions. Write *Why don't you get* + object pronoun + object noun on the board. Brainstorm some sentences that use the pattern. For example, *Why don't you get her tickets?* Write them on the board.
- Have students look at the pictures and describe the things they see. Then have students complete the exercise individually. Go over the answers as a class.
- Have students work in pairs to read the speech balloons and *Why don't you . . . ?* questions as conversations. For example, for the first item:
  A: Tomorrow is my parents' anniversary.
  B: Why don't you get them a travel book?
- Have students find new partners and practice the conversations again, this time substituting their own gift ideas.

Exercise 4: Editing

- Have students complete the exercise individually. Go over the correct answers as a class.

- Have students use the invitation in this exercise as a model and write an invitation to a real or imaginary event. Have students work in groups of three to read their invitations and give feedback to each other. Circulate as students are reading, making corrections as needed.
- Have a few students read their invitations to the class.

Go to **www.myfocusongrammarlab.com** for additional grammar practice.

Step 4: Communication Practice
(pages 244–245)

See the general suggestions for Communication Practice on page 5.

Exercise 5: Listening

A
- Go over the instructions and play the audio. Elicit the answer.

B
- Have students complete the exercise. Then go over the answers as a class.
- Play the audio for clarification as needed.
- ⏱ Provide students with the audioscript and have them practice the conversation in pairs.

Exercise 6: Pronunciation

A
- Play the audio and have students read along in their books. Point out the sentences in brackets near each example conversation. Explain that these explain the meaning implied by the stressed words.
- Play the audio again and have students repeat the example conversations.
- Read the example conversations with a student. Have the student read line A while you read line B. For example:
  A: Is that your CD?
  B: No, it's **my cousin's** CD.

  A: Is that your CD?
  B: No, it's my **video game**.

B
- Play the audio and have students complete the exercise individually. Then have them check their answers in pairs.
- Call on pairs to share their answers with the class. Play the audio again if needed.

C
- Have students practice the conversations in pairs. Make sure each student practices both roles.

Exercise 7: Choose Gifts

- Have students work individually on their lists and then discuss their ideas in pairs, using the example conversation as a model.
- Call on pairs to role-play their conversations for the class. If you have students whose language is very limited, you may want to have them write out their conversations first.

Exercise 8: Writing

A

- Have students complete the task individually. If needed, brainstorm ideas with the class and write them on the board.

B

- Have students use the Editing Checklist to correct each other's work in pairs. Then have them take turns reading their paragraphs to each other.
- Call on students to read their paragraphs to the class.

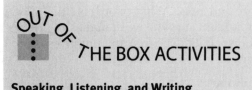

OUT OF THE BOX ACTIVITIES

Speaking, Listening, and Writing

- Bring in pictures from newspapers, magazines, or catalogs that show people giving, receiving, or opening gifts. You will need one picture for each student or pair of students.
- Distribute the pictures to individuals or pairs. Have students make up a story about the scene in the picture using subject and object pronouns. For example:
The girl's parents are giving her a bicycle for her birthday. They bought it on sale at Sports R 4 U. It's purple, and purple is her favorite color. She's telling them that she loves the bicycle. She wants to show it to her brother. He got one for his birthday, too.
- Have students write an imaginary letter about the gift and the picture. For example:
Dear Uncle Ramon and Aunt Maya:

Mom and Dad gave me a bicycle for my birthday. I love it! It's purple, and the seat is silver. They bought it at Sports R 4 U. I rode it to school. My friend Lise thinks it's awesome. All my friends have bicycles. Now we can all ride them to school.

I hope you both can visit soon.

Love,
Ana

Speaking and Listening

- Bring in a variety of catalogs: clothing, cars, gardening supplies, furniture, housewares, etc. You'll need one catalog for every four students.
- Have students work in groups of four. Give each group a catalog. Tell each group that the task is to pick out a birthday gift for someone everyone knows. It could be you, another teacher, a student who is absent, or someone in another group.
- Set a time limit. Have students use Exercise 7 on page 245 as a model for their discussion. When time is up, have each group tell the class which gift they selected for the person and why.

Go to **www.myfocusongrammarlab.com** for additional listening, pronunciation, speaking, and writing practice.

Note:
- See the *Focus on Grammar Workbook* for additional in-class or homework grammar practice.

Unit 25 Review (page 246)

- Have students complete the Review and check their answers on Student Book page UR-4. Review or assign additional material as needed.

Go to **www.myfocusongrammarlab.com** for the Unit Achievement Test.

Grammar: UNIT 26 *How much / How many;* QUANTITY EXPRESSIONS

Unit 26 focuses on the meanings and uses of *How much* and *How many*.

- Use *How much* with non-count nouns to ask about an amount.
- Use *How many* with plural count nouns to ask about a quantity.
- Use *How much* to ask about the cost of something.

The unit also introduces meanings and uses of quantifiers.

- *A lot, a few, a little, not many,* and *not much* are general expressions that tell about quantity and amount.
- *A lot* tells that an amount is large.
- *A few, a little, not many,* and *not much* tell that amounts are small.
- Numbers can also give information about quantity. Numbers give an exact amount.

Theme: A TRIP TO THE GALÁPAGOS ISLANDS

Unit 26 focuses on language that is used to talk about a vacation or trip.

Step 1: Grammar in Context (pages 247–249)

See the general suggestions for Grammar in Context on page 1.

Before You Read

- If you have students from Ecuador or Central or South America, they may have visited or even lived on the Galápagos. Have them share what they know about the Galápagos with the class.
- You may also want to ask students about other islands that they know and the capital cities of their home countries or provinces.

Read

- To encourage students to read with a purpose, write these questions on the board:
  1. Where did Jessica and Tim go? *(Ecuador)*
  2. How many days were they away? *(ten)*
  3. Which places did they visit? *(the capital, Quito, and the Galápagos Islands)*
  4. Where did they sleep? *(on a boat)*
  5. Was the trip expensive? *(yes)*
- Have students read each of the questions on the board. Have students keep these questions in mind as they read and listen to the conversation.

- Play the audio and have students read along in their books. Have students discuss the questions in pairs or groups of three. Call on pairs or groups to share answers with the class.
- Point out the expression *Nothing beats travel* and the footnote that gives the explanation on page 247.

After You Read

A. Practice

- Circulate as students practice the conversation.
- Call on students from different groups to read each person's part in the conversation and perform it for the class.

B. Vocabulary

- Play the audio and have students repeat each word.
- Have students work in pairs to take turns practicing identifying and spelling the vocabulary words. One student points to a picture and asks, "What (word) is this?" The other student says the word and asks, "How do you spell it?" The first student gives the spelling.

C. Vocabulary

- Have students complete the exercise and check their answers in pairs.
- Have pairs practice the conversation two times, changing roles after the first practice.

D. Comprehension

- Remind the students that the opening conversation is on page 247. Have students complete the exercise. Go over the answers as a class. Have one student read the question and call on another student to respond to it.

Go to **www.myfocusongrammarlab.com** for an additional reading, and for reading and vocabulary practice.

Step 2: Grammar Presentation (pages 249–250)

See the general suggestions for Grammar Presentation on page 3.

Grammar Charts

- Have students look at the chart. Ask these questions to help students identify the use of *how many* and *how much*:
  — What kind of noun comes after *how many? (plural count)*
  — Which words and expressions can we use to answer a question with *how many? (a lot, not many, a few, or a number)*

— What kind of noun comes after *how much? (non-count)*
— Which words and expressions can we use to answer a question with *how much? (a lot, not much, a little, a number + a noun)*
— Is it necessary to put a noun after *how much* or *how many? (no)*

Grammar Notes

Note 1
• Make a list of count and non-count nouns from previous units. Do a drill so students can practice *how much* and *how many*. You give a cue and choose a student to make a question. For example:
T: flowers
S1: How many flowers do you want?

T: roast beef
S2: How much roast beef did you buy?
• As an alternative, have students write a list of six to eight foods they ate or drank in the past two days. Have them work in pairs to take turns asking and answering questions about how much they ate. For example:
S1: How much milk did you drink?
S2: Two glasses.
S2: How many cookies did you eat?
S1: About 12!

Note 2
• Write these words on the board in random order: *a lot, a few, some, a little, not much, not many.*
• Have students fold a piece of paper lengthwise to make two columns. At the top of the left column, have them write *Count.* At the top of the right column, have them write *Non-count.* Have students put the words on the board in order from the largest to the smallest quantity in the correct column of the chart. Point out that *much* is not usually used in affirmative statements.

Count	Non-count
a lot	a lot
some	some
a few	a little
not many	not much

• Write a mix of plural count and non-count nouns on the board, for example: *free time, money, friends, CDs, pairs of shoes,* etc. Have students work in pairs and take turns asking and answering questions with *how much* + non-count noun and *how many* + count noun. Partners should answer truthfully using the quantifiers in the chart they made.

Note 3
• With the class, brainstorm a list questions that can have a wide range of answers. For example:
How many cousins do you have?
How many pairs of shoes do you own?
How many books did you read last year?
How many movies did you see last year?
• Have students form a single line. If you have a large class, have them form lines with several students in each line. The student at the front of the line asks the other students a question with *how many.* Students in line answer with a number and line up from the smallest to the largest number.

Note 4
• Bring in (or have students bring in) pictures of various consumer items from magazines or catalogs. You will need one picture for each student in the class. Hand out the pictures. Have students pretend they own the item in their picture and to imagine what it cost.
• Have students mingle to ask and answer questions about the cost of "their" items. Encourage them to explain their answers. For example:
S1: How much was your watch?
S2: $125. How much did your shoes cost?
S1: Only $25. I got them on sale.
• You may also want to point out to students that many people think it is impolite or rude to ask a friend or acquaintance about the cost of something.

🕐 **Identify the Grammar**: Have students identify the grammar in the opening conversation on page 247. For example:
How many days were you away?
How much time did you spend there?
How many people were on the boat?

Go to **www.myfocusongrammarlab.com** for grammar charts and notes.

Step 3: Focused Practice (pages 250–253)
See the general suggestions for Focused Practice on page 4.

Exercise 1: Discover the Grammar
• Have students complete the exercise and work in pairs to check their answers.
• Divide the class into two groups and practice the conversations two times, changing roles after the first practice.

Exercise 2: *How much / How many*

- Go over the answers to the exercise as a class. Have one student read a question and choose another to answer it.
- Then have students work in pairs to take turns asking the questions in random order and giving the answers.

Exercise 3: *How much / How many*

- Have students complete the exercise. Call on students to write their questions on the board and explain why *how much* or *how many* is correct in that question.
- Have students work in pairs to practice the conversation two times. Have them change roles after the first practice.

Exercise 4: Editing

- Call on students to write their corrected sentences on the board and explain the error and their corrections.
- Discuss the answers as a class.
- Have pairs practice reading the corrected version of the conversation.

Go to **www.myfocusongrammarlab.com** for additional grammar practice.

Step 4: Communication Practice

(pages 253–255)

See the general suggestions for Communication Practice on page 5.

Exercise 5: Listening

A

- Go over the instructions and choices. Then play the audio. Elicit the correct answer from the class.

B

- Have students complete the task. Then have them check their answers in groups.

C

- Play the audio again. Have students answer the question individually and compare them in groups.

Exercise 6: Pronunciation

A

- Play the audio. Have students listen and repeat.

B

- Have students underline the words individually.
- Play the audio and have students listen and repeat.

C

- Have students practice the sentences and questions in pairs.

- ⏱ Write the words from Part A on the board. Dictate a simple sentence that contains each of the words and have students write the sentences. Then call on students to write their sentences on the board.

Exercise 7: Ask and Answer

A

- Read the instructions and go over any unfamiliar vocabulary in the box.
- Have two students read the example conversation. Then have them ask and answer questions in groups.

B

- Explain the task. Have students complete the task individually.

Exercise 8: Writing

A

- Explain the task. If needed, model the task with a place you visited. Then have the students complete the task in pairs.

B

- Have students complete the task individually.

C

- Have students use the Editing Checklist to correct their work.
- **Note:** For variation, students can complete this exercise as an interview. Have pairs ask each other the questions. Then have each student write about his or her partner.

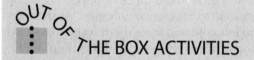

OUT OF THE BOX ACTIVITIES

Speaking and Listening

- Have students bring in photos from a memorable trip that they have taken.
- Brainstorm a list of topics that people would talk about in describing a trip to a friend or relative. Write the topics on the board. Have them work in groups of three to take turns telling about their trip and answering the other students' questions about it. Have students use the topics listed on the board. They can also use the opening conversation on page 247 of this unit as a model.

Reading, Listening, Speaking, and Writing

- Have students interview each other about their lifestyles. They can work in pairs or in small groups.

- Brainstorm a list of healthy and unhealthy things people consume, eat, drink, or do. For example: fish, fat, vegetables, red meat, soda, sleep, water, exercise. Have students interview one another by asking questions beginning with *How much / many* _____ *do you get / have / eat / drink /*, etc.? For example, "How much stress do you have in your life?"
- Have each student write a paragraph about another student's lifestyle, using the information from the interviews. They can start with the topic sentence: "I think _____ has a(n) _____ lifestyle."
- Have students review their writing, using the Editing Checklist on page 255 and revise as needed. Have students read their paragraphs to the person they wrote about. Call on a few students to read their paragraphs to the class.

Go to **www.myfocusongrammarlab.com** for additional listening, pronunciation, speaking, and writing practice.

Note:
- See the *Focus on Grammar Workbook* for additional in-class or homework grammar practice.

Unit 26 Review (page 256)

Have students complete the Review and check their answers on Student Book page UR-4. Review or assign additional material as needed.

Go to **www.myfocusongrammarlab.com** for the Unit Achievement Test.

UNIT 27 OVERVIEW

Grammar: *There is / There are*

Unit 27 focuses on the meanings and uses of *There is* and *There are*.

- Use *there is* or *there's* to state facts about a person or a thing.
- Use *there are* to talk about a plural noun.
- We often use *there is* or *there are* to talk about the location of things or people.
- Use *there isn't a / an* or *there aren't any* to state a negative fact.
- To make a question, put *is* or *are* before *there*.
- Use *there* in both questions and short answers.

Theme: DESCRIBING PLACES

Unit 27 focuses on language that describes businesses, buildings, or other places an area does or does not have.

Step 1: Grammar in Context (pages 257–259)

See the general suggestions for Grammar in Context on page 1.

Before You Read
- You may want to encourage students to ask one question to each member of the group about the place they named. For example:
  S1: There's a beautiful waterfall near my hometown. It's 50 meters high.
  S2: Do a lot of people go there?
  S1: Yes. It's a very famous waterfall.
- Have students complete the exercise. Then call on students to share information about someone in their group with the class.

Read
- To encourage students to read with a purpose, write these questions on the board:
  1. What state did Josh and Amanda go to on their vacation? *(South Dakota)*
  2. Why did they go there? *(to see Mount Rushmore)*
  3. Why is Mount Rushmore famous? *(because it has the heads of American presidents carved into it)*
  4. What national park did Josh and Amanda visit? *(the Badlands National Park)*
- Go over the questions with the class. Have students read and listen to the conversation, then have them work in pairs to answer the questions on the board.

After You Read

A. Practice
- Point out the word *carved* and the footnote on page 257.
- Have groups practice the conversation four times so that each person has an opportunity to read each role.
- Call on students from different groups to read each part and perform the conversation for the class.

B. Vocabulary
- Have students listen to and repeat the vocabulary words and write new words in their notebooks. Have them compare the new words they wrote in pairs.
- Have students name a few places where you might see a snack bar. *(an airport, a bus station, or a train station)* Ask what the difference is between a snack bar and a restaurant. *(Snack bars serve fast food such as soup and sandwiches; you usually eat at a counter, not a table; there are no servers that come to your table. Sometimes you buy the food at the counter and sit somewhere else to eat it, often outside.)*
- Then have them practice using the vocabulary words in original sentences and asking each other questions. For example:
  S1: I stayed at a bed and breakfast last year.
  S2: Where was it?
  S1: In Florida.
  S2: I went to an amusement park last summer.
  S1: Who did you go with?
  S2: My roommate and her family.

C. Vocabulary
- Have students complete the exercise. Call on a few students to share information about their partner's neighborhoods with the class.

D. Comprehension
- Remind students that the opening conversation is on pages 257–258. Have students complete the exercise. Go over the answers as a class.
- Then have students work in pairs to write three more true or false statements about the conversation. Have them use the questions in this exercise as a model.
- Have two pairs work together. Have them exchange their statements, answer them, and correct all of the false statements in the exercise that their partners wrote. Call on pairs to read the false statements and their corrections to the class.

Go to **www.myfocusongrammarlab.com** for an additional reading, and for reading and vocabulary practice.

Step 2: Grammar Presentation (pages 259–260)

See the general suggestions for Grammar Presentation on page 3.

Grammar Charts
- Have students look over the first chart. Ask these questions to help students understand the grammar:
  — What kind of noun comes after *there is*? *(singular count or non-count)*
  — What is the negative form of *there is*? (there isn't)
  — What kind of noun comes after *there are*? *(plural)*
  — How do we form the negative? (there is *or* there are + not)
- Call on two students to read the questions and answers from the second chart. Then ask these questions:
  — What is the word order in *yes / no* questions? (Is / are + there + *noun*)
  — How do we form affirmative short answers? (Yes, there is / there are)
  — How do we form negative short answers? (No, there isn't / there aren't)

Grammar Notes

Notes 1 and 5
- Explain to students that *There is / There are* are often used to say that something *is* or *exists*.
- Have students look over Notes 1 and 5.
- Model a few sentences about the room you are in. For example:
  There are two doors in our room. There's a white board. There is also a bulletin board.
- Have students make more sentences that tell about the room.

Note 2
- Repeat the same activity from Note 1 on this page but make negative statements about the room. Model a few negative statements to start. For example:
  There isn't a television in our room. There aren't any sofas.
- Have students work in pairs to make more negative statements.

Notes 3–4
- Have one student read Note 3 and another read Note 4. Ask: "What are the different ways to give negative answers with *there is*?" (*No, there isn't. / No, there's not.*)

- Have students work in pairs to ask and answer questions about their hometowns or countries. For example:
  S1: Are there any mountains near your town?
  S2: No, there aren't. Is there a national park in your country?
  S1: Yes, there is. It's near my hometown. How many national parks are there in your country?
  S2: There are two. There's one in the north and one in the south.

Note 6
- Choose a room in your home and have the class ask you questions about it using *Is there / Are there*. Answer using *it* or *they*. For example:
  S1: Is there a television in your living room?
   T: Yes, it's in the corner.
  S2: Are there tables in your living room?
   T: Yes. They are next to the sofa.
- Point out the difference between *there* and *they're*. Say a sentence with *there are* and ask a student to write it on the board. Then say a sentence with *they're* and ask another student to write it on the board. For example:
  There are two books on my desk. They're both books about English.
- Have students work in pairs or small groups and have them ask about things in a room in another student's home. They can talk about a room in their parents' home or the place where they are now living.

🕐 **Identify the Grammar**: Have students identify the grammar in the opening conversation on pages 257–258. For example:
  Isn't there something famous about Mount Rushmore?
  Yes, **there is**. **There are** four presidents' **heads** carved into the mountain.
  What else **is there** to see in the area?

Go to **www.myfocusongrammarlab.com** for grammar charts and notes.

Step 3: Focused Practice (pages 260–262)

See the general suggestions for Focused Practice on page 4.

Exercise 1: Discover the Grammar
- Have students complete the exercise. Go over the answers as a class.
- Have students work in groups of three to practice the conversation.
- Call on students from each group to read each role and perform the conversation for the class.

Exercise 2: *There is / There are / They are*
- Have students complete the exercise and work in groups of three to check their answers.
- Have groups practice the conversation three times, changing roles after each practice.

Exercise 3: *There / It / They*
- Have students complete the exercise. Call on students to write their answers on the board and explain them to the class.
- Call on pairs to read the conversations aloud to the class.

Exercise 4: Editing
- Have students work in pairs to check their work. Discuss the answers as a class.
- Have pairs practice reading the corrected letter to each other.

Go to **www.myfocusongrammarlab.com** for additional grammar practice.

Step 4: Communication Practice
(pages 263–265)

See the general suggestions for Communication Practice on page 5.

Exercise 5: Listening

A
- Explain the task and ask the question. Play the audio and elicit the answer.

B
- Play the audio again. Have students complete the task and check their answers in pairs. Play the audio again if needed.
- 🕐 Have pairs correct the false statements. Go over their corrections as a class.
- 🕐 Give students the audioscript for this exercise. Have them practice the conversation in groups of four.

Exercise 6: Pronunciation

A
- Play the audio and have students complete the exercise. Go over the answers as a class. Play the audio again for clarification as needed.
- Have students close their books. Tell students that you are going to read each of the questions and responses from this exercise. Their task is to write only the responses. Read each question and response. Pause after the responses to give students time to write.
- Have students open their books to page 264, Exercise 6B. Have students work in pairs to exchange papers and check their answers using the responses in Exercise 6B.

B

- For variation, you may want to have students complete this exercise in groups of four. Two students read A's role together, and two students read B's.
- Then have groups split into two pairs and practice the conversation again.

Exercise 7: Game

- Set up this activity so that the two teams are standing and facing each other.
- When a person on a team misses, he or she sits down, and the next person on the opposite team goes next.
- The team with the most people standing at the end of the game wins.

Exercise 8: Writing

A

- Have students read the example description. Then have them write the description individually.

B

- Have students check each other's work in pairs and revise their paragraphs if needed.
- ⏱ Have students form groups of four. Have each student read his or her paragraph to the rest of the group. The group asks the reader questions with *Is there / Are there*.

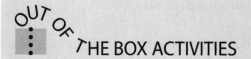

OUT OF THE BOX ACTIVITIES

Listening, Speaking, and Writing

- Make copies of a picture that shows a lot of people doing different things. Have students form pairs and give each pair a copy of the picture, face down.
- Tell students that at your signal, they will turn the picture over and have 15 to 30 seconds to study it. Have students turn over the pictures and study them, then call time and have students turn the pictures face down again. Each pair of students writes as many sentences about the picture as they can, using *There is*, *There are*, *It is*, and *They are*. The pair that has the most correct sentences wins.

Speaking and Listening

- Create or find two versions of a simple drawing. The scene is the same, but the details are different. You can usually find these in children's magazines or puzzle books. You can also use the pictures on page 144 of Unit 15 or page 174 of Unit 18.

- Have students work in pairs. Each student in the pair has one version of the picture. If you are using the pictures from Unit 15 or 18, have students put a piece of paper over the picture they are not using. They should be close enough to be able to communicate verbally, but not so close that they can see each other's pictures.
- Students must find a specific number of differences in their pictures by asking and answering questions with *Is there / Are there*. For example:
  S1: How many people are there in your picture?
  S2: There are five people. How many are there in your picture?
  S1: Five, so that's the same. Are there men in your picture?
  S2: Yes. There are three men and two women.
  S1: There are three women and two men in my picture. That's different.
- Set a time limit. The pair that finds the most differences in the time allowed wins. As an alternative, tell students that the first pair to find the specified number of differences wins.

Go to **www.myfocusongrammarlab.com** for additional listening, pronunciation, speaking, and writing practice.

Note:
- See the *Focus on Grammar Workbook* for additional in-class or homework grammar practice.

Unit 27 Review (page 266)

Have students complete the Review and check their answers on Student Book page UR-4. Review or assign additional material as needed.

Go to **www.myfocusongrammarlab.com** for the Unit Achievement Test.

From Grammar to Writing (page FG-8)

See the general suggestions for From Grammar to Writing on page 9.

Go to **www.myfocusongrammarlab.com** for an additional From Grammar to Writing Assignment, Part Review, and Part Post-Test.

MODIFIERS; COMPARISONS; PREPOSITIONS OF TIME

UNIT	GRAMMAR FOCUS	THEME
28	Noun and Adjective Modifiers	Personal Characteristics
29	Comparative Adjectives	Planning a Get-together
30	Prepositions of Time: *In, On, At*	Leisure Activities

Go to **www.myfocusongrammarlab.com** for the Part and Unit Tests.

Note: PowerPoint® grammar presentations, test-generating software, and reproducible Part and Unit Tests are on the *Teacher's Resource Disc.*

Grammar: NOUN AND ADJECTIVE MODIFIERS

Unit 28 focuses on the meanings and uses of noun and adjective modifiers.

- Adjectives can modify (describe) nouns. They give more information about that noun.
- Nouns can also modify nouns.
- Adjectives can come after the verb *be* or before a noun.
- Adjectives can have different endings such as *-ic, -ing, -ly,* and *-ed.*
- Some adjectives are two or more words.
- Do not add *-s* to an adjective or noun modifier.

Theme: PERSONAL CHARACTERISTICS

Unit 28 focuses on language that is used to talk about qualities and characteristics of people.

Step 1: Grammar in Context (pages 268–270)

See the general suggestions for Grammar in Context on page 1.

Before You Read

A

- Explain the task and go over any unfamiliar vocabulary. Then have students complete the exercise individually.

B

- Go over any unfamiliar vocabulary. Have students complete the task individually.

C

- Have students compare their answers in groups. Then ask the groups which answers were most popular.

Read

- To encourage students to read with a purpose, write these questions on the board:
  Which man or woman . . .
  . . . is a chemistry professor? *(man 3)*
  . . . enjoys fast cars? *(woman 5)*
  . . . likes jazz bands? *(man 1)*
  . . . is young and artistic? *(woman 4)*
  . . . is rich? *(man 2 and woman 6)*
- Call on students to read the questions for the class. Have students keep these questions in mind as they read and listen to the conversation.
- Play the audio and have students follow along in their books. Have students discuss the questions in pairs or groups of three. Call on pairs or groups to share answers with the class.

After You Read

A. Practice

- Go over the words in bold in the opening reading. Have students repeat them after you say them.
- Have students take turns reading the numbered items.

B. Vocabulary

- Play the audio and have students repeat each word. Have students work in pairs to compare the new words that they wrote in their notebooks.
- Have pairs take turns practicing the words. One student points to a picture and the other student says the word. Then the second student points to a picture and the first student says the word. Have students select the pictures randomly rather than in order.

C. Vocabulary

- Have students complete the exercise. Then call on students to share their answers with the class. Correct pronunciation as needed.

D. Comprehension

- Go over the example with the students. Point out that in order to get the answer, students need to make an inference, or guess, based on the things the man in personal ad number 3 likes. Have students find the information in the man's profile that helps them make this inference. (*I enjoy bird-watching and long walks in the country.*)

- Remind students that the opening reading is on page 268. Have students complete the exercise. Then have students work in pairs to check their answers.

Go to **www.myfocusongrammarlab.com** for an additional reading, and for reading and vocabulary practice.

Step 2: Grammar Presentation (pages 270–271)

See the general suggestions for Grammar Presentation on page 3.

Grammar Charts
- Write one example sentence from each chart on the board. Ask questions to help students identify the various ways the nouns and adjectives can combine.
- Point to each word in the sentences on the board and ask students what each one is. For example:
  This woman is artistic. (This [or demonstrative adjective] + noun + be + adjective.)
- As students respond, ask them to help you write "formulas" on the board to describe the combinations. For example:

  This woman is artistic.   be + adjective
  She is an artistic woman.   adjective + noun
  We saw a spy film.   noun + noun
  He's a young computer   adjective + noun
    scientist.   + noun

- Have students look at the charts and confirm that the formulas are correct.
- Have students work in pairs or groups and find two examples of each formula in the opening reading. Have pairs or groups share their examples with the class.

Grammar Notes

Note 1
- Have a student read Note 1.
- To reinforce the information, write a noun on the board. Quickly point to students around the room and have them say different adjective + noun phrases. For example: for the noun *music: soft music, loud music, rap music, classical music.*
- Be prepared to explain that in noun + noun combinations, the first noun acts as an adjective.

Note 2
- Read the explanation and have students read the example sentences aloud.
- Write the example sentences on the board with blanks instead of adjectives:

She is _____ .
She's a / an _____ woman.
- Call on students to complete the sentences with appropriate adjectives. For example: *She is tall. She is a tall woman.*

Note 3
- Students will probably ask you about the difference between *interesting / interested, bored / boring,* etc. To explain, provide a pair of sentences like these:
  The movie was interesting.
  I was interested in the movie.
- Ask students questions to clarify: What was interesting? Who was interested? Provide other examples such as these:
  The lesson was boring. / I was bored.
  John was excited about the trip to Disneyland. / The trip was exciting.

Note 4
- For multiword adjectives, explain that the hyphen connects all the words and makes them function as one.

Note 5
- Have students close their books. On the board, write:
  1. He likes fast cars.
  2. He likes fasts cars.
- Ask: "Which sentence is correct?" (*sentence 1*) Ask: "Why is it correct?" (*singular and plural nouns take the same adjective form in English*)
- Have students open their books. Read the note aloud and have students read the correct example sentences aloud.

Note 6
- On the board, write these column headings: Pronoun / Noun Subject, *a / an*, Adjective, Singular or Plural Noun. Brainstorm words that could go in each column, including vocabulary items from page 269. For example:

Pronoun / Noun Subject	a / an	Adjective	Singular or Plural Noun
I		honest	man
you		artistic	woman
he		happy	student
she		terrific	person
it		interesting	actor
we		lively	professor
they		famous	teacher
Mei Ling		great	artist
Paulina		rich	writer
Paulo		funny	friend
Nessa		warm	roommate
Luba		smart	singer
Tom and Amy		shy	musician
		young	

- Establish a time limit and have students work in pairs or groups to write as many sentences as they can using the words from both columns and the two patterns that are explained in this note. Call on students to share their sentences with the class. The pair or group with the most sentences wins. For example:

Mei Ling is fun.

Mei Ling is an honest woman.

Mei Ling is an honest person.

Note 7

- Read the note aloud and write the example sentences on the board. Ask: "Which words are adjective modifiers?" *(new, good)* "Which are noun modifiers?" *(leather, tennis)*
- On the board, write the sentence: "I like music." Elicit adjectives and nouns that could modify *music*. For example: *loud, soft, American, French* (adjectives); *rock, jazz, rap, disco* (nouns).
- Have students work in pairs to expand the sentence on the board with an adjective and a noun modifying *music*. For example: "I like American rap music." Call on pairs to write their sentences on the board. Make sure the adjective modifier comes before the noun modifier.

- ⏱ **Identify the Grammar**: Have students identify the grammar in the opening reading on page 268. For example:

Are you interested in a **35-year-old, fun-loving** man?

I enjoy **jazz** bands and **sandy** beaches.

I'm looking for a **kind, sensitive** woman.

I'm a **rich, healthy, active, 80-year-old** man.

Go to **www.myfocusongrammarlab.com** for grammar charts and notes.

Step 3: Focused Practice (pages 272–273)

See the general suggestions for Focused Practice on page 4.

Exercise 1: Discover the Grammar

- Have students complete the exercise. Go over the answers as a class.
- Have students practice saying the sentences as a class after you say them.

Exercise 2: Modifiers

- Have students complete the exercise individually and work in pairs to check their answers.
- Go over the answers as a class. Ask students to explain why they ordered the adjectives as they did.

- Have pairs work together to take turns practicing the entire conversation. Have students choose who will be Speaker A and who will be Speaker B. Have them switch roles and practice again, then repeat with a new partner.

Exercise 3: Modifiers

- Have students read the words in the box aloud. Ask: "Do you see any words that go together?" Give them an example: The words *coffee* and *shop* go together to make the phrase *coffee shop*. Brainstorm other combinations and write them on the board. For example: *blueberry pancakes, computer science major, delicious pancakes, orange juice*.
- Have students complete the exercise individually.
- Play the audio so students can check their answers. If needed, play the audio again, pausing so students have time to write.
- Have students check their work in pairs.
- ⏱ Have students practice the conversation twice, changing roles.

Exercise 4: Editing

- Have students complete the exercise individually. Then call on students to write their corrected sentences on the board.
- Have each student explain the error and the correction.

Go to **www.myfocusongrammarlab.com** for additional grammar practice.

Step 4: Communication Practice

(pages 274–276)

See the general suggestions for Communication Practice on page 5.

Exercise 5: Listening

- Have students complete the exercise individually and compare answers in pairs.
- Have each pair join another pair and practice describing some of the other people in the picture. Circulate as students are practicing. Provide help as needed with descriptive words. For example, students may not know *checked, polka dot / polka dotted*, and *striped*.

Exercise 6: Pronunciation

A

- Play the audio and have students follow along in their books.

B

- Have students listen and complete the exercise. Then have them take turns practicing the sentences in pairs.

- (!) Have each pair write five more sentences with the same pattern. Have pairs exchange sentences and take turns practicing the new ones. Call on pairs to share their sentences with the class.

C
- Go over the example and have students complete the exercise. Circulate and make corrections as needed.
- Have each pair join another pair and repeat the activity. For variation, partners can talk about each other's likes. For example: *Maya likes history and geography. She likes blue and green.*

Exercise 7: Describe People
- As an extension for this exercise, have students work in small groups. Give each group a picture from a magazine or catalog. You can have the whole group use one or give one picture to each student in the group.
- Have students describe the people in the pictures to their group members, or have groups share their descriptions with another group. Call on groups to share descriptions with the class.

Exercise 8: Describe Things

A
- Have students look up the vocabulary in class or for homework.

B
- Have students complete the exercise in pairs. Then elicit the answers and write them on the board.

C
- Elicit examples of adjectives and write them on the board. Then have students add adjectives to the phrases in pairs.

D
- Have students write sentences individually. Then have them share their sentences in groups.
- Call on groups to share their ideas with the class. For example:
  S1: Won Il, I think you're wearing an interesting leather belt.
  S2: Thanks. What's in your purple nylon backpack, Paulo?

Exercise 9: Writing

A
- Explain the task and have students read the example. Then have them write their response.

B
- Have students correct their work using the Editing Checklist and make revisions as needed.
- (!) As a variation, tell students to sign their responses with an imaginary name like the one in the example. Then collect all of the papers and redistribute them making sure that no student gets his or her own paper. Have each student read the response, guess who wrote it, and say why they think so. For example:
  S1: I think Paulo is "You're for Me" because he is a great artist. He also loves good jazz, and he takes long walks on the beach.
  S2: Are you sure? I don't think it's Paulo. He doesn't like . . .

OUT OF THE BOX ACTIVITIES

Speaking, Listening, Reading, and Writing
- Have students work in groups of three or four. Have them reread Rosa's letter to Dahlia on page 273, Exercise 4, Editing. Have each group brainstorm a list of all possible solutions to Rosa's problem. For example: break up with Joe and find a generous man, be generous and pay for their dates, talk to one of Joe's good friends and ask him to talk to Joe, talk to Joe and tell him how she feels.
- Have each group choose the solution they think is best and write an answer to Rosa. Have them use nouns and adjective modifiers in the letter. Call on a student from each group to read the letter to the class or have two groups share their letters with each other.
- For an alternative, have each of the students in the groups choose the solution he or she likes best and write his or her own letter to Rosa. Post the letters around the classroom and give students time to walk around and read them.

Speaking and Listening

- Have students work in pairs or groups to discuss the question, "What's important to you in love?"
- Brainstorm a list of topics for the discussion and write them on the board. For example:
  — age (*young, middle-aged, old,* etc.)
  — looks (*tall, dark hair, beautiful, handsome, brown eyes, great smile,* etc.)
  — personality (*kind, thoughtful, friendly, happy, romantic, quiet, serious,* etc.)
  — professions (*athlete, engineer, professor, dancer, musician,* etc.)
  — likes and dislikes (*likes classical music, good mystery books; dislikes rock music, biographies, swimming, pizza*)
- Tell students they are going to describe their dream person to the rest of the group. For example:
  My dream man is tall with dark hair and blue eyes. He is serious, thoughtful, and kind. He can be a professor or a classical musician. He likes good mystery books and tennis. He doesn't like rock music, and he hates pizza. He loves Japanese food and quiet, romantic dinners.

Writing, Reading, Speaking, and Listening

- Have students work in pairs to write a letter to an advice columnist. They can use Rosa's letter to Dahlia on page 273, Exercise 4, Editing as a model.
- Have pairs exchange letters and write a response.
- Call on pairs to read their letters and responses to the class.

Go to **www.myfocusongrammarlab.com** for additional listening, pronunciation, speaking, and writing practice.

Note:
- See the *Focus on Grammar Workbook* for additional in-class or homework grammar practice.

Unit 28 Review (page 277)

Have students complete the Review and check their answers on Student Book page UR-4. Review or assign additional material as needed.

Go to **www.myfocusongrammarlab.com** for the Unit Achievement Test.

UNIT 29 OVERVIEW

Grammar: COMPARATIVE ADJECTIVES

Unit 29 focuses on the meanings and uses of comparative adjectives.

- To form the comparative of one-syllable adjectives, add *-er* to the adjective. If the adjective ends in *-e*, just add *-r*.
- To form the comparative of two-syllable adjectives that end in *-y*, change the *y* to *i* and add *-er*.
- For many adjectives with two or more syllables, we use *more* before the adjective.
- Some adjectives, such as *good* and *bad*, have irregular comparative forms.
- You can use the comparative form of an adjective + *than* to compare two people, places, or things.
- Use *which* to ask about a comparison of things or places. Use *who* to ask about people.

Theme: PLANNING A GET-TOGETHER

Unit 29 focuses on language used to plan a social get-together or party.

Step 1: Grammar in Context (pages 278–280)

See the general suggestions for Grammar in Context on page 1.

Before You Read

- Have students discuss the questions in pairs. Elicit the answers and write types of music on the board.

Read

- To encourage students to read with a purpose, write these questions on the board:
  1. When is the party? (*Saturday night at about 8:00*)
  2. How many people are coming? (*fifteen*)
  3. What kind of music is good for dancing? (*pop or hip-hop*)
  4. What food do they decide to have? (*pizza*)
  5. What kind of entertainment do they choose? (*games*)
- Have students read the questions. Have them think about the questions as they read and listen to the conversation.
- Play the audio and have students read along in their books. Have students discuss the questions as a class.

After You Read

A. Practice
- Review information about intonation of questions and statements. (*Statements and Wh- questions have falling intonation at the end. Yes / No questions have rising intonation at the end.*)
- Point out that one of the questions in the conversation is really a statement with a rising intonation. Ask them which one it is. (*We want to dance, right?*) Explain that *right* at the end of this sentence is really a shortened form of a *yes / no* question: *Isn't that right?*
- Have students practice the conversations in pairs. Have them switch roles and practice again.

B. Vocabulary
- Play the audio and have students repeat each word.
- Write this question stem on the board:
- How do you spell _____?
- Have students work in pairs to take turns spelling the words using the question stem.

C. Vocabulary
- Have students complete the exercise. Go over the answers as a class. Call on students to read the sentences aloud including the correct word.

D. Comprehension
- Have students complete the exercise individually and work in pairs to check their answers.
- Have pairs work together to take turns creating *Wh-* questions for each statement in the exercise. One student makes a question and the other answers it. Then they switch. Tell them not to follow the order of the statements in the book. For example:
  S1: What kind of music is worse than rap for dancing?
  S2: Ken says metal is worse than rap.
  S2: What food is quicker to prepare than steak?
  S1: Pizza is quicker to prepare than steak.

Go to **www.myfocusongrammarlab.com** for an additional reading, and for reading and vocabulary practice.

Step 2: Grammar Presentation (pages 280–281)
See the general suggestions for Grammar Presentation on page 3.

Grammar Charts
- Have students look at the charts and the example sentences and answer these questions:
  — If an adjective has one syllable, how do we form the comparative? (*add -er*)
  — If an adjective is longer than one syllable, how do we form the comparative? (*more + adjective*)
  — Which word often comes after the adjective? (*than*)

Grammar Notes

Notes 1–2
- Write a set of one-syllable adjectives on the board, e.g., *fast, slow, tall, short, quick, young, old.*
- Using facts about students in the class, model several sentences with comparative adjectives. For example: "Irma is taller than Lei. She's also younger."
- Name other pairs of students and elicit sentences from the class.

Note 3
- Provide or brainstorm a list of adjectives that end with *-y* and write them on the board. For example: *funny, easy, dirty, pretty, sunny, rainy, happy, busy, friendly, messy.*
- Have one student use comparative adjectives to make sentences about people, places, or things. Invite a second student to disagree with the first. For example:
  S1: Pizza is messier than fried chicken.
  S2: I disagree. I think fried chicken is messier.

Note 4
- Repeat the procedure from Note 3 but have the second student add information. Here are some adjectives you can use: *interesting, beautiful, difficult, expensive, crowded, dangerous, famous, serious, intelligent.* For example:
  S1: Tokyo is more expensive than Houston.
  S2: It's also more crowded.

Notes 5 and 6
- Have students write two lists of items: things they like and things they don't like.
- Have students work in pairs. Have students take turns asking and answering questions using *better* or *worse* and the words in their lists. For example:
  S1: Which is better, steak or chicken?
  S2: I think steak is better.

  S2: Which is worse, rain or snow?
  S1: For me, rain is worse.

- Circulate as students are practicing. Give help and make corrections as needed.

⏱ **Identify the Grammar:** Have students identify the grammar in the opening conversation on page 278. For example:

Rap is bad for dancing, and heavy metal is **worse**.

Any other kind of pop music is **better** for dancing.

My **older** brother has a lot of hip-hop CDs.

It's **easier** and **quicker than** steak.

Games are **more interesting than** DVDs, at a party.

Go to **www.myfocusongrammarlab.com** for grammar charts and notes.

Step 3: Focused Practice (pages 281–283)

See the general suggestions for Focused Practice on page 4.

Exercise 1: Discover the Grammar

A

- Remind students that the opening conversation is on page 278. Have students complete the exercise. Then have them extend each list with other adjectives they know.
- Have students work in pairs to compare their lists. Call on pairs to share with the class some of the other adjectives they added. You may want to record these on a large poster and hang it in the room.

B

- Have students complete the exercise individually. Then have pairs work together to check their answers.

Exercise 2: Comparative Adjectives

- Have students complete the exercise. Then call on students to write their answers on the board. Have each student read aloud the sentence he or she wrote and explain the answer to the class. For example:
  S1: Marty is older than Ken. *Old* is a one-syllable adjective, so I added *-er*.
- Have students work in groups to continue making comparisons about the people in the picture. For example: *Laura's hair is curlier than Mi Young's.* Call on students from each group to share some of their comparisons with the class.

Exercise 3: Comparative Adjectives

- Have students complete the exercise. Then call on students to give their answers.

- Divide the class into two groups. Have one group ask the questions chorally and the other respond. Then have the groups switch roles and practice again.

Exercise 4: Editing

- Have students complete the exercise individually. Call on students to write their answers on the board.
- Have each person read his or her sentence to the class and explain the error and the correction.

Go to **www.myfocusongrammarlab.com** for additional grammar practice.

Step 4: Communication Practice
(pages 284–286)

See the general suggestions for Communication Practice on page 5.

Exercise 5: Listening

A

- Explain the task. Play the audio and elicit the answer.

B

- Explain the task and play the audio again. Have students complete the exercise individually. Then have them check their answers in pairs.
- ⏱ Have students correct the false statements individually. Call on students to share their corrections with the class. Play the audio again as needed.

Exercise 6: Pronunciation

A

- Have students listen to and read the Pronunciation Note. Have them place one hand on their throats over the larynx and say all of the words with the voiced *th* sound: *this, that, these,* and *those*. Then have them say all of the words with the voiceless *th* sound: *think, tooth,* and *thing*.
- Ask students for which set of words they could feel the vibration. (this, that, these, *and* those—*the words with the voiced* th *sound*)

B

- As students work through this exercise, encourage them to keep their hands on their throats as they repeat the sentences.
- You may need to pause the audio after each sentence and/or play the audio more than once.

C

- Have students take turns saying each sentence to one another and then switch, so each student says all of the sentences.
- Circulate as students are practicing. Make corrections as needed.

Exercise 7: Compare People and Things

A

- Read the instructions. Go over the chart and the example with the class. Brainstorm some examples and questions and write them on the board.
- Have students complete the chart with examples and write questions. Call on a few students to share their topics and questions.

B

- Have students ask and answer the questions in groups of four.

C

- Have groups record and tally the numbers. Then have them share their numbers and results with the class.

Exercise 8: Writing

A

- Have students write paragraphs individually.

B

- Have students correct each other's work in pairs using the Editing Checklist.
- ⏱ Have students revise their paragraphs. Then post them around the room and give students time to walk around and read them.

OUT OF THE BOX ACTIVITIES

Reading, Speaking, Listening, and Writing

- Have students work in groups of three. Each group will plan an imaginary get-together. Students can use the opening conversation as a model for their discussion.
- Assign each group a different type of event to plan. If you have a large class, some groups may plan the same event. Some suggested events are: a summer picnic or barbecue, a party for teenagers, a birthday party, a wedding reception, a going-away luncheon, a welcome-home party, etc. Each group should discuss food, drinks, decorations, entertainment, and the guest list. Have them brainstorm and write lists of possible choices for each category.

- Set a time limit for the discussion. Circulate and make students use comparatives in their discussion. They can take notes if they want to. Have each group tell the class (or another group if time is limited or you have a large class) about the event and why they made their choices. Each person in the group should report on at least one of the categories.

Go to **www.myfocusongrammarlab.com** for additional listening, pronunciation, speaking, and writing practice.

Note:

- See the *Focus on Grammar Workbook* for additional in-class or homework grammar practice.

Unit 29 Review (page 287)

Have students complete the Review and check their answers on Student Book page UR-4. Review or assign additional material as needed.

Go to **www.myfocusongrammarlab.com** for the Unit Achievement Test.

UNIT 30 OVERVIEW

Grammar: PREPOSITIONS OF TIME: *In, On, At*

Unit 30 focuses on the meanings and uses of some common prepositions of time: *in, on,* and *at.*

- Use *in* with years, months, parts of the day, and some time expressions such as *in a few minutes*. Use *at*, not *in*, to talk about *night: at night*.
- Use *on* with days of the week and dates, and in expressions such as *on weekends, on weekdays,* and *on weeknights*.
- Use *at* with times and expressions such as *at lunch* or *at dinnertime*.

Theme: LEISURE ACTIVITIES

Unit 30 focuses on language that describes a leisure activity such as a barbecue.

Step 1: Grammar in Context (pages 288–290)

See the general suggestions for Grammar in Context on page 1.

Before You Read

- You may want to provide additional practice with these prepositions of time. Write this sentence stem and these time expressions on the board:
  What do you usually do _____?

  in the morning
  in the afternoon
  at night
  at 6:00 P.M.
  on weekends
  on your birthday?

- Have a student ask you a question using the sentence stem and one of the expressions. Be sure to use the time expression in your answer. Have students work in small groups to take turns asking and answering the questions.

Read

- To encourage students to read with a purpose, write these questions on the board:
  1. Where and when did Tim and Felix meet? *(on the train to Seattle in June)*
  2. Why is Felix calling? *(to invite Tim and his wife to a barbecue)*
  3. When is it? *(on Saturday the 20th)*
  4. Is the barbecue in the afternoon or at night? *(It's in the afternoon, starting at 1:00; they're eating at 2:00.)*

- Have students read the questions aloud. Establish a purpose for reading. Have students think about the questions as they read and listen to the conversation.
- Have students read the conversation and work in pairs to discuss the questions. Call on pairs to share their answers with the class.

After You Read

A. Practice

- Have students find three *yes / no* questions in the conversation. *(Do you remember me? Can I call you back? Can we bring anything?)* Ask students if the intonation at the end of these questions should be rising or falling. *(rising)* Have students repeat each of these questions after you say it. Exaggerate the rising intonation at the end of each question.
- Ask students about the intonation for *Wh-* questions. *(It rises around the middle of the question but falls at the end.)* Have students identify three *Wh-* questions and write them on the board. Have students repeat each of the questions after you say it.

- Have students practice the conversation. Call on pairs to read the conversation for the class. Have the rest of the class pay particular attention to the intonation of the questions.

B. Vocabulary

- Have students write the words that are new for them in their notebooks and compare their lists in groups of three.

C. Vocabulary

- Read the instructions. Have students look at the vocabulary words in Part B. Ask: "Which words are activities?" *(have a barbecue, play volleyball, go shopping, go to a play)* Explain that students will rank the activities from 1 to 4. They should give 1 to the activity they like the most and 4 to the one they like the least. Write on the board:
  I love / like / don't like / hate to _____ .
  I gave it a (number).

- Have students write down their statements and share their answers in groups. You may need to model the first one for them. Use the language on the board. For example: *I love to go shopping. I gave it a 1. It's fun to go shopping for new clothes with friends.*
- Call on students from each group to share their answers with the class.

D. Comprehension

- Remind students that the opening conversation is on pages 288–289.
- Have students complete the exercise and work in pairs to check their answers. Call on pairs to share their corrections of the false statements with the class.

Go to **www.myfocusongrammarlab.com** for an additional reading, and for reading and vocabulary practice.

Step 2: Grammar Presentation (page 290)

See the general suggestions for Grammar Presentation on page 3.

Grammar Charts

- Have students look over the grammar chart. Then have students look back at the opening conversation on pages 288–289 and find examples of time expressions with *in, on,* and *at. (in June, on Saturday, in the afternoon, on the 20th, at 1:00, on Saturday at 1:00)*

- Call on students to come to the board and show the class an example of each target structure in the lines from the conversation. Help students explain why it is correct. You may want to point out similar examples in the grammar chart. For example: *The opening conversation says* in June *and the grammar chart uses the example* in January.

Grammar Notes

Note 1

- Have students write a year, a month, and one or two parts of the day in their notebooks. Tell them that these should be meaningful to them in some way.
- Call on a student to write his or her times on the board. Ask that student questions about each of the times. For example:
  T: Tetsu, what happened in 1997?
  S: My brother was born in 1997.

  T: Is your birthday in June?
  S: No, my birthday is in July. I graduate in June.
- Draw attention to the *Be Careful!* note. Have students work in pairs or groups of three. Ask them to exchange notebooks. Have them take turns asking and answering questions about the times they wrote.

Note 2

- Repeat the procedure from Note 1 but have students write expressions with *on*.

Note 3

- Repeat the procedure from Notes 1 and 2 but have students write expressions with *at*.

🕐 **Identify the Grammar:** Have students identify the grammar in the opening conversation on pages 288–289. For example:
  We met **in June** on the train to Seattle.
  When is it? **On Saturday, the 20th, in the afternoon**.
  We're free **on the 20th**.
  Why don't you come **at 1:00**?

Go to **www.myfocusongrammarlab.com** for grammar charts and notes.

Step 3: Focused Practice (pages 291–292)

See the general suggestions for Focused Practice on page 4.

Exercise 1: Discover the Grammar

- Have students complete the exercise. Go over the answers as a class.

- Have students work in pairs to take turns using the grammar chart and notes on page 290 to explain why each preposition is correct.

Exercise 2: *In, On,* and *At*

- Have students complete the exercise and work in groups of four to check their answers.
- Have groups practice reading the conversation four times, changing roles after each practice.

Exercise 3: *In, On,* and *At*

- Have students complete the exercise. Call on students to write their questions and answers on the board. Discuss them as a class.
- Have pairs work together to practice asking and answering their questions.

Exercise 4: Editing

- Have students work in groups to correct their work.
- Call on groups to share their corrections with the class and explain the correction.

Go to **www.myfocusongrammarlab.com** for additional grammar practice.

Step 4: Communication Practice
(pages 293–294)

See the general suggestions for Communication Practice on page 5.

Exercise 5: Listening

A

- Play the audio and have students complete the task. Then have them compare their answers in pairs.

B

- Play the audio again, pausing as needed to give students time to complete the chart. Have students complete the chart. Then play the audio again so they can check their work.
- 🕐 For additional listening practice, play the audio again and have students write down the days, departure times, arrival times, and destinations for all of the flights mentioned in the audio. Then give students the audioscript and go over the answers as a class.

Exercise 6: Pronunciation

A

- Have students listen to the Pronunciation Note. Then have students place their hands on their jaw. Say the words *cat* and *pot* several times. Exaggerate the vowel sounds as you say the words. Explain to students that their jaws should move more for the /æ/ sound.

B

- Play the audio and have students complete the task. Then have them compare answers in pairs.

C

- Have students take turns reading the sentences in pairs. Have students place their hands on their jaws before reading each sentence. Circulate and make corrections as needed.

Exercise 7: Ask and Answer

- Once students complete the chart, have two groups work together to share one thing they learned about someone else in the group.
- Have that larger group work with another larger group and share something different that they learned.
- Continue the process until the class is one big group. Call on students to share something interesting they learned.

Exercise 8: Writing

A

- Explain the task and have students read the example. Have students write their letters. Circulate and give help as needed.

B

- Divide the class into small groups. Have group members exchange papers and use the Editing Checklist to correct each other's letters.
- ⏱ Call on students to read their letters to the class.

OUT OF THE BOX ACTIVITIES

Reading, Writing, Listening, and Speaking

- Have students find out some important events that occurred on their birthday or another day they choose. Have students do an Internet search for "this date in history." There are quite a few sites of this kind. Have them choose a site and select the date they want to read about. Have them record at least three events that occurred on the date they chose. For example, they could write down someone who was born on that day, someone who died, and another important event.

- Have students work in groups and have them report on what they found using *in*, *at*, and *on*. Explain that they should begin like this: *Several important things happened on January 18. First, I was born at 11:20 A.M. in 1982. Also, . . .*

Reading, Writing, Speaking, and Listening

- Have students work in groups of four. If possible, have students from the same country work together. Have each group pick one holiday that people celebrate in their country. If your students are all from the same culture, be sure that each group picks a different holiday.
- Prepare the following as a handout and give it to each student or write these questions on the board:
  1. When is the holiday? Give the date and month.
  2. What happens at different times of the day?
  3. What clothes do people wear?
  4. What foods do people eat?
  5. What are some other customs and traditions that people follow?
- Have groups work together to prepare a presentation to the class about the holiday. Encourage them to bring in photos or maybe even wear the traditional clothing when they give their presentation. Each student in the group must talk about one aspect of the holiday.
- Have each group give a presentation to the class. If you have a large class, groups can give presentations to each other. If you are in a building where there are other classes, you may want to invite another class to listen to the presentations.

Go to **www.myfocusongrammarlab.com** for additional listening, pronunciation, speaking, and writing practice.

Note:
- See the *Focus on Grammar Workbook* for additional in-class or homework grammar practice.

Unit 30 Review (page 295)

Have students complete the Review and check their answers on Student Book page UR-4. Review or assign additional material as needed.

Go to **www.myfocusongrammarlab.com** for the Unit Achievement Test.

From Grammar to Writing (page FG-9)

See the general suggestions for From Grammar to Writing on page 9.

Go to **www.myfocusongrammarlab.com** for an additional From Grammar to Writing Assignment, Part Review, and Part Post-Test.

UNIT 31 OVERVIEW

Grammar: FUTURE WITH *Be going to*: STATEMENTS

Unit 31 focuses on the meanings and uses of *be going to* to express the future in affirmative and negative statements. It also introduces future time expressions.

- Use *be going to* to talk about the future.
- To form the future with *be going to*, use *am, is,* or *are + going to* + the base form of the verb.
- To make a negative sentence, place *not* before *going to*. Use contractions in conversation and informal writing.

Theme: SPORTING EVENTS

Unit 31 focuses on language that is used to talk about sporting events that are going to take place in the future.

Step 1: Grammar in Context (pages 298–300)

See the general suggestions for Grammar in Context on page 1.

Before You Read

- Have students discuss their answers in groups. Call on groups to share their answers with the class. Do a quick tally on the board to see which event is the favorite.
- Have students work in their groups to ask each other why that particular event is their favorite. For example:
  S1: Why is the Super Bowl your favorite sports event?
  S2: It's my favorite because I like football. I also like the halftime show.

Read

- To encourage students to read with a purpose, write these questions on the board:
  1. Where are Laura and Ken going? *(to a soccer game)*
  2. Who's playing? *(Sam, Laura's brother)*
  3. Does Ken need his umbrella? *(no)*
  4. What is the most popular game in the world? *(soccer)*
- Have students look over the questions. Have them think about the questions as they read and listen to the conversation.
- Play the audio and have students follow along in their books. Have students discuss the questions in pairs or groups of three. Call on pairs or groups to share answers with the class.

After You Read

A. Practice

- Go over some of the expressions that students may not know, such as *how come, do the speed limit, chill out,* and *giant*. Point out the line in which Ken says, "But how come you like soccer so much?" Have students tell you another way to ask that question. *(But why do you like soccer so much?)* Point out to students that the expression "How come?" is often used in speech to replace "Why?" Point out the expression <u>do the speed limit</u>. Tell students that it's also correct to say *drive the speed limit* or *go the speed limit*. Ask students what *chill out* means. *(It is an idiom used mainly by young people in the United States. Sometimes it is shortened to "chill.")* Ask students what Laura means when she says, "You don't have to be a giant." *(In this context, a giant means very tall or very big.)*

- Have students practice the conversation in pairs. Have students practice both parts of the conversation. Then have them find new partners and repeat.

B. Vocabulary
- Play the audio and have students repeat each word or phrase. Have students share the words they wrote in their notebooks with a partner.
- Have pairs work together to practice spelling the vocabulary items. If needed, write this sentence stem on the board:
  How do you spell _____?

C. Vocabulary
- Call on students to share their answers with the class.
- Have students explain why they rated their favorite and least favorite as they did.

D. Comprehension
- Have students complete the exercise individually. Then have them compare answers in pairs.
- Call on pairs to share their answers with the class by reading the correct sentences aloud.

Go to **www.myfocusongrammarlab.com** for an additional reading, and for reading and vocabulary practice.

Step 2: Grammar Presentation (pages 300–301)
See the general suggestions for Grammar Presentation on page 3.

Grammar Charts
- Read the example sentences aloud and have students repeat. Have students look for similar sentences in the opening conversation on page 298. Write those sentences on the board.
- Model the pronunciation that is accepted in the community where you teach. In North America *going to* is almost always pronounced *gonna*.
- To help students notice the grammar, ask questions such as these:
  — Which forms of *be* can we use with *going to*? (all forms: am, is, are, etc.)
  — How do we form the negative of *be going to*? (place *not* after *be*)
  — Which kind of word comes after *to*? (base form of the verb)
  — Which time expressions can we use with *be going to*? (soon, this afternoon, tonight, tomorrow, today, later, any specific future time)

Grammar Notes
Notes 1–4
- You may want to explain that *be going to* is used most often to make predictions and to talk about planned actions.
- Model the target grammar by pretending you are a fortune teller. Call up a student and pretend to tell his or her fortune. For example: *You're going to be the first female president of your country. You're going to win a million dollars in the lottery.*
- Write a variety of singular and plural nouns on the board. Include names of athletes and sports teams the students know. List other subjects students may enjoy talking about. Have the students make affirmative predictions with *be going to*.
- Model negative predictions. Have students make negative predictions about the subjects you wrote on the board.
- To model the use of *be going to* for planned actions, show a page from a planner or make a list of activities you plan to do the next day or on the weekend. Model sentences about your planned activities. For example: *Saturday morning I'm going to work in my garden. I'm going to have lunch with my mother on Sunday.*
- Go around the room and have students say one sentence about something they are planning to do the following day, next weekend, etc. For an alternative, pick one day and time, for example, Friday evening, and have students say what they're going to do at that time.
- Point out the first example in Note 4: "The game's going to start soon." Ask students what the contraction means. *(The game is going to start soon.)* Point out that a subject contracted with a form of *be* (for present time frames) is common in speech but is not usually used in writing.

🕐 **Identify the Grammar:** Have students identify the grammar in the opening conversation on page 298. For example:
  We**'re going to be** late!
  I think they**'re going to win**.
  It**'s not going to rain**.
  The game**'s going to start** soon.

Go to **www.myfocusongrammarlab.com** for grammar charts and notes.

Step 3: Focused Practice (pages 301–303)
See the general suggestions for Focused Practice on page 4.

Exercise 1: Discover the Grammar
- Have students complete the exercise and compare their answers in pairs. Then review the correct answers as a class.
- Have pairs practice asking and answering the questions two times, changing roles after the first practice.

Exercise 2: *Be going to*
- Have students complete the exercise, then call on students to write their answers on the board and read them to the class.
- Ask the class if they agree with the answer. If not, have dissenters give their answers. Then have students look back at the grammar charts and notes to determine which is the correct answer.
- Have students practice reading the paragraph aloud to each other.

Exercise 3: *Be going to*
- Have students complete the exercise and check their answers in pairs.
- Have each pair take turns reading each of the items aloud.
- Have pairs write one more sentence about each picture using *be going to* + base form. For example, for the first picture: *Skier 34 isn't going to lose. Skier 21 isn't going to finish last*. Call on pairs to share sentences with the class.

Exercise 4: Editing
- Have students complete the exercise individually.
- Call on students to write their corrected sentences on the board. Have each student explain the error and the correction.

Go to **www.myfocusongrammarlab.com** for additional grammar practice.

Step 4: Communication Practice
(pages 303–305)

See the general suggestions for Communication Practice on page 5.

Exercise 5: Listening
A
- Ask the class: *What is happening in the picture?*
- Read the instructions and question. Play the audio and elicit the answer.

B
- Play the audio again and have students complete the exercise. Then have them check their answers in small groups.

- Have students correct the false statements individually and compare corrections as a group.

Exercise 6: Pronunciation
A
- Have students complete the exercise.
- Have pairs work together to check their answers.
- Play the audio again to clarify answers as needed.

B
- Have students practice the sentences two times, changing roles after the first practice.
- Do a quick drill using the sentences from this exercise. Call on a student and say either "going to" or "gonna." The student must say the sentence as you directed. Have the class raise their hands if they think the pronunciation was correct.
- Have that student select someone else and say "going to" or "gonna." The second student reads the next sentence as directed. The class raises their hands if they think the pronunciation is correct. In cases where there is dissent, have the first student repeat the directive and the second student repeat the sentence. Have the class raise their hands to provide feedback.

Exercise 7: Memory Game: *I'm Going to Take . . .*
- To set up this exercise, have students form a standing circle. Give the student who begins a bean bag, tennis ball, or crumpled sheet of paper.
- The first student makes the *I'm going to take . . .* statement and throws the bean bag (or ball) to someone else in the circle.
- If a person forgets to include something, he or she sits down.

Exercise 8: Writing
A
- Explain the task and go over the topics in the box. Brainstorm additional topics with the class.
- Have students read the example. Then have them write their paragraphs individually.

B
- Have students use the Editing Checklist to correct each other's work in pairs. Then have them revise the paragraphs as needed.
- ⏱ Have students form new pairs and read their paragraphs to each other. Call on students to read their paragraphs to the class.

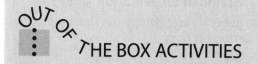

OUT OF THE BOX ACTIVITIES

Reading, Listening, and Speaking

- Bring in copies of the sports section from a local newspaper. You can also bring in the television listings and have students look for a sports program they want to watch.
- Have students work in pairs. Give a newspaper to each pair. Have students work together to find articles or announcements about local sports events. Have them choose one event they would like to attend together. They should note the day, time, and location of the event. They should also give some additional information using the future with *be going to*. Each pair of students should then tell the class about the event they chose.
- Model the activity with a student. For example:
We're going to go to a tennis tournament. It's going to be at the university on Sunday at 3 P.M. We're going to ask Pietro and Non to go with us. First, we're going to meet for lunch at the Campus Grill. Then we're going to walk to the tennis tournament. If it's raining, we're not going to go.

Writing, Reading, Speaking, and Listening

- Have each student write a note to a friend or family member inviting that person to an event in the future. They can use the letter in Exercise 4 on Student Book page 303 as a model.
- Have students use the Editing Checklist on Student Book page 305 to revise and rewrite their work as needed.
- Have students work in groups to read their invitations to each other.

Go to **www.myfocusongrammarlab.com** for additional listening, pronunciation, speaking, and writing practice.

Note:

- See the *Focus on Grammar Workbook* for additional in-class or homework grammar practice.

Unit 31 Review (page 306)

Have students complete the Review and check their answers on Student Book page UR-5. Review or assign additional material as needed.

Go to **www.myfocusongrammarlab.com** for the Unit Achievement Test.

UNIT 32 OVERVIEW

Grammar: FUTURE WITH *Be going to*: QUESTIONS

Unit 32 focuses on the meanings and uses of questions in the future with *be going to*.

- For *yes / no* questions with *be going to*, put *am, is,* or *are* before the subject.
- We usually use contractions in negative short answers.
- For a *Wh-* question with *be going to*, use a *Wh-* word + the correct form of *be* + subject + *going to* + the base form of the verb.
- For a *Wh-* question about the subject, use *who* or *what* + *is* + *going to* + the base form of the verb.

Theme: CAREER PLANS AND GOALS

Unit 32 focuses on language that is used to talk about career plans and goals.

Step 1: Grammar in Context (pages 307–308)

See the general suggestions for Grammar in Context on page 1.

Before You Read

- Have pairs ask and answer all of the suggested questions.
- Then have two pairs form a group and tell each other their partners' answers to all of the questions. Have students choose the most interesting answer to report to the class.

Read

- To encourage students to read with a purpose, write these questions on the board:
  1. What are the speakers doing? (*eating dinner*)
  2. Who called Jessica? (*a TV producer*)
  3. What did he want? (*He wanted Jessica to be in a new news program.*)
  4. What is Jessica's new job going to be? (*the star*)
- Have students read the questions on the board. Have them think about these questions as they read and listen to the conversation. Then have students read the conversation. Discuss answers to the questions as a class.

After You Read

A. Practice

- Ask students if they remember what the spoken form of *going to* often sounds like in North American English. *(gonna)*
- Remind students that this pronunciation is well accepted but quite informal. Explain that in the context of a dinner conversation at home such as this family is having, *gonna* is acceptable. It may not, however, be as well accepted in a more formal setting.
- Have students practice the conversation in groups. Have them switch roles and practice again until each student has done each role.

B. Vocabulary

- You may want to point out the distinction between a TV producer and director. A producer controls all aspects of the show. He or she often helps develop the idea of a show, checks facts, and hires actors for the show. A producer is responsible for the quality of the show. A director is the person who decides where the cameras are placed and supervises other elements such as lighting and sound.
- Play the audio and have students repeat each word or phrase. Then have students repeat the words and phrases again as you say them.

C. Vocabulary

- Have students complete the exercise individually. Go over the answers as a class by calling on students to read each sentence aloud.

D. Comprehension

- Have students complete the exercise individually and then compare their answers in pairs or groups of three.
- Have students take turns reading the corrected statements aloud in their pairs or groups.
- As an alternative, have pairs or groups take turns making questions based on the statements in the exercise and answering them. For example:
  S1: Is Dan Evans a movie producer?
  S2: No, he's not. He's a TV producer. When does the new program start?
  S1: Not for a long time.

Go to **www.myfocusongrammarlab.com** for an additional reading, and for reading and vocabulary practice.

Step 2: Grammar Presentation (page 309)

See the general suggestions for Grammar Presentation on page 3.

Grammar Charts

- Have students look at the example sentences in the grammar charts. Then ask these questions:
  — What is the word order for *yes / no* questions with *be going to*? (*be + subject + going to + verb*)
  — What is the difference in word order for regular *Wh-* questions and *Wh-* questions about the subject? (*In regular* Wh- *questions the word order is* Wh- *word +* be *+ subject + going to + base form of the verb. In questions about the subject the order is* Who *or* What *+ be going to + base form of the verb.*)

Grammar Notes

Notes 1–2

- Drill the form of *yes / no* questions and negative short answers with *be going to*. Write a verb phrase on the board, for example: *have dinner with parents*. Say different noun and pronoun subjects and have students form the questions. For example:
  T: you
  S1: Are you going to have dinner with your parents?
  T: No, I'm not.

  T: Ho and Chen
  S2: Are Ho and Chen going to have dinner with their parents?
  T: No, they're not. / No, they aren't.
- Have students brainstorm a list of phrases that involve actions and write those on the board. Have students work in groups of three to continue making *yes / no* questions with *be going to* using the list of phrases on the board and noun and pronoun subjects they think of. Remind them to vary their answers when there are two correct forms. Circulate as students are practicing. Make corrections as needed.

Note 3

- Make five columns on the board:
  Question words
  be
  Pronoun / Noun
  be going to
  Action

- Brainstorm words that can go in each column and write them on the board. For example:

Question Words	be	Pronoun/ Noun	be going to	Action

Where
How
When
How
  long
Why
What
Who
	am
	is
	are
		I
		you
		he
		she
		it
		we
		they
		Paolo
		Hong
		Ken and
		  Amy
			be
			going
			to
				go
				call
				see
				stay
				leave
				arrive
				read
				write
				meet
				start

- Have students work in pairs, small groups, or as a class to ask and answer as many different questions as they can using the chart. Circulate and make corrections as needed.
- For variation, do this as a written activity for pairs. Have each pair write ten to twelve questions. Then have them exchange questions with another pair and write answers for the questions they got. Have pairs share some of their questions and answers with the class.

Note 4
- Repeat the procedure above, but elicit from students the number of columns and the order of the heads in the chart. *(Who / What; Be; Going to; Actions)*

🕐 **Identify the Grammar:** Have students identify the grammar in the opening conversation on page 307. For example:
  Are you going to have a big part?
  When are you going to begin?
  Are you going to travel a lot?
  Who's going to help me with my homework?

Go to **www.myfocusongrammarlab.com** for grammar charts and notes.

Step 3: Focused Practice (pages 309–311)

See the general suggestions for Focused Practice on page 4.

Exercise 1: Discover the Grammar
- Have students complete the exercise and work in pairs to check their answers.
- Go over the answers as a class and answer any questions about the exercise.
- Have students continue working in pairs to take turns asking and answering the questions.

Exercise 2: *Be going to*
- Have students complete the exercise and go over the answers as a class.
- Have students work in pairs to take turns practicing the conversations twice, changing roles after the first practice.
- Call on pairs to read each of the conversations to the class.

Exercise 3: *Be going to*
- Have students complete the exercise individually. Call on students to write their questions on the board and read them aloud to the class. Have students make corrections as needed.
- Have female students read Jessica's thoughts chorally. Have male students read Tim's.

Exercise 4: Editing
- Have students complete the exercise individually. Call on students to write their corrected sentences on the board. Have each student explain his or her correction to the class.

Go to **www.myfocusongrammarlab.com** for additional grammar practice.

Step 4: Communication Practice
(pages 312–313)

See the general suggestions for Communication Practice on page 5.

Exercise 5: Listening

A
- Explain the task and go over the two choices. Play the audio and elicit the answer.

B
- Play the audio again and have students complete the exercise. Go over the answers as a class.

C
- Play the audio again, replaying as needed. Elicit the answer.
- 🕐 Give students the audioscript for this exercise. Have them work in groups of three to practice the conversations in Parts A and B. Call on groups to role-play the conversations for the class.

Exercise 6: Pronunciation

A

- Have students listen to and read the Pronunciation Note.
- Have them place their hands on their throats over the larynx. Say /b/ and /v/ several times and have students repeat so they can feel the vibration when saying them.

B

- Have students complete the exercise. Go over the answers as a class. Play the audio again as needed for clarification.

C

- As students listen to the audio, have them correct their answers in Part C.

D

- Play the audio, pausing as needed for students to complete the task.
- Review each sentence again with the class. Have students identify and say the words with voiced /b/ and /v/. Remind students that the sounds may not always be at the beginnings of the words, as *have* in the third question.

Exercise 7: What Are They Going to Do?

- For variation, bring in photos from magazines or catalogs that show people in action. Have each student or pair of students select a photo. Have students write as many sentences about the photo as they can using *be going to*. For added challenge, have students talk about the picture rather than writing about it.
- Have students share their photos and sentences in pairs or groups. Call on a few pairs to show their photos and read their sentences to the class. Have students ask questions about the photo using *be going to*.

Exercise 8: Writing

A

- Encourage students to add some sentences about themselves to the email message. For example:

  Dear _____,
  Congratulations on getting a job at Goodbuys. When are you going to begin? Are you going to work evenings?

I'm going to look for a job soon. After the semester ends, I'm going to go home for two weeks. My sister and her husband are going to visit my parents while I'm there. We're going to go to the beach for two or three days. It's the first time that I'm going to see their new baby.

Good luck on your first day. You're going to be awesome!

B

- Have students correct their work using the Editing Checklist. Then have them trade papers with another student and correct each other's work using the Editing Checklist.
- Have pairs discuss any errors they found and have the students make corrections as needed.
- Have students form new pairs and read their email messages to each other.

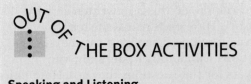

OUT OF THE BOX ACTIVITIES

Speaking and Listening

- Do an Internet image search for "messy room." Print out three or four different pictures or cartoons. Each student gets a different picture of a messy room.
- Have students work in groups of three or four. Students need to decide whether to keep or throw away items as part of an imaginary cleaning of their messy room. Explain to students that they are going to pretend that this is their room, and their classmates are going to help them clean it up. Students take turns showing the picture of their room to the group. The classmates ask questions, and the "owner" of the room answers. For example:

S1: Are you going to keep this pizza box or throw it away?
S2: I'm going to throw it away.
S3: What are you going to do with this old sofa?
S2: I'm going to keep it. It's really comfortable.
S4: Where are you going to put this soccer ball?
S2: In the closet.

Go to **www.myfocusongrammarlab.com** for additional listening, pronunciation, speaking, and writing practice.

Note:
- See the *Focus on Grammar Workbook* for additional in-class or homework grammar practice.

Unit 32 Review (page 314)

Have students complete the Review and check their answers on Student Book page UR-5. Review or assign additional material as needed.

Go to **www.myfocusongrammarlab.com** for the Unit Achievement Test.

From Grammar to Writing (page FG-10)

See the general suggestions for From Grammar to Writing on page 9.

Go to **www.myfocusongrammarlab.com** for an additional From Grammar to Writing Assignment, Part Review, and Part Post-Test.

STUDENT BOOK AUDIOSCRIPT

UNIT 1

EXERCISE 5 (page 7)

A: Yuan, are you in this photo?

B: Yes, I am. See, I'm on the left. And this is my teacher in the middle. He's from Canada. His name is Mr. Singer. He's a wonderful teacher. I'm happy to be in his class. And this is my friend, Hai, on the right.

A: Where is he from?

B: China, just like me.

EXERCISE 6 (page 7)

1. This is my friend.
2. These are my photos.
3. This is our ticket.
4. These are my sisters.
5. Are these your keys?

UNIT 2

EXERCISE 6 (page 16)

ELENA: Judy, these glasses are dirty.

JUDY: You're right, Elena. And these spoons are dirty too.

ELENA: This restaurant is dirty.

JUDY: Well, let's go home. Our apartment is clean.

UNIT 3

EXERCISE 6 (page 26)

C

1. We're happy to be here.
2. They are from the capital.
3. He's a chef.
4. She's a student.
5. I am her cousin.
6. It's delicious.

EXERCISE 7 (page 26)

MATTEO: Nice to meet you. I'm Matteo Milano.

AMY: Nice to meet you. Are you from around here?

MATTEO: No, I'm from Italy. What about you?

AMY: I'm from Australia. But my parents are from Italy.

MATTEO: Oh, really? Are you a student?

AMY: I am. What about you?

MATTEO: I'm a chef.

AMY: Italian food?

MATTEO: Of course.

AMY: I love Italian food. It's very popular in Australia.

MATTEO: I think it's popular everywhere.

AMY: You're right. It's not expensive and it's delicious.

MATTEO: It's healthy, too. Come to my restaurant. Try my pasta.

AMY: Thanks. I'd love to.

MATTEO: Well, here's my business card with the address.

UNIT 4

EXERCISE 6 (page 35)

B

1. Those children are Ben, Annie, and Jeremy. They're Jessica's children.
2. And that's Bozo. He's their dog.
3. Do you have your camera with you?
4. Steve, everybody thinks you're a good photographer.
5. I like Seattle. It's a beautiful city.
6. Every city has its problems, even Seattle.

EXERCISE 7 (page 35)

JUDY: Glad to meet you, Jessica. Wow, what nice pictures! Are those your children?

JESSICA: Yes. The boys are our sons, Jeremy and Ben. And that's our daughter, Annie.

JUDY: And is that their cat?

JESSICA: Yes. Her name is Fluffy.

JUDY: Who are those other kids?

JESSICA: Those are their friends from school.

UNIT 5

EXERCISE 6 (page 44)

B

1. Are you here for the wedding?
2. What about you?
3. Who's that man with Steve?
4. Is he single?

5. What does he do?
6. Who's that woman with Amanda?
7. Is she married?
8. Is she a travel agent?

EXERCISE 7 (page 44)

A: Hi, Ahmed. Nice wedding, right?

B: It sure is. Say, Diego, who's that woman?

A: That's my friend Mai. She's a writer.

B: Is she married?

A: No, she's single.

B: Oh. And who are those people?

A: They're my cousins, Jaime and Carlos. They're brothers.

B: And who's *that* woman?

A: That's my wife, Alicia.

B: She looks nice.

A: She is.

UNIT 6

EXERCISE 6 (page 54)

MAN: Excuse me. Where's the nearest supermarket?

WOMAN: It's on the northeast corner of Washington Street and First Avenue. This is Washington Street and Second Avenue. Walk down Washington one block. The supermarket is across from the post office.

MAN: Thanks. One more thing. Do they sell flowers in that supermarket?

WOMAN: Uh, yes, they do. But walk down Second Avenue one block and there's a big flower shop on the northeast corner of Main and Second. The flowers there are beautiful.

MAN: Thanks.

EXERCISE 7 (page 54)

C
1. **A:** Where's the doctor's office?
   B: It's in room 15 on the 2nd floor.
   A: Fifteen or fifty?
   B: Fifteen.
2. **A:** How old is your son?
   B: He's fourteen
   A: Fourteen or forty?
   B: Fourteen. I'm just 45 years old.
   A: Just kidding.
3. **A:** Where's the number fifty bus?
   B: Was that fifteen or fifty?
   A: Fifty.

4. **A:** Where's the library?
   B: It's 60 Main Street.
   A: Was that sixteen or sixty?
   B: Sixty.

UNIT 7

EXERCISE 6 (page 64)

A
1. I wasn't at school yesterday.
2. It was hot yesterday.
3. They weren't at the rock concert last night.
4. My friend wasn't with me at the movies.
5. She wasn't asleep at midnight.
6. We were at the soccer game.

EXERCISE 7 (page 65)

MARK: Hello. This is Mark. Sorry I can't take your call right now. Please leave a message.

JOSH: Hi, Mark. This is Josh. Hey, where were you last night? Amanda and I were at the movies. We saw *Spider-Man 3*. It was really interesting. It was exciting, too. Call me, OK? Bye.

UNIT 8

EXERCISE 6 (page 73)

MARK: Hey, Jason. How are you? How was your weekend?

JASON: It was great.

MARK: Where were you?

JASON: At the beach.

MARK: How was the weather?

JASON: Nice. It was sunny and hot. How was your weekend?

MARK: So-so. I was home all weekend. I was busy with school work.

JASON: Sorry to hear that.

MARK: Well, it's done. And there's always next weekend.

UNIT 9

EXERCISE 6 (page 83)

NEW STUDENT: Excuse me, where's the library?

OLD STUDENT: Go down the hall. Then turn right. It's between the cafeteria and the computer lab. There's a sign that says "Library" on the door.

NEW STUDENT: Thanks. And where's the main office?

OLD STUDENT: It's on the first floor. Go down one flight. Turn left. It's next to the student lounge.

NEW STUDENT: Thank you.

EXERCISE 7 (page 84)

B

1. Don't eat the cake.   eat
2. It's for the party.   It's
3. Don't sit there.   sit
4. Where's your seat?   seat
5. Turn on the heat.   heat
6. Keep your cellphone on.   Keep
7. Please walk Kip.   Kip
8. He's my brother.   He's
9. Don't take his bike.   his

UNIT 10

EXERCISE 6 (page 93)

MAN: Is anyone sitting here?

TIM: No. Have a seat, please.

MAN: Oh! I'm really tired. . . . Are you going to Seattle?

TIM: Yes, I am. You, too?

MAN: Yes. When are we due in Seattle?

TIM: Let's see . . . About seven-thirty, I think. . . . Are you from around here?

MAN: Actually, I'm not. I come from Romania. I live in Bucharest.

TIM: Romania? Hmm. Your English is really good.

MAN: Thanks very much.

TIM: Do people speak English in Romania?

MAN: A lot of people know some English. Some people speak it. In my family everyone speaks three languages.

TIM: Really?

MAN: Yes. My parents were at the United Nations. So we speak English, French, and Romanian, of course.

TIM: That's great! I don't speak any languages besides English. Just a little Spanish.

EXERCISE 7 (page 94)

B

TIM: Do you live in Seattle?

MAN: For the moment. My wife has a teaching job at the university this year.

TIM: Oh. What does she teach?

MAN: She teaches European literature. She also writes novels.

TIM: That sounds interesting.

MAN: Yes, it is. But it's also difficult. She watches TV and movies in English a lot, so she understands American English, but she doesn't speak it too well yet. What about you? What do you do?

TIM: I'm a graphic artist. I work for an advertising agency. My wife works for a TV station.

UNIT 11

EXERCISE 6 (page 104)

JUDY: Are you going to the game?

MARK: No. It's my grandmother's birthday and I need to get a gift. Do you have any ideas?

JUDY: Let's see. Does she like music?

MARK: I don't know.

JUDY: Well, does she like to read?

MARK: I don't really know.

JUDY: Does she like chocolate?

MARK: I think so. But I'm not sure.

JUDY: I've got it. I know the perfect gift.

MARK: You do? What?

JUDY: Spend the day with her.

MARK: That's not a gift.

JUDY: Yes, it is. Your time is a gift. I'm sure she'll love it.

UNIT 12

EXERCISE 5 (page 112)

MARGARET: Excuse me. Is anyone sitting here?

JASON: No. Sit down, please.

MARGARET: Are you new here?

JASON: Yes. Today's my first day on the job.

MARGARET: Oh. Welcome to the company. My name's Margaret Boyd.

JASON: Nice to meet you, Margaret. I'm Jason Mendoza.

MARGARET: Nice to meet you too, Jason. What do you do?

JASON: I'm an accountant. What about you?

MARGARET: I'm a writer. I write advertisements for the company.

JASON: Oh. That's interesting. Well, this is a good company, I think. The only problem is the traffic. I live in Belmont. It takes more than an hour to get here.

MARGARET: Really? I live in Belmont too. But I take the bus—it's usually about half an hour.

JASON: That sounds good. Where do you catch the bus?

MARGARET: At Tenth and Maple.

JASON: Really? I live near there.

MARGARET: Why don't you take the bus tomorrow? I catch the eight o'clock bus.

JASON: Great idea. See you then.

UNIT 13

EXERCISE 5 (page 123)

MARK: So tell me about your friend,

JUDY: Well, Olivia's a jazz musician.

MARK: Really? That's interesting.

JUDY: Uh-huh. She's about twenty-five. She's single.

MARK: Is she from around here?

JUDY: No. She's from Canada. She's performing here this week.

MARK: Is she from Montreal?

JUDY: Uh-huh. She's a student at McGill.

MARK: Oh. What does she look like?

JUDY: She's average height and weight. She's attractive.

MARK: What color hair does she have?

JUDY: She has dark brown hair. It's very long. She's a great saxophone player. Here. There's a photo of her and her band on the Internet.

MARK: Let me see. Hmm. I'd love to hear them play.

UNIT 14

EXERCISE 5 (page 132)

KEN: Hello?

GRANDMA: Hi, Kenny. How's my favorite grandson? And happy birthday.

KEN: Oh, hi, Grandma. Thanks a lot. But it's not until tomorrow.

GRANDMA: I know. But I'm usually early. So how are you?

KEN: Well, pretty good, but . . .

GRANDMA: But what?

KEN: Well, I'm always tired. I have a new job, and . . .

GRANDMA: That's good. But why are you tired so much? Are you eating your vegetables? Getting enough sleep?

KEN: Well, maybe I have too much to do. I usually start work at 1:30, and I never have time for lunch.

GRANDMA: Kenny! No! You have to eat lunch. And what about sleep?

KEN: Well, sometimes I stay up late to study.

GRANDMA: How much sleep are you getting?

KEN: Usually about five or six hours.

GRANDMA: Kenny! That's not enough.

KEN: I know, Grandma, but . . .

GRANDMA: But nothing. You need to take a lunch with you to work. And you need to get eight hours of sleep every night.

KEN: Well . . .

GRANDMA: Promise me.

KEN: OK, Grandma.

EXERCISE 6 (page 132)

B

1. west	3. tired	5. run	7. sure	9. white
2. rest	4. tied	6. one	8. shoe	10. right

UNIT 15

EXERCISE 5 (page 143)

STEVE: What are you looking at?

JESSICA: Photos of Lauren's visit. Here's one of the two of you.

STEVE: Let me see. Oh yeah. We're in the park. We're watching a race.

JESSICA: A race?

STEVE: Uh-huh. A race to help fight cancer.

JESSICA: That jacket is long on Lauren.

STEVE: It's my jacket. It was rainy and cool.

JESSICA: She's a lot of fun.

STEVE: You know, I'm planning to go to New York in May.

JESSICA: Really? To see Lauren?

STEVE: Maybe. There's a journalism conference. I'm writing a paper for it now.

JESSICA: Good luck with the paper.

STEVE: Thanks. Are there other pictures of Lauren and me?

JESSICA: I think so. Let me check. . . . Here's one of Lauren, you, and Jeremy.

STEVE: Oh, yeah. She's talking to Jeremy about New York University.

JESSICA: Why?

STEVE: I think he wants to go there for college.

JESSICA: Really? He's talking to Lauren about college. He never talks to me about college.

STEVE: Well she's not his mom.

JESSICA: Oh.

UNIT 16

EXERCISE 5 (page 153)

B
1. Are you washing them?
2. Please match them.
3. What's a dish?
4. Are they buying chips?
5. How do you spell "sheep"?

EXERCISE 6 (page 153)

STEVE: Hello.

JESSICA: Hi, Steve.

STEVE: Jessica! Hi. How are you?

JESSICA: Great. How about you? How are you doing?

STEVE: Busy. Very busy. Hold on. I'm teaching an online course, and I'm preparing for it now. Let me turn off the computer . . . This term I'm also writing articles for the *Daily Times*. I don't have much free time.

JESSICA: Boy, you *are* busy. Try to relax. Listen. Thanks again for the model ship for Ben.

STEVE: Is he really enjoying it?

JESSICA: He loves it. He's working on it right now.

STEVE: I'm glad. How's Annie?

JESSICA: Great. Guess what she's doing at school?

STEVE: I don't know. Is she acting in the school play?

JESSICA: No.

STEVE: Is she playing basketball?

JESSICA: No. She's writing for her school paper!

STEVE: That's my girl.

JESSICA: Come for dinner this weekend. We miss you.

STEVE: I'll be there.

UNIT 17

EXERCISE 6 (page 161)

MARK: Hello?

NICK: Hi, little brother. It's me again. What are you doing?

MARK: Hey, big brother! Well, I'm watching a DVD.

NICK: What are you watching?

MARK: *2012*.

NICK: Are you watching it alone?

MARK: Well, no.

NICK: Who are you watching it with?

MARK: My friend Kathy.

NICK: Hmm. Very interesting.

MARK: What about the job interview? How was it?

NICK: Really good.

MARK: So what are you planning to do?

NICK: Visit you. And think about the job.

MARK: Where are you staying? Are you still in Denver?

NICK: Yeah—I'm at a Super 8 Motel.

MARK: When will you be here?

NICK: Friday, the 15th, at 4 P.M. Can you pick me up at the train station?

MARK: I sure can. What time?

NICK: 4:00 in the afternoon. See you then, little brother.

UNIT 18

EXERCISE 6 (page 172)

B
1. That's my mother's magazine.
2. My father's car is across from the restaurant.
3. Those are their children's CDs.
4. That's my boss's office.
5. Are these your roommate's glasses?
6. No, they're Chris's glasses

EXERCISE 7 (page 173)

JUDY: So how did dinner with Kathy's parents go?

MARK: It went well, I think. Her dad's a really nice guy.

JUDY: What did you talk about?

MARK: His boat. That's his passion.

JUDY: Do you know anything about boats?

MARK: A bit. My friend's dad has a boat and I'm often invited.

JUDY: That's good. And what's Kathy's mom like?

MARK: She seemed nice too, but she was quiet. Kathy's aunt, her mom's sister, is in the hospital. I think Kathy's mom was worried about her.

JUDY: Is she very sick?

MARK: No, but Kathy's mom is still worried.

JUDY: I can understand. Did anyone say anything about your goatee?

MARK: Kathy did. She doesn't like it. She misses my beard.

JUDY: Oh, well.

MARK: But she liked my tie and suspenders.

JUDY: I guess you'll have to grow back your beard and keep borrowing your roommate's clothes.

EXERCISE 5 (page 183)

WAITER: May I help you?

MARK: Yes. Can we order lunch?

WAITER: I'm sorry. We serve lunch at 11:00. It's only 10:30. How about a snack?

JUDY: Well, all right. Some chips and salsa for me, and a cup of coffee, please.

WAITER: I'm sorry. The coffee machine is broken.

JUDY: Broken? Well, how about tea?

WAITER: All right. What kind?

JUDY: Iced tea.

WAITER: Sorry, no iced tea. All we have is hot tea.

JUDY: OK. A cup of hot tea and chips and salsa.

WAITER: I'm sorry, ma'am, but we're out of salsa. I can bring you some chips. . . . And for you, sir?

MARK: Some mineral water, please.

WAITER: Sorry, sir. We don't have any mineral water. All we have is lime soda. Or regular water.

MARK: Hmm. OK. Lime soda, please.

WAITER: All right, sir. There's just one thing. The soda isn't cold.

MARK: No kidding!

JUDY: I can't believe this place!

UNIT 20

EXERCISE 5 (page 192)

JOSH: Amanda, let's go out tonight.

AMANDA: OK. What do you want to do?

JOSH: Let's go to a concert. There are two or three good ones downtown.

AMANDA: What are they?

JOSH: Well, there's a rock concert, and a classical concert, and a Latin concert.

AMANDA: Let's go to the Latin concert. You know how much I like Latin music. But Josh, what about the dog?

JOSH: Let's take him to my Mom's. She wants to see him.

AMANDA: OK. Hey, here's an idea. Let's take her a photograph of the house.

JOSH: Good idea. How about this one?

AMANDA: Fine. That one looks great. OK, let's go. . . . Uh-oh. It's raining. Bring an umbrella.

JOSH: OK. The big one or the small one?

AMANDA: The big one.

JOSH: It's still in the car.

AMANDA: OK. Let's go.

UNIT 21

EXERCISE 5 (page 202)

B

1. **A:** We can't understand you.
   B: Sorry. I'll speak slowly.
2. **A:** We can understand you now.
   B: That's good.
3. **A:** I can't pronounce that word.
   B: I can't either. It's hard for me to say words that begin with "S-C-R."
4. **A:** I can pronounce that word.
   B: I can too. It's easy to pronounce.
5. **A:** I can't see the letters.
   B: Maybe you need glasses.
6. **A:** I can see the letters.
   B: Good. Please read them to me.

EXERCISE 6 (page 202)

JESSICA: How was your Spanish presentation?

JEREMY: OK. Jorge was a big help.

JESSICA: Great.

JEREMY: But I still can't understand my teacher's Spanish, and my pronunciation is still not so good.

JESSICA: But you're improving and that's the main thing. What about Jorge? How's his math?

JEREMY: Amazing. He can do everything. On our last test, he was second best in the class.

JESSICA: Wow. He must be happy about that. Now he can stay on the team.

JEREMY: He's happy and the basketball team is happy too. I'm their hero.

JESSICA: That's great.

JEREMY: Maybe I can be a math tutor.

JESSICA: Really?

JEREMY: Uh-huh. Then if I make a lot of money, I can buy another computer.

JESSICA: Oh, no. Where will we put it?

UNIT 22

EXERCISE 5 (page 214)

1. **ANNE:** Hi, Judy. This is Anne. Thanks for the flowers. They arrived yesterday, just in time for my birthday. They're beautiful.

2. **MARK:** Hi, Judy. This is Mark. I'm still at work. I finished my report last night, but I still have calls to make. Let's meet at 7:00, not 6:00.

3. AMANDA: Hi, Judy. This is Amanda. Josh and I watched a really good movie on TV a couple of days ago. It's on again tonight. Watch Channel 6 at 8 o'clock. Don't miss it.

EXERCISE 6 (page 215)

C

1. He graduated from college last year.
2. They started a business 10 years ago.
3. They worked for 10 hours yesterday.
4. They hired many people last month.
5. They learned a lot last year.
6. A company wanted to buy their business three years ago.
7. They agreed to the sale yesterday afternoon.

UNIT 23

EXERCISE 5 (page 224)

TEACHER: Class, today we're interviewing Yoshio Tanaka. Yoshio is our exchange student at Redmond High this year. Everybody ready? Who has the first question?

STUDENT 1: I do. Yoshio, when did you come to the United States?

YOSHIO: I came in July. That was four months ago.

TEACHER: OK. Next question?

STUDENT 2: Where are you from in Japan, Yoshio? Tokyo?

YOSHIO: Well, I was born in Tokyo, but my family moved to Hamamatsu when I was four. It's a city south of Tokyo.

STUDENT 3: Did you play sports in high school?

YOSHIO: Yes, I did. I played soccer. But my favorite sport was karate. I did karate for a long time, and I got a black belt.

STUDENT 1: Wow! . . . What else did you do when you were in school?

YOSHIO: Mountain climbing. I climbed Mt. Fuji when I was 14.

STUDENT 2: Why did you want to be an exchange student?

YOSHIO: Well, my family and I took a trip to the United States when I was 10. We went to a lot of places—New York, Los Angeles, Florida. After that I always wanted to come back.

STUDENT 3: Did you visit Seattle on that trip?

YOSHIO: No, we didn't. But I always wanted to come to Seattle.

STUDENT 1: Do you like it here?

YOSHIO: Yes, I really do. Everyone is friendly. And I love the water and the mountains.

UNIT 24

EXERCISE 5 (page 234)

C

1. Where'd it happen?
2. When'd it happen?
3. How'd it happen?
4. What'd the police do?
5. How'd the drivers look?

EXERCISE 6 (page 234)

AMANDA: Hi Rob.

ROB: Hey Amanda. How's it going?

AMANDA: Good. How's everything with you? What did Dad say about the car?

ROB: Well, at first he was pretty angry. But then I promised to pay for the damage.

AMANDA: You did? How can you do that?

ROB: I got a part-time job. I'm a cashier at BG Drugstore.

AMANDA: Great. When did you start?

ROB: A couple of days ago. It's not bad.

AMANDA: What are your hours?

ROB: They're different on different days. Yesterday I worked from 9:00 to 5:00. The day before I worked from 9:00 to 12:00.

AMANDA: How's the pay?

ROB: So-so. But it's a job.

UNIT 25

EXERCISE 5 (page 244)

TIM: Oh, no! Jessica! I need help.

JESSICA: What's the matter?

TIM: I wrapped all the gifts. But who are they for? I don't remember.

JESSICA: Well, let's see. What's in the long, red box?

TIM: A tennis racquet.

JESSICA: So that's for your cousin Martha, right?

TIM: Yeah, that's right. It's for her.

JESSICA: OK. Now, what's in the small green envelope?

TIM: Let me think . . . Oh, I remember. Concert tickets.

JESSICA: Are they for Steve?

TIM: No, they're not for a jazz concert. They're tickets for a Broadway musical.

JESSICA: Oh. So they're for Mom and Dad.

TIM: Yeah, right. They're for them.

JESSICA: So what about Jeremy?

TIM: Uh . . . oh, yeah. It's the orange box. It's a DVD.

JESSICA: Good. Now, what about this big white box? What's in it?

TIM: Um . . . oh, yeah. It's a game. Ben and Annie love games.

JESSICA: Right. OK. Now . . . what's in this small blue box?

TIM: Don't touch that!

JESSICA: Why not?

TIM: Because it's something special.

JESSICA: Oh, I see. Is it for me?

TIM: Yep.

UNIT 26

EXERCISE 5 (page 253)

STEVE: What are you listening to?

JESSICA: The news.

STEVE: Oh. Turn it up.

NEWSCASTER: I'm Rich Williams with tonight's local news. Good evening everyone. Last Monday travel writer John Phillips died at the age of 92. He was the author of more than thirty popular books. Phillips had four children and ten grandchildren, but in a surprise move, he left his six million dollars to his assistant, his gardener, his cook, and his housekeeper. Today Phillips's lawyer, Dan Evans, read a letter dated two months ago. In it Phillips wrote, "My family spends very little time with me. They really don't know me or care about me. These four employees are my real family. Each one is a special person. I want them to have my money." Phillips's family plans to contest the will.

UNIT 27

EXERCISE 5 (page 263)

AMANDA: Uh-oh. There aren't any empty tables.

JOSH: Maybe we could join that couple there. . . . Excuse me, would you mind if we joined you?

MARTIN: Not at all. Please do. . . . I'm Martin Jones, and this is my wife, Helen.

JOSH: Good to meet you. I'm Josh Wang, and this is my wife, Amanda.

MARTIN: Glad to meet you both.

AMANDA: Nice to meet you.

HELEN: Nice to meet you.

AMANDA: You two must be from Britain. Is that right?

HELEN: Yes, we are—from London. I suppose you can tell from our accents.

AMANDA: Yes. Actually, we love the British accent.

MARTIN: You know, we just arrived yesterday. We're going to Mount Rushmore tomorrow on a tour, but we have a free day today. Can you recommend something?

JOSH: Well, what about Wall Drug Store?

HELEN: Wall Drug Store? What is it?

AMANDA: It's a gigantic drugstore in a little town called Wall. It's about 60 miles east.

MARTIN: What is there to see?

AMANDA: Well, it's probably the biggest drugstore in the world. It has everything – books, clothes, souvenirs. . . . There are even restaurants inside the drugstore.

JOSH: And if you go to Wall, you can stop at Badlands National Park—on the way or on the way back. There are beautiful rock formations and flowers in the park. But leave early. There are often traffic jams later in the day.

HELEN: That sounds really good. Let's do that, Martin.

MARTIN: All right, let's. Thanks for the suggestion.

EXERCISE 6 (page 263)

1. **A:** What can we see in this area?
   B: There are caves nearby.
2. **A:** How are the people at your bed and breakfast?
   B: They are great.
3. **A:** Are there any good hotels in this town?
   B: Yes, there are several.
4. **A:** What are Lead and Deadwood?
   B: They are old mining towns.
5. **A:** Where are Judy and Elena?
   B: They aren't here yet.
6. **A:** Let's go to a movie.
   B: There aren't any theaters nearby.

UNIT 28

EXERCISE 5 (page 274)

BRIAN: Hey Ken, how's it going?

KEN: Fine, man. What's up?

BRIAN: Well, I borrowed some CDs from Mia Klein. I want to return them, but I'm too busy today. Can you give them to her? She's in your history class.

KEN: Sure, but I don't know her. What does Mia look like?

BRIAN: Oh, she's very tall and thin. She has long dark hair. She usually wears jeans, a black turtleneck, and interesting earrings. She's cute, but she never smiles. She's very serious.

KEN: Oh. I think I know her.

BRIAN: Good. Thanks a lot.

KEN: No problem.

UNIT 29

EXERCISE 5 (page 284)

GRANDMA: Hello?

KEN: Hi, Grandma. This is your favorite grandson. How's my favorite grandma?

GRANDMA: Kenny! What a nice surprise. How are you doing? What are you up to?

KEN: Well, I'm pretty busy. My classes are harder than they were last semester. I'm taking chemistry and physics.

GRANDMA: How are you doing?

KEN: OK. The thing is, I have a problem about next term. I can take art or music. I love music, but the music teacher is very tough. I'm not very good at art, but the art teacher is really cool. Her tests are a lot easier than the music teacher's. She gives less homework and higher grades. So, what do you think?

GRANDMA: I say, take the art class. I remember you were very good at art as a child.

KEN: Hmm. Maybe you're right. A good teacher makes a big difference. So, how are you? Is everything OK?

GRANDMA: Yes, dear. I'm doing just fine. Today my reading group is coming here. I'm making my strawberry cheese cake.

KEN: They're lucky . . . Well . . . I guess you're pretty busy, so I'll let you go. Anyway, It's almost time for me to go to work. Talk to you soon, Grandma.

GRANDMA: Yes. Bye, Kenny. Thanks for calling.

UNIT 30

EXERCISE 5 (page 293)

AGENT: World Airlines. How may I help you?

FELIX: I'd like to make a reservation for a flight to Bucharest, Romania. My name is Felix Maxa.

AGENT: Yes, Mr. Maxa. When would you like to leave?

FELIX: On Thursday, January 30th.

AGENT: There's a flight leaving Seattle at noon on Thursday, with a connecting flight in New York. It's a direct flight from New York to Bucharest, leaving at 10:30 P.M. and arriving in Bucharest at 5:05 P.M. the next afternoon.

FELIX: Are there any other options?

AGENT: Yes, there's another flight leaving Seattle at 6:30 in the evening, arriving in New York at 2:30 A.M. But there's no direct flight to Bucharest until 10:00 the next morning.

FELIX: I think the noon flight is better.

AGENT: OK. Is this one-way or round trip?

FELIX: Round trip. I'd like to be back in Seattle on Friday, February 7th.

AGENT: All right, Mr. Maxa. How would you like to pay for that?

UNIT 31

EXERCISE 5 (page 303)

KEN: Hey, this is pretty exciting after all.

LAURA: I told you.

KEN: Yeah, you did. But look at those clouds. I still think it's going to rain.

LAURA: Don't worry. It's not going to rain. Take my word for it.

KEN: Hmm. OK . . . . The score's 2–2. Do you still think Sam's team is going to win?

LAURA: I think so. Hey, Sam's going to take a penalty kick.

KEN: So what does that mean?

LAURA: He's going to kick the ball. If it goes in, his team wins.

KEN: Wow! That was pretty cool! He did it.

LAURA: I told you. So do you want to go to another soccer game sometime?

KEN: Well, sure!

UNIT 32

EXERCISE 5 (page 312)

A

JOSH: Hello.

AMANDA: Hi, Josh. It's me.

JOSH: Hi, Amanda. How are you? What did the doctor say?

AMANDA: I'm fine.

JOSH: Great.

AMANDA: And I have some wonderful news. I was right. Josh, we're going to be parents next July!

JOSH: Oh . . . my . . . gosh! I can't believe it! That's pretty soon.

AMANDA: Well, in seven months or so you're going to be a daddy.

JOSH: That's terrific!

AMANDA: Listen, Josh. I have to go back to work now. See you tonight.

JOSH: Bye, honey. Take care. I love you.

AMANDA: I love you, too.

B

JOSH: Hey guys. I'm going to be a father!

JASON: Congratulations! Are you going to move?

JOSH: Are you kidding? Not right away. We're not going to buy a house for a few years.

JASON: Is Amanda going to stay home with the baby?

JOSH: Only for the first three months. Then her mom's going to watch the baby. Her mom's great with kids.

JASON: That's terrific, but did you know it's going to cost $200,000 to raise a child born next year?

JOSH: Well, are you guys going to start a collection for me?

EXERCISE 6 (page 312)
B

1. big	**3.** fat	**5.** bin	**7.** few
2. pig	**4.** vat	**6.** pin	**8.** view

STUDENT BOOK ANSWER KEY

In this answer key, where the short or contracted form is given, the full or long form is also correct (unless the purpose of the exercise is to practice the short or contracted form). Where the full or long form is given, the contracted form is also correct.

UNIT 1 (pages 2–8)

AFTER YOU READ
C. 2. d   **3.** b   **4.** f   **5.** c   **6.** a
D. 2. F   **3.** F   **4.** T   **5.** T

EXERCISE 1
2. d   **3.** f   **4.** c   **5.** a   **6.** e

EXERCISE 2
2. This   **4.** This   **6.** These   **8.** Are these
3. These   **5.** This   **7.** Is this

EXERCISE 3
2. They   **4.** you   **6.** They   **8.** We
3. It   **5.** I   **7.** I   **9.** he

EXERCISE 4
2. A: ~~This~~ *These* are my brothers.
   B: Hello. Nice to meet you.
3. A: This *is* my partner, Ahmed.
   B: Hi, Ahmed.
4. A: ~~Is~~ *Are* these your books?
   B: No, they *'re* not.

EXERCISE 5
A. left picture: Yuan
   middle picture: Mr. Singer
   right picture: Hai
B. 1. a   **2.** b   **3.** a   **4.** b

EXERCISE 6
A. 2. These   **3.** This   **4.** These   **5.** These

UNIT 2 (pages 10–17)

AFTER YOU READ
D. 1. a   **2.** a   **3.** a   **4.** b

EXERCISE 1
A. knife, kitchen
B. apple, egg, oven
C. Brazil, Elena, Johnson, Judy

EXERCISE 2
2. eggs   **4.** apples   **6.** muffins
3. chicken   **5.** muffins   **7.** packages

EXERCISE 3
3. notebooks   **5.** apples   **7.** a banana
4. a dictionary   **6.** an orange

EXERCISE 4
2. Elena is from ~~brazil~~ *Brazil*.
3. She wants ~~a~~ *an* orange.
4. These ~~banana~~ *bananas* are good.
5. This is *a* toaster.

EXERCISE 5
C. o•range toast•er ba•na•na um•brel•la dic•tion•ar•y

EXERCISE 6
A. c
B. glasses, spoons, restaurant

UNIT 3 (pages 20–28)

BEFORE YOU READ
A. 1. big   **2.** an island   **3.** Sydney

AFTER YOU READ
C. 2. friendly   **4.** reasonable   **6.** awful
   3. popular   **5.** delicious   **7.** good

D. 2. vacation   **4.** Steve   **6.** cities   **9.** a great
   3. cousin   **5.** Mark   **8.** clean

EXERCISE 1

2. A   **3.** A   **4.** N   **5.** N   **6.** N

EXERCISE 2

A. 2. They are   **3.** It is   **4.** We are   **5.** He is
B. 1. She's from Australia.   **4.** We're in room 2.
   2. They're in Seattle on   **5.** He's in Seattle.
     vacation.
   3. It's in Australia.

EXERCISE 3

A. Answers **2, 3, 5,** & **8** will vary. Check **7**.
4. The Sydney Opera House is not in Canberra.
6. Our school is not in Australia.
B. Answers **2, 3, 5,** & **8** will vary.
4. The Sydney Opera House isn't in Canberra.
6. Our school isn't in Australia.

EXERCISE 4

2. 're not   **4.** 's   **6.** are   **8.** is   **10.** 're
3. 're   **5.** 's not   **7.** 's   **9.** 's   **11.** are

EXERCISE 5

2. A: My cousin ~~'s~~ from Tokyo. She's a student.
   B: I'm from Tokyo. I ~~no am~~ 'm not a student.
3. A: Seattle is a big city in California.
   B: No, ~~it's~~ it isn't. Seattle is in Washington.
4. A: The people ~~is~~ are friendly here.
   B: I know. They're great.
5. A: I ~~be~~ 'm from a big city.
   B: I'm not. I 'm from a small town.

EXERCISE 6

C. 2. full form   **4.** contraction   **6.** contraction
   3. contraction   **5.** full form

EXERCISE 7

A. 1
B. 2. F   **3.** T   **4.** NI   **5.** T

UNIT 4 (pages 30–36)

AFTER YOU READ

D. 1. F   **2.** T   **3.** T   **4.** T
E. Space Needle

EXERCISE 1

Possessive adjectives: 2. his   **3.** your   **5.** your
   a. our, our   **b.** Their   **c.** Its   **e.** my
   2. e   **3.** b   **4.** c   **5.** f   **6.** a

EXERCISE 2

2. those   **3.** that   **4.** Those   **5.** that   **6.** those

EXERCISE 3

2. our   **3.** her   **4.** his   **5.** my, its   **6.** their

EXERCISE 4

2. our   **3.** their   **4.** his   **5.** Its   **6.** his   **7.** her

EXERCISE 5

1.   they're
   B: No, ~~they~~ her keys.
      That
2. A: ~~Those~~ is my daughter.
   B: She's a beautiful woman.
      Is
3. A: ~~Are~~ that your child?
   B: Yes. That's our son.
      That
4. A: ~~Those~~ cat is very cute.
      Its
   B: ~~It~~ name is Tiger.

EXERCISE 6

B. 2. a   **3.** a   **4.** b   **5.** b   **6.** a

EXERCISE 7

2. b   **3.** b   **4.** a   **5.** b

UNIT 5 (pages 38–46)

AFTER YOU READ

D. 2. b   **3.** a   **4.** b   **5.** b

EXERCISE 1

2. d   **3.** e   **4.** f   **5.** a   **6.** b

EXERCISE 2

2. What   **3.** Who   **4.** Who   **5.** What   **6.** What

EXERCISE 3

2. A. Is the game today?   **B.** Yes, it is.
3. A. Are they cousins?   **B.** No, they aren't.
                        They're brothers.
4. A. Who is that man?   **B.** He's my teacher.
5. A. Is Seattle hot?   **B.** No, it isn't.

EXERCISE 4

1. **A.** woman   **A.** Is she   **B.** she's not
2. **A.** Is he   **B.** Yes . . . is
   A. writer   **B.** not . . . He's.

EXERCISE 5

1. **B:** Yes, ~~I'm.~~ *I am*
2. **A:** Is she single?
   B: No, ~~she~~ not. *she's*
3. **A:** ~~They~~ students? *Are they*
   B: No, they ~~are.~~ *aren't*

4. **A:** Is he a mechanic?
   B: No, ~~he's.~~ *he's not*
5. **A:** Is your car new?
   B: No, ~~it~~ old. *it's*
6. **A:** Is he a dentist?
   B: No, he's not. ~~He~~ a writer. *He's*

EXERCISE 6

2. down   4. up   6. down   8. up
3. down   5. down   7. up

EXERCISE 7

A. 1. No, she isn't. OR No, she's not.
2. No, she isn't. OR No, she's not.
3. No, they aren't. OR No, they're not.
4. No, she isn't. OR No, she's not.
B. 1. Diego   2. Jaime and Carlos   3. Alicia

UNIT 6 (pages 48–55)

AFTER YOU READ

D. 10 First Avenue

EXERCISE 1

1. c   2. a   3. b

EXERCISE 2

1. in Seattle, Washington   3. 10 First Avenue
2. First   4. on the second

EXERCISE 3

1. b   2. d   3. c   4. a

EXERCISE 4

A. 1. Is this Main Street?
2. Is it on Main Street?
3. Where's First Avenue?
4. Turn right at the corner.
B. The man and woman are on Main Street near Second Avenue.

EXERCISE 5

1. **B:** I'm from Bogotá.
   A: Where is Bogotá?
   B: It's ~~on~~ Colombia. *in*
2. **A:** Is your apartment ~~in~~ this floor? *on*
   B: No, it's on the ~~eight~~ floor. *eighth*
3. **A:** Where's the bookstore?
   B: It's ^ First Avenue. *on*
   A: Is it next ^ the museum? *to*
   B: Yes, it is.
4. **A:** Is the supermarket on First ~~in~~ Main and Washington? *between*
   B: No, it's between Main and Jackson.

EXERCISE 6

A. b
B. The supermarket is on the northeast corner of Washington and First. The flower shop is on the corner of Second and Main.

EXERCISE 7

C. 1. a   2. a   3. b   4. b

UNIT 7 (pages 58–66)

AFTER YOU READ

D. 2. F   3. T   4. F   5. F

EXERCISE 1

A.

_d_ 1. Were (you) at home yesterday?
_e_ 2. Was (he) in class yesterday?
_a_ 3. Was the (concert) good?
_f_ 4. Was the (movie) interesting?
_b_ 5. Was (Susan) at the library yesterday?
_c_ 6. Were (you) at the ball game last night?

a. No, (it) wasn't. The (music) was pretty bad.
b. Yes, (she) was. (We) were both there.
c. Yes, (I) was. (It) was a really exciting game.
d. No, (I) wasn't. (I) was at a concert.
e. No, (he) wasn't. (He) was sick.
f. Yes, (it) was. Johnny Depp is a great actor.

B.

Judy,
   You didn't call me last night. Where <u>were</u> (you)? <u>Were</u> (you) out? (I) <u>was</u> at home from 6:00 on. I tried you a couple of times. We need to talk.
Please call soon.
Ken

EXERCISE 2

2. were at home home **4.** was at a soccer game **6.** was at a party
3. was at a concert **5.** were at a play

EXERCISE 3

2. was **4.** wasn't **6.** Were **8.** were
3. Were **5.** was **7.** weren't

EXERCISE 4

2. I wasn't . . . I was at home.
3. we weren't . . . We were at a play.
4. she wasn't . . . She was at a soccer game.
5. we were . . . the film was boring.
6. he was . . . he was there

EXERCISE 5

Mark,
   wasn't   *was*
 Sorry I ~~was~~ home last night. I ~~am~~ at a
         were
basketball game. Amanda and Josh ~~was~~ with me.
 was
It ~~were~~ really exciting.
 Where were you on Tuesday afternoon? Susan
      were
and Brent and I ~~are~~ at the soccer game, but you
weren't *was*
~~were~~ there. Too bad. It ~~is~~ really exciting.
 I'll talk to you soon. Call me.
         Kathy

EXERCISE 6

A. 2. A; was **4.** N; wasn't **6.** A; were
3. N; weren't **5.** N; wasn't

EXERCISE 7

2. T **3.** F **4.** F **5.** F **6.** T **7.** NI

UNIT 8 (pages 68–75)

AFTER YOU READ

D.
        hot   *cool*
 The weather was sunny and ~~cool~~, but it was ~~hot~~ at
  parents
the beach. Jason's ~~cousins~~ were in Spain last month.
    hot
The weather was ~~rainy~~ then. The food in Spain was
delicious. Mark's trip was great. Amanda's friend
       Barcelona
Kathy was his guide. She was in ~~Madrid~~ for a month.

EXERCISE 1

b **1.** (Where) were you last night?
   a. It was warm.
e **2.** (Who) was with you?
   b. I was at a soccer game.
f **3.** (How) was the game?
   c. Two hours.
c **4.** (How long) was the game?
   d. He was on vacation in Miami.
a **5.** (How) was the weather?
   e. My sister.
d **6.** (Where) was your brother?
   f. Exciting.

EXERCISE 2

1 **B:** It was great.
2. **A:** Where were you **B:** At a jazz concert
3. **A:** When was the concert **B:** It was last night
4. **A:** Who was the musician **B:** It was Diana Krall
5. **A:** How long was the concert **B:** It was two hours

EXERCISE 3

2. **A:** Who was
3. **A:** Where was
4. **A:** When was the party
5. **A:** Who were Mark and Jason with
6. **A:** How long was
7. **A:** Where were his parents
8. **A:** How was your guide

EXERCISE 4

1. were you
2. was it OR was the wedding
3. were you in London
4. was the weather

EXERCISE 5

    was
1. **A:** How ~~were~~ your weekend?
 B: Saturday evening was great.
    were
 A: Where ~~was~~ you?
 B: At a soccer game.
    was
 A: How ˄ the game ~~was~~?
 B: Exciting and long.
     was
 A: How long ~~were~~ it?
 B: Three hours.

    was
2. **A:** How ~~were~~ your vacation?
 B: OK.
    were you
 A: Where ~~you were~~?
    I was
 B: ˄ ~~Was~~ at the beach.
    was
 A: How ˄ the weather?
 B: Cool and rainy.
 A: That's too bad.

EXERCISE 6

A. 1. a   **2.** c
B. 1. a   **2.** b   **3.** c   **4.** b

EXERCISE 7

3. When   **4.** What   **5.** What

UNIT 9 (pages 78–85)

AFTER YOU READ

D.

Mark's route: From the spot at "You are here" to the corner of Fifth and Jackson, left on Jackson, down Jackson to Third, right on Third, stop. Draw an "X" on the restaurant on the corner of Jackson and Third.

EXERCISE 1

_c_ **1.** Don't walk.
_d_ **2.** Don't park there.
_a_ **3.** My hands are full.
_b_ **4.** Don't turn left at the corner.
_f_ **5.** Don't worry.
_e_ **6.** Please hand me the dictionary.

EXERCISE 2

1. Turn left.
2. Don't park here.
3. Make a U-turn.
4. Turn right.

EXERCISE 3

2. Listen to this CD.
3. Close the window, please.
4. Don't read this book.
5. Please don't smoke.
6. Please turn to page six.
7. Don't go in the deep water.
8. Try this cake.

EXERCISE 4

Don't   *door*
A. ~~Do not~~ (open) the ~~window~~.
Don't open the door.

Please don't   *garage*
B. ~~Do not~~ park in the ~~driveway~~.
Please don't park in the garage.

EXERCISE 5

Don't
2. ~~You no~~ sit here. It's not your seat.

Please study OR *Study page 3, please.*
3. ~~Study please~~ page 3.

Complete
4. ~~Completes~~ the sentences.

Please don't
5. ~~Don't please~~ drive fast.

Don't
6. ~~No~~ close the window. Keep it open.
7. Don't ~~to~~ turn left. Turn right at the corner.

EXERCISE 6

A. library, main office
B. 2. right   **5.** the first   **8.** next
   3. cafeteria   **6.** one   **9.** student
   4. computer lab   **7.** left

EXERCISE 7

B.

	/ I / (b<u>i</u>t, h<u>i</u>t)	/ i / (b<u>ea</u>t, h<u>ea</u>t)
2.	√	
3.	√	
4.		√
5.		√
6.		√
7.	√	
8.		√
9.	√	

EXERCISE 9

A. 1

UNIT 10 (pages 87–95)

AFTER YOU READ

D. 2. F   **3.** T   **4.** T   **5.** F   **6.** T

EXERCISE 1

A. 3, 4, 6, 7
B. 3, 4, 5, 7

EXERCISE 2

2. Ali lives in Amman, Jordan. He speaks Arabic.
3. Antonio and Rosa live in Salvador, Brazil. They speak Portuguese.
4. Elena lives in Santiago, Chile. She speaks Spanish.
5. Maureen and James live in Dublin, Ireland. They speak English.

EXERCISE 3

2. wants   **4.** want   **6.** wants   **8.** don't want
3. don't want   **5.** want   **7.** wants   **9.** want

EXERCISE 4

2. doesn't like pizza, likes salad
3. needs water, doesn't need ice cream
4. doesn't want tea, wants coffee

EXERCISE 5

Dear Mary,
    Spain is great. The Spanish people are very
friendly, but they ~~speaks~~ *speak* so fast. Jim ~~speak~~ *speaks* Spanish
very well. He ~~don't~~ *doesn't* understand everything, but he
~~understand~~ *understands* a lot. I speak a little Spanish. I don't
understand much yet.
    It's rainy here! People say it ~~don't~~ *doesn't* usually rain
much in the summer here. We're at my cousin's
house. He and his wife ~~lives~~ *live* in a beautiful
apartment in Madrid. Juan ~~work~~ *works* in an office
downtown. His wife Alicia ~~no~~ *doesn't* work. She
stays at home with the children.
    See you soon.
    Rose

EXERCISE 6

A. 2. c   **3.** a   **4.** a   **5.** c   **6.** b
B. is really good

EXERCISE 7

B.
teaches	/ɪz/
writes	/s/
sounds	/z/
watches	/ɪz/
understands	/z/
works	/s/

EXERCISE 8

False statements: 3, 4, 5, 6
Corrected statements:
  3. People in Japan drive on the left.
  4. People in Great Britain drive on the left.
  5. People don't live at the North Pole.
  6. Penguins don't live in deserts.

UNIT 11 (pages 98–105)

AFTER YOU READ

D. 2. No   **4.** No   **6.** Yes
    3. I don't know   **5.** Yes   **7.** No

EXERCISE 1

_b_ **1.** Do you want a TV?   **a.** Yes, we do, but there's a $50 charge. Do you have a big car? We can help you get it in.

_d_ **2.** Do these TVs cost $1000?

_c_ **3.** Does that TV have a warranty?   **b.** Yes, we do, Our old TV doesn't work.

                       c. Yes, it does. It comes with a 90-day warranty.

_a_ **4.** Do you deliver?   **d.** No, they cost $850. They're on sale. Do you like them? They're very popular.

EXERCISE 2

2. Does . . . cost   **4.** Does . . . live   **6.** Do . . . use
3. Do . . . need   **5.** Does . . . like   **7.** Does . . . mean

EXERCISE 3

2. Do you know a good electronics store?
3. Does your family have a lot of electronics?
4. Do your friends spend a lot of time online?
5. Do your friends spend a lot of money on electronics?
6. Does your cell phone have a case?

EXERCISE 4

2. A: Does Jeremy use the phone for different things?
    B: Yes, he does.
3. A: Does Jeremy check email from the phone?
    B: Yes, he does.
4. A: Does Jeremy listen to music from the phone?
    B: Yes, he does.
5. A: Does Jeremy watch TV shows from his phone?
    B: No, he doesn't.
6. A: Do Jeremy and his friends send text messages?
    B: Yes, they do.
7. A: Do Amanda and Josh live near Jeremy?
    B: Yes, they do.

EXERCISE 5

B: Yes, I do. It's on Main Street.

A: Does it ~~stays~~ *stay* open late?

B: Yes, it ~~do~~ *does*.

A: What's the name of the store?

B: Goodbuys.

A: Do you ~~spells~~ *spell* it G-O-O-D-B-U-Y?

B: Uh-huh, but it has an *s* at the end.

A: ~~Costs electronics~~ *Do electronics* at Goodbuys *cost* a lot?

B: No, they don't. Everything there is a good buy.

A: That's terrific.

EXERCISE 6

A. c

B. 1. b **2.** b **3.** b **4.** a

EXERCISE 7

B. 2. Does he <u>want</u> a <u>phone</u>?
   3. Do you <u>sell</u> <u>cameras</u>?
   4. Do you <u>have</u> a <u>computer</u>?
   5. Do they <u>use</u> their <u>GPS</u>?

EXERCISE 8

2. Do you have a GPS?
3. Do you like electronics?
4. Do you play computer games?
5. Do you send e-cards?
6. Do you shop online?

UNIT 12 (pages 107–115)

AFTER YOU READ

D. 2. F **3.** T **4.** F **5.** F **6.** T

EXERCISE 1

What do you mean?
What time do you go to bed?
Who wakes you up?
What do you talk about?

EXERCISE 2

2. What time do you start work?
3. What do you do in your job?
4. Who do you work with?
5. How late do you stay up on weeknights?
6. What sport do you really like?
7. Why do you like it?
8. When do you play it?

EXERCISE 3

2. what time do you go to bed
3. how do you feel
4. why do you play soccer
5. what does *fascinating* mean
6. How do you spell *sleepy*
7. who wakes your father up in the morning

EXERCISE 4

A: At a bookstore.

B: What *do* you do?

A: I'm a salesperson.

B: What time ~~you do~~ *do you* start?

A: Eight-thirty in the morning.

B: How ~~does~~ *do* you like the work?

A: It's challenging.

B: *Challenging*? I don't know that word. What ~~means challenging~~ *does challenging mean*?

A: It means "hard but interesting."

EXERCISE 5

A. 3

B. 2. He's an accountant.   **6.** They live in Belmont.
   3. She's a writer.   **7.** She takes the bus.
   4. Yes, he does.   **8.** She catches the bus
   5. He dislikes the traffic.   at eight o'clock.

EXERCISE 6

2. you   **4.** bus   **6.** bus   **8.** bus
3. catch   **5.** tomorrow   **7.** take

UNIT 13 (pages 117–124)

AFTER YOU READ

D. 2. No, she doesn't.
   3. No, it isn't.
   4. No, they aren't.
   5. Yes, they are.
   6. Yes, she is.
   7. No, she doesn't.

EXERCISE 1

_c_ **1.** How old <u>is</u> he?
_f_ **2.** <u>Does</u> he <u>have</u> short hair?
_a_ **3.** Who <u>has</u> the tickets?
_e_ **4.** <u>Is</u> she in your class?
_d_ **5.** <u>Do you have</u> a music class?
_b_ **6.** <u>Are</u> those girls pregnant?

a. He <u>has</u> them.
b. Yes, they <u>are</u> both in their eighth month.
c. He's 20.
d. No, I <u>don't have</u> music this year.
e. Yes, she's in my music class
f. No, it's long.

EXERCISE 2

2. am   **4.** am   **6.** have   **8.** have   **10.** is
3. am   **5.** is   **7.** is   **9.** are

EXERCISE 3

2. Where is she from?
3. Is she in Japan now?
4. Does she have any sisters or brothers?
5. Is he a violinist?
6. Does Midori have other interests?

EXERCISE 4

MARK: Twenty-five.
JUDY: Where _is_ he from?
MARK: São Paulo.
JUDY: Is he a writer like you?
MARK: No. He _'s_ a musician. He plays the guitar.
JUDY: _Is he_ ~~He~~ cute?
MARK: Yes, he is. He looks like me.
JUDY: Does he _have_ ~~has~~ a girlfriend?
MARK: Yes, he _does_ ~~do~~.
JUDY: That's too bad.

EXERCISE 5

A. 1. She's a jazz musician.
   2. She's from Canada.
B. average, dark brown, long, great, player
Circle the saxophone player.

UNIT 14 (pages 126–133)

AFTER YOU READ

D. 2. after   **4.** sometimes   **6.** a little
   3. always   **5.** rarely

EXERCISE 1

Josh Wang has an active life. He (usually) gets up at 6:00 A.M. He (always) runs 2 or 3 miles with his dog. (Sometimes) he feels tired, but he still runs. When he gets home from running, he has breakfast. He (often) has eggs, juice, toast, and coffee, but (sometimes) he has cereal and fruit. Then Josh goes to work, and he's (never) late. He works from 9:00 until 5:00. He (rarely) stays late. In the evening, Josh (always) has a healthy dinner. He (often) has fish with rice and vegetables. He (never) has fast food. He (rarely) eats sweets. After dinner, Josh (sometimes) reads. Josh is also an artist, so (sometimes) he paints. He's (always) in bed by 10:30.

EXERCISE 2

1. B: Yes, I often do.
2. A: Are you ever tired in the morning?
   B: Yes, I'm always tired then.
3. A: How often do you exercise?
   B: I usually exercise five times a week.
4. A: What do you usually do in the evening?
   B: I often practice the piano.

EXERCISE 3

1. Jessica always takes a shower.
2. Jessica never drives to work.
3. Jessica usually arrives at work on time.
4. Jessica sometimes cooks dinner.

EXERCISE 4

DOMINGO: I exercise six or seven days a week.
JESSICA: Do _you ever_ ~~ever you~~ get tired of exercising?
DOMINGO: Sure I do. But _I always do_ ~~always I do~~ it.
JESSICA: OK. How often do you travel?
DOMINGO: I travel a lot—at least three times a month.
JESSICA: _Does your wife ever get_ ~~Does ever your wife get~~ unhappy because you travel so much?
DOMINGO: No, _she never gets_ ~~never she gets~~ unhappy. She _usually travels_ ~~travels usually~~ with me.
JESSICA: That's great, Domingo. Now, good luck in your next game.

EXERCISE 5

A. 2, 3

EXERCISE 5

B. 2. early   **4.** 1:30   **6.** to study   **8.** 8 hours
   3. tired   **5.** for lunch **7.** 5 or 6 hours

EXERCISE 6

B. 2, 3, 5, 7, 10

UNIT 15 (pages 136–145)

AFTER YOU READ

D. 2. c   **3.** d   **4.** e   **5.** f   **6.** a

EXERCISE 1

Underline: It's snowing, I'm looking, Tim isn't wearing, I'm wearing, I'm just kidding.

EXERCISE 2

  2. am wearing OR 'm wearing
  3. am not wearing OR 'm not wearing
  4. are playing
  5. is sitting OR 's sitting
  6. is losing OR losing
  7. is not enjoying OR isn't enjoying OR 's not enjoying
  8. is thinking OR 's thinking

EXERCISE 3

  2. Jessica is wearing a brown jacket.
  3. Lauren and Jessica are standing near the baggage carousel.
  4. Jessica is not sitting. OR Jessica isn't sitting.
  5. Jessica is looking for someone.
  6. Lauren is calling someone.
  7. Lauren and Jessica are not smiling. OR Lauren and Jessica aren't smiling.

EXERCISE 4

  2. We ~~no are~~ [aren't] looking for a taxi.
  3. They're ~~wait~~ [waiting] for a relative at the airport.
  4. He [᾽s] watching a ball game. His team [᾽s] losing.
  5. It ~~no is~~ [isn't] raining today.
  6. They're playing cards and ~~are~~ watching TV at the same time.
  7. He's ~~text~~ [texting] me now.

EXERCISE 5

A. a
B. 1. a. F   **b.** T   **c.** F   **d.** T
   2. a. F   **b.** T   **c.** T

EXERCISE 6

D. 1. a   **2.** a   **3.** b   **4.** a

EXERCISE 8

Difference between the two pictures:
Picture A
Tim Olson is cooking hot dogs.
The man with Tim Olson and Bill Beck is holding a can.
Three children (Annie, Ben, and Jeremy) are playing soccer.
Three teenagers are sitting.
The woman sitting near Jessica isn't wearing any glasses.
Mary isn't wearing a hat.

Picture B
Tim Olson is cooking chicken.
The man (with Tim Olson and Bill Beck) isn't holding anything.
The three children are playing volleyball.
The two teenage girls are sitting, but the boy is standing.
The woman sitting near Jessica is wearing sunglasses.
Mary is wearing a hat.

UNIT 16 (pages 147–154)

BEFORE YOU READ

T, F, T

AFTER YOU READ

C. 2. getting a haircut   **5.** with
   3. is babysitting   **6.** is not worrying OR
   4. helping   isn't worrying OR 's not worrying

D. 2. b **3.** a **4.** a **5.** b **6.** b **7.** b **8.** a

EXERCISE 1

A.
√ **2.** *d*
√ **3.** *f*
√ **4.** *e*
√ **5.** *b*
__ **6.** *c*

B. *Suggested answers:*
  Dennis is doing the babysitter's job. OR The babysitter is sleeping but Dennis isn't.

EXERCISE 2

2. We're watching a DVD
3. Are you watching a romance
4. We're watching
5. Is Jeremy wearing his cool basketball jacket
6. I'm kidding
7. Jeremy's not sitting OR isn't sitting
8. We're not watching a DVD
9. are playing

EXERCISE 3

1. **B:** isn't . . . He's washing the car
2. **A:** Are the kids eating chips
   B: they aren't
3. **A:** Is it raining
   B: it is
4. **A:** Is uncle Steve getting a haircut
   B: he is
5. **A:** Are Tim and Jessica celebrating
   their anniversary
   B: they are

EXERCISE 4

1. **B.** Yes, I am. Is that OK?
2. **A:** ~~They~~ *Are they* celebrating Tim's birthday?
   B: No. They're celebrating Tim and Jessica's anniversary.
3. **A:** Is he ~~gets~~ *getting* a haircut now?
   B: Yes, he is. He likes his hair short.
4. **A:** Are the children eating chips?
   B: No, ~~they~~ *they're* not. They're eating sandwiches.
5. **A:** Is *it* raining?
   B: Yes, ~~it's~~ *it is*.
6. **A:** Are you ~~wash~~ *washing* the dishes?
   B: Yes, I am.

EXERCISE 5

B. 2. match   **3.** ditch   **4.** chips   **5.** sheep

EXERCISE 6

A. a
B. 2. No, he isn't.
   3. Yes, he is.
   4. No, she isn't.
   5. No, she isn't.
   6. No, she isn't.
   7. Yes, she is.

UNIT 17 (pages 156–163)

AFTER YOU READ

D. 2. a   **3.** b   **4.** b   **5.** b   **6.** a

EXERCISE 1

2. Who; b   **3.** How; d   **4.** Where; c   **5.** Why; a

EXERCISE 2

1. Why are you wearing a suit? b
2. Who is taking him to Colorado? c
3. How is Nick traveling to Denver? d
4. Where is Jerry teaching? a

EXERCISE 3

2. Why are you staying
3. What is Mark doing
4. How are you feeling
5. Who is Mark dating

EXERCISE 4

1. **B:** ~~He~~ *He's* not feeling well.
2. **A:** ~~Who~~ *Who's (Who is)* driving Nick to Colorado?
   B: ~~Jerry's~~ *Jerry is*.
3. **A:** Why ~~you are~~ *are you* studying, Judy?
   B: I have a history test tomorrow.
4. **A:** Why ^ *are* you wearing a suit today?
   B: I have a job interview.
5. **A:** Who ^ *are* you talking to?
   B: Nick. He's coming to Seattle.
6. **A:** What ^ *is* he wearing?
   B: A blue suit.

EXERCISE 5

B. 2. ↓   **3.** ↑   **4.** ↓   **5.** ↑   **6.** ↓   **7.** ↓   **8.** ↑

EXERCISE 6

A. 3
B. 2. He is watching a DVD.
   3. He is watching *2012*.
   4. He is with Kathy.
   5. He is planning to visit Mark and think about the job.
   6. He is staying in Denver.
   7. He is planning to travel by train.

AFTER YOU READ

C. 1. sports jacket **3.** go well with
   2. slacks **4.** dress shoes

D. 2. mother and father **6.** dress
   3. expensive **7.** goatee
   4. brother's **8.** artist
   5. roommate's

EXERCISE 1

_c_ **1.** Let's visit Kathy's grandmother.
_e_ **2.** Are those your father's slacks?
_a_ **3.** This is my sister's friend Melanie.
_b_ **4.** What color are your roommate's dress shoes?
_d_ **5.** Bob's son has a broken leg.

  a. Nice to meet you. I'm Kathy's friend Mark.
  b. They're black.
  c. That's a good idea. She loves visitors.
  d. That's too bad.
  e. No, they're not. They're my brother's. These are my father's.

EXERCISE 2

A. 1. these **3.** That, This **5.** those
   2. that **4.** This, these

B. 1. women's **2.** parents' **3.** Kathy's

EXERCISE 3

  2. Steve Beck's mother
  3. Kathy White's mother
  4. husband's name
  5. Kathy's sister

EXERCISE 4

  1. That's great. **3.** That's right.
  2. That's too bad. **4.** That's a good idea.

EXERCISE 5

    My family loves to eat out. On my ~~parents~~ _parents'_ anniversary we go to a Chinese restaurant. That's because my ~~parent's~~ _parents_ love Chinese food. On my ~~brother~~ _bother's_ birthday we go to an Italian restaurant. My brother loves Italian food. On my ~~sister~~ _sister's_ birthday we go to a Mexican restaurant. ~~That~~ _That's_ because her favorite food comes from Mexico. And on my birthday, we go to a different restaurant every year because I like to try different places. ~~These~~ _This_ year I want to try a Brazilian restaurant.

EXERCISE 6

B.

Possessive Noun	/s/	/z/	/ɪz/
2. father's		√	
3. children's		√	
4. boss's			√
5. roommate's	√		
6. Chris's			√

C. 2. parents' **4.** boss's **6.** friend's
   3. teacher's **5.** roommate's

EXERCISE 7

A. b.
B. 1. a **2.** a **3.** c **4.** a

AFTER YOU READ

D. 2. b **3.** c **4.** a **5.** a **6.** c

EXERCISE 1

  Count nouns: crackers, vegetables, carrots, peas, beans, a cookie, an orange, an apple, a banana
  Non-count nouns: soup, meat, rice, fruit, ice cream, coffee, tea

EXERCISE 2

  2. some **5.** some **8.** some **11.** some
  3. a cup of **6.** Ø **9.** Ø **12.** a glass of
  4. a **7.** some **10.** a slice of

EXERCISE 3

  2. any soda **6.** some black olives
  3. any chips **7.** any green olives
  4. some fruit **8.** any OR some candy
  5. some olives **9.** some chocolate candy

EXERCISE 4

  1. B: No, I don't. But I like ~~a sandwich~~ _sandwiches_.
  2. A: Can I bring you some coffee?
     B: No, thanks. I don't drink X coffee.
  3. A: Are we having ~~egg~~ _eggs_ for lunch?
     B: Yes, we are. We're also having X yogurt.
  4. A: Do we need milk?
     B: No, we don't need ~~some~~ _any_ milk.

EXERCISE 5

A. 2, 4

B. 2. T
  3. F. The restaurant doesn't have iced tea.
  4. NI
  5. T
  6. F. The restaurant doesn't have mineral water.
  7. NI
  8. F. Mark and Judy don't like the restaurant.

EXERCISE 6

B. 2. eggs   **5.** slices   **8.** Bananas
  3. oranges   **6.** chips   **9.** Vegetables
  4. olives   **7.** sandwiches   **10.** pancakes

C.

/s/	chips	fruits	pancakes
/z/	*bagels*	eggs	olives	vegetables
/ɪz/	oranges	slices	sandwiches

UNIT 20 (pages 187–194)

AFTER YOU READ

D. 2. b.   **3.** b.   **4.** a.   **5.** b.

EXERCISE 1

1. B. a hat in general
2. A. one
  B. one
3. A. a car in general
  B. a car in general
4. A. a jacket in general
  B. a specific jacket

EXERCISE 2

2. The **3.** the **4.** the **5.** The **6.** the **7.** an

EXERCISE 3

2. e, ones **3.** a, ones **4.** b, one **5.** d, ones

EXERCISE 4

Dear Kathy,

                  The
    Josh and I have a great house! House isn't very

     an   *a*
big, and it's also ~~a~~ old one. It needs work. It has ~~the~~
nice living room, but the colors are terrible. Each

   a   *an*   *a*
wall is ~~the~~ different color. There's ~~a~~ orange wall, ~~an~~

               a
yellow wall, a blue wall, and ~~the~~ red wall. We need to
repaint.

             the
    We want you to see͜ house. Give me a call.
Love,
Amanda

EXERCISE 5

A. 3, 4
B. 2. one   **4.** one   **6.** one
  3. more than one **5.** more than one

EXERCISE 6

B. 2. an **4.** a   **6.** an, interview **8.** a
  3. a **5.** an, old **7.** a   **9.** an, expensive

UNIT 21 (pages 196–205)

AFTER YOU READ

C. 2. star **3.** pass **4.** fluent **5.** coach
D. 1. b   **2.** a   **3.** a   **4.** a

EXERCISE 1

 a **2.** I can't (understand)
 b **3.** can I (remember)
 c **4.** can (meet)
 e **5.** can (do)

EXERCISE 2

1. JORGE: can't help / can try
2. JORGE: can't do / Can . . . explain
  JEREMY: Can . . . understand
  JORGE: can / can't get
3. JEREMY: can't remember
  JORGE: can keep / can review
4. JORGE: can play
  JEREMY: can't / can play

EXERCISE 3

1. Can . . . open
2. can't see / Can . . . change
3. can't work / Can . . . show
4. can't speak
5. can't understand

EXERCISE 4

          speak
2. Mei Liang can't ~~speaks~~ English. She can ~~to~~
  speak Mandarin Chinese.

        work
3. Can they ~~working~~ this weekend?

      can I
4. How ~~I can~~ get to the library?

       teach
5. Can she ~~teaches~~ us Portuguese?

  can
6. He͜ speak Spanish fluently.

EXERCISE 5

B.

	1.	2.	3.	4.	5.	6.
can		√		√		√
can't	√		√		√	

C. 2. can   **3.** can't   **4.** can   **5.** can't   **6.** can

EXERCISE 6

A. a

B. 2. not so good   **4.** can do   **6.** can tutor
   3. is improving   **5.** can stay

UNIT 22 (pages 208–216)

AFTER YOU READ

C. convention, checked in, presentations, stayed, enjoyed

D. 1. a   **2.** a   **3.** b   **4.** b

EXERCISE 1

A. was, finished, started, worked, hired, fired, improved, offered, agreed, ended, used

B. be, finish, start, work, hire, fire, improve, offer, agree, end, use

EXERCISE 2

2. graduated   **4.** stayed   **6.** opened
3. worked   **5.** learned

EXERCISE 3

2. stayed   **6.** didn't enjoy   **10.** played
3. cleaned   **7.** didn't rain   **11.** enjoyed
4. watched   **8.** didn't stay
5. didn't play   **9.** didn't clean

EXERCISE 4

2. Hi, Ted. This is Al. I ~~am~~ arrived at the hotel this morning. My phone number is 555-9090.

3. Hello, Ted. This is Melissa. I ~~yesterday~~ *Yesterday* talked to Ellen. She loved your presentation.

4. Hi, Ted. This is Judy. Sorry I ~~was~~ missed your call. Call me. I have some exciting news.

5. Hi, Uncle Ted. This is Mickey. I received ~~this morning~~ *this morning* your gift. It's awesome. Thank you so much. I love the game.

6. Hi Teddy. This is Mom. I arrived in Miami last night. I didn't ~~stayed~~ *stay* at Aunt Sophie's house. She has the flu. I'm staying with Sara.

7. Hi, Ted. This is Justino. Warren ~~did~~ checked in at the Grand Hotel today. His presentation is tomorrow. He wants to have lunch with us after his presentation. Call me.

EXERCISE 5

1. *Anne*   Thanks for the _flowers_ . They _arrived_ yesterday.

2. *Mark*   I'm still _at work_ . Let's meet at _7:00_ , not _6:00_ .

3. *Amanda*   I _watched_ a really good _movie_ a couple of _days_ _ago_ . It's on tonight on Channel _six_ at _eight_ o'clock .

EXERCISE 6

B.

Sentence	Base Form of Verb
2. started , ago	start
3. worked , yesterday	work
4. hired , last	hire
5. learned , last	learn
6. wanted , ago	want
7. agreed , yesterday	agree

C.

	/t/	/d/	/ɪd/
2.			√
3.	√		
4.		√	
5.		√	
6.			√
7.		√	

UNIT 23 (pages 218–226)

AFTER YOU READ

C. 2. give up   **4.** was born   **6.** moved
   3. acted   **5.** injured . . . died

D. 2. a   **3.** a   **4.** b   **5.** a

EXERCISE 1

Did you get up late? Did you stay up late last night? Did you write your paper for the drama class?
got, drank, had, did, had, took, was, went, wrote

EXERCISE 2

2. went **6.** became **10.** drank
3. had **7.** got **11.** was
4. saw **8.** didn't eat **12.** fainted
5. gave **9.** ate **13.** didn't give up

EXERCISE 3

2. Did she write
3. Did it take
4. Did Christopher Reeve go
5. Did Reeve play
6. Did Reeve have

EXERCISE 4

1. B: Yes, I ~~do~~ *did*. I stayed up until 2 A.M.
2. A: Tim, ~~Jeremy finished~~ *did Jeremy finish* his drama paper?
   B: Yes, and he ~~does~~ *did* a good job.
3. A: How many *Superman* movies did Reeve make?
   B: He ~~maked~~ *made* four of them.
4. A: ~~Christopher Reeve had~~ *Did Christopher Reeve have* a long life?
   B: No, he ~~doesn't~~ *didn't*. He ~~dead~~ *died* at the age of 52.

EXERCISE 5

A. Yoshio likes the Seattle area.
B. 2. False **5.** True **8.** No information
   3. No information **6.** False **9.** False
   4. True **7.** False

EXERCISE 6

B. In sentences 3, 6, 7, and 9 the last "d" in *did* is pronounced as /dʒ/

UNIT 24 (pages 228–235)

AFTER YOU READ

C. 2. A: dent
   B: an auto repair shop
   3. A: headlight
   4. B: slippery
D. 2. b **3.** a **4.** b **5.** b

EXERCISE 1

Where did you see him?
What time did you see him?
What did he look like?
What did he say?

EXERCISE 2

2. Why did you drive there
3. What happened
4. How long did the drive take
5. What did your parents say

EXERCISE 3

2. Who ate kimchee last night?
3. Who taught you to drive?
4. Who came late today?
5. Who visited you last weekend?
6. Who gave you a special gift last year?

EXERCISE 4

A: At 9:30 this morning.
B: Where did it ~~happened~~ *happen*?
A: It ~~did happen~~ *happened* on Oak Street between First and Second Avenues.
B: How ~~it did~~ *did it* happen?

A: A cat ran into the street. The car ahead of me ~~stop~~ *stopped* suddenly. The road was slippery, and I hit the car. My headlights are broken. There's a dent in the other car's bumper.

B: Thank you for reporting the accident.
C: What *did* the insurance company say?

A: Just "Thank you for reporting the accident."

EXERCISE 5

C. 2. When did it happen?
   3. How did it happen?
   4. What did the police do?
   5. How did the drivers look?

EXERCISE 6

A. b
B. 1. the damage to Rob's father's car
   2. a couple of days ago (two or three days ago)
   3. 8 hours
   4. 3 hours

UNIT 25 (pages 238–245)

AFTER YOU READ

C. 2. a gift certificate **4.** DVD **6.** chocolates
   3. a ride **5.** flowers
D. 2. False **4.** True **6.** False
   3. False **5.** True

EXERCISE 1

Steve: Well, <u>we</u>'re having a party on Sunday at my apartment. <u>You</u> and Josh are both invited. Are <u>you</u> free at three o'clock?

Amanda: <u>I</u> think so. What's the occasion?

Steve: <u>It</u>'s Jessica's birthday, but <u>I</u> don't know what to get (her.) What's a good gift? Any ideas?

Amanda: How about tickets for a concert? Does <u>she</u> like music?

Steve: Yes. <u>She</u> listens to (it) all the time.

Amanda: Good. Get (her) some tickets. Or else get (her) a gift certificate. Now, tell (me) again. What's your new address?

Steve: 14 Vine Street, Apartment 202.

Amanda: OK. See (you) then.

EXERCISE 2

1. **B:** She
2. **B:** he . . . him
3. **A:** you . . . us
   B: you
4. **A:** them
   B: They
5. **A:** it
   B: it
6. **A:** They
   B: them

EXERCISE 3

1. Why don't you get them a travel book?
2. Why don't you get her a tennis racquet?
3. Why don't you get him a vest?
4. Why don't you get me a DVD?

EXERCISE 4

Dear Sarah,

          I
    Jim and ~~me~~ are having a party on Saturday,
              It's
June 10, at 3:00. ~~Is~~ for our son, Bob, and our daughter, Sally. They both have birthdays in June.
                       them
You and Stan are invited. Please don't bring ~~they~~
        We're
any presents. ~~Us are~~ just having a band and lots of
                            me
food, but no gifts. Please come! Give Jim and ~~I~~ a call if you can make it.
    you both
See ~~both you~~ soon,
Doris

EXERCISE 5

A. Tim or Tim wrapped them.
B.

Color of Package	Who is it for?	Gift
red	Cousin Martha	*a tennis racquet*
green	Mom and Dad	tickets
orange	Jeremy	a DVD
white	Ben and Annie	a game
blue	Jessica	something special

EXERCISE 6

B. 2. wife   **3.** Josh   **4.** chocolates   **5.** Grants

UNIT 26 (pages 247–255)

AFTER YOU READ

C. 2. island   **4.** plants   **6.** animals
   3. flight   **5.** Only
D. 2. 10 days   **4.** 12 people
   3. A lot   **5.** Two—Quito and the Galápagos Islands

EXERCISE 1

2. **A:** <u>How many</u> (seats) are available on Flight 1 to Quito?
   B: <u>Not many</u>. You need to make a reservation now.
3. **A:** <u>How much</u> (time) does it take to get to the airport?
   B: <u>Not much</u>. Only about <u>30 minutes</u>.
4. **A:** <u>How much</u> (money) does the flight cost?
   B: About <u>$360</u>.
5. **A:** <u>How many</u> (tourists) visit the Galápagos Islands in May?
   B: <u>A lot</u>. Most tourists go there in April, May, and November.
6. **A:** Is there <u>a lot of</u> (rain) in July?
   B: No, there isn't, just <u>a little</u> (mist) called "garua."

EXERCISE 2

2. c   **3.** e   **4.** a   **5.** d

EXERCISE 3

1. How much does the trip cost
2. How many days is the trip
3. How many meals do they include **or** are included
4. How many people do they put in a room **or** How many people in a room **or** How many people are there in a room

EXERCISE 4

1. **B:** Only one other person, but we met a ~~little~~ *few* people on the trip.

2. **A:** How many ~~day~~ *days* were you away?

   B: Not ~~much~~ *many*, only three days. But we were on a small island.

3. **A:** How much time did you spend in your hotel room?

   B: Not ~~many~~ *much* time. We left early and returned late.

4. **A:** How ~~much~~ *many* trips do you usually take in a year?

   B: Two or three. I love to travel.

EXERCISE 5

A. b

B. 2. How many   **5.** How many
   3. How many   **6.** How much
   4. How much

C. 2. 4   **5.** 4
   3. 10   **6.** Very little
   4. 6 million dollars

EXERCISE 6

B. 2. yams   **4.** Jess, Yale   **6.** jams
   3. yellow   **5.** jail   **7.** Jell-o

UNIT 27 (pages 257–265)

AFTER YOU READ

D. 2. F. There are statues of four presidents on Mount Rushmore.
   3. T
   4. T
   5. F. Wall has a drugstore. OR There's a drugstore in Wall.

EXERCISE 1

JOSH: Thank you. We're glad there's a room for us.

MRS. GRANT: Actually, there are two rooms to choose from, one on the second floor and one on the third. The one on the third floor has a nice view

of the waterfall, but there isn't an elevator, unfortunately.

AMANDA: Oh, that's fine. We'd like the one with the

nice view. Is there a bath in the room?

MRS. GRANT: No. ~~Sorry about that.~~ There's just one bathroom per floor. But we don't have many guests. So, let's see . . . breakfast is from 7:00

until 9:00. There's coffee in your room, ~~and~~ there are also crackers and cookies. Your room is up that stairway over there. We'll see you in the morning.

JOSH: Thanks a lot. See you then.

EXERCISE 2

2. there is   **5.** there's   **8.** There are
3. there's   **6.** there are   **9.** they're
4. Are there   **7.** There's

EXERCISE 3

2. it   **4.** there   **6.** they
3. It   **5.** there   **7.** they

EXERCISE 4

Dear Kathy,
   Greetings from South Dakota. We're having a
There are
wonderful time. ~~It is~~ so many interesting things to see and do here! Right now we're in Deadwood,
There
an old mining town. ^ are interesting little shops
there
on every street, and ^ is a lot of fun stuff to buy. I
There are
hope my suitcase is big enough. ~~Are~~ ^ also a lot of

beautiful landmarks to see; we went to Mount Rushmore yesterday, and we're going to the Crazy Horse monument today. We're staying at a really
It is
nice bed-and-breakfast called Calamity Jane's. ~~Is~~ ^

a nice, comfortable place, and there are lots of interesting people from different places staying here.
   I have to sign off now; we're ready to go to Crazy Horse. Say hi to Mark and everyone else.
Love,
Amanda

EXERCISE 5

A. They're from Britain.
B. 2. T   **4.** NI   **6.** T   **8.** T   **10.** T
   3. F   **5.** NI   **7.** F   **9.** NI

EXERCISE 6

A. 2. they are   **4.** they are   **6.** there aren't
   3. there are   **5.** they aren't

AFTER YOU READ

C. **2.** computer science major
 3. fun-loving man
 4. spy movies
 5. chemistry professor
 6. artistic woman
 7. honest man
D. West Park: 1
 Cineplex: 6, 5
 Art Museum: 4
 Trip to Westville Falls: 2

EXERCISE 1

Underline: same, similar
Circle: jazz, grammar, gift, movie, chicken, spy, cotton
2. a **4.** b **6.** e **8.** g **10.** h
3. f **5.** d **7.** i **9.** j

EXERCISE 2

 2. black cotton T-shirts
 3. baggy jeans
 4. black sports car
 5. small brick house
 6. beautiful rock garden
 7. old spy movies

EXERCISE 3

A. **2.** shop **6.** orange **10.** major
 3. blueberry **7.** juice **11.** blue
 4. pancakes **8.** hungry **12.** nice
 5. delicious **9.** computer science **13.** polite

EXERCISE 4

Dear Dahlia,
My boyfriend, Joe, is wonderful. He's ~~a~~ kind,
 a good job
honest, and intelligent. He has ~~an job good~~ and a
 kind heart
~~heart kind~~. There's only one problem. He doesn't
like to spend money. We always watch TV at his
 cable TV
house, and he doesn't even have ~~TV cable~~.
 free
Sometimes we go to ~~frees~~ concerts and picnics. I
 different
have fun with Joe, but I want to do ~~differents~~
things. Do you have any suggestions?

Sincerely,
Rosa

EXERCISE 5

A. a
B. Circle the third woman from the left.

EXERCISE 7

A. **2.** f **3.** a **4.** d **5.** c **6.** e

AFTER YOU READ

C. **2.** a list **5.** game **8.** Snacks
 3. an invitation **6.** beverages
 4. Desserts **7.** entertainment
D. **2.** Pizza **4.** heavy metal
 3. Steak **5.** games

EXERCISE 1

A.

Short Adjectives	Adjectives That End in -y	Long Adjectives	Irregular Adjective Forms
older quicker cheaper faster smarter	easier funnier	more interesting	*worse* better

B. **2.** c **3.** a **4.** e **5.** b **6.** d

EXERCISE 2

 2. Marty is older than Ken.
 3. Ken's clothes are more colorful than Marty's clothes.
 4. Laura is shorter than Mi Young.
 5. Mi Young's hair is darker than Laura's hair.
 6. Lisa is better than David at dancing.
 7. Jason is worse than Maia at singing.

EXERCISE 3

 1. B: I think cafeteria food is worse.
 2. A: Are you taller than your father?
 B: Yes, but he's heavier.
 3. A: Are games more fun than DVDs?
 B: Yes, games are more fun than DVDs.
 4. A: Which is better for a party, pop music or jazz?
 B: I think pop music is better.

EXERCISE 4

> ### Dogs Rule
>
>   *better*
> In my opinion, a dog is a ~~gooder~~ pet than a cat.
> I know because we have a dog and a cat at home.
>   *friendlier*
> Here are my reasons. First, a dog is ~~friendly~~ than a
>   *happier*
> cat. My dog is ~~more happy~~ to see me when I come
> home. My cat just doesn't care. Second, a dog is
> *more active*
> ~~activer~~. I always take my dog for a walk. I can't do
> that with my cat. She only wants to sleep. Third,
>   *more*   *more playful*
> a dog is interesting than a cat. My dog is ~~playfuler~~
>   ^
> than my cat. He knows a lot of tricks. My cat
> doesn't know any tricks at all. She's boring. Last, a
>   *protective*
> dog is more ~~protectiver~~ than a cat. My dog barks if
> anyone comes to the house. The cat just runs and
> hides. I think dogs rule.

EXERCISE 5

A. chemistry and physics.
B. 2. NI **3.** T **4.** T **5.** T **6.** F **7.** F **8.** F

EXERCISE 6

B. 2. The weather is better this month than last
    month.
  3. The exercise on page thirty-two is easier than
    the exercise on page thirty-one.
  4. Beth is thinner than my mother.
  5. Their brothers are older than our brothers.
  6. Let's go to another movie that's more
    interesting.
  7. They're luckier than we are.
  8. Kathy's toothache is getting worse, and it's
    bothering her a lot.

UNIT 30 (pages 288–294)

AFTER YOU READ

D. 2. T
  3. F. The barbecue is on Saturday afternoon.
  4. F. They live on 40th Avenue.
  5. T
  6. T
  7. F. They're going to play volleyball.

EXERCISE 1

Hi Honey, I couldn't reach you on the phone. Do
you remember Felix Maxa? I met him on the train
<u>in June</u>. Felix called and invited us to a barbecue at
their house near the university. The barbecue is <u>on
the 20th</u>, <u>at 1:00</u>. I know we're going to a play <u>on
Sunday afternoon</u>, but I think we're free <u>on Saturday</u>.
Are we free? Please get back to me right away. Love,
Tim

EXERCISE 2

  2. in   **4.** at   **6.** in   **8.** on
  3. at   **5.** at   **7.** at   **9.** in

EXERCISE 3

  1. B: Dinner is usually at 7:00 or 7:30.
  2. A: What time do people start work in the morning?
      B: People usually start work at 8:00.
  3. A: What do people do in the evenings?
      B: They often watch TV in the evenings.
  4. A: What do people do on the weekends?
      B: They often go shopping on the weekends.

EXERCISE 4

                              on
  1. Daniela is leaving Seattle ~~in~~ Monday,
                at
    January 25, ~~on~~ 12:00 noon.
                                     in
  2. Her flight arrives in Chicago at 6:00 ~~at~~ the
    evening.
                           at
  3. Her flight to London leaves at 7:30 ~~in~~ night.
                         at
  4. Flight 774 arrives in London ~~in~~ 11:30 in the
    morning.
                        at   *on*
  5. Her flight to Bucharest leaves ~~in~~ 2:00 P.M. ~~in~~
    January 26.
                         in
  6. It arrives in Bucharest at 6:05 ~~at~~ the evening.

EXERCISE 5

A. Bucharest, Romania
B.

Day, month, and date Felix leaves Seattle	Time first flight leaves Seattle	Time second flight leaves Seattle	Day, month, and date Felix returns to Seattle
on Thursday, January 30th	At noon on Thursday, January 30th	At 6:30 P.M. on Thursday, January 30th	On Friday, February 7th

EXERCISE 6

B. 2. Bob has a snack every morning(at)eleven o'clock.

3. Nancy usually has a sandwich in the early (afternoon.)

4. The party starts(at)six-thirty(and)will be(at)Robert's house.

5. John(and)I plan to watch the play(after)we go shopping.

6. (Alice)can't be here(at)six, but Margaret can.

UNIT 31 (pages 298–305)

AFTER YOU READ

D. 2. is   **4.** isn't   **6.** don't have to be   **8.** are not
3. is   **5.** isn't   **7.** is

EXERCISE 1

_e_ **1.** Josh, do I need my heavy coat?

_f_ **2.** Dad, what <u>are</u> we <u>going to do</u> tonight?

_d_ **3.** Mom, where's Dad going?

_b_ **4.** Do you think Mark and Kathy <u>are going to get married</u>?

_c_ **5.** What<u>'s going to happen</u> next June?

_a_ **6.** Does Jason do gymnastics?

a. Yes. Actually, he<u>'s going to compete</u> in a match tonight.

b. Probably. They're a great couple.

c. Judy<u>'s going to graduate.</u>

d. He and Ben <u>are going to swim</u> for an hour or so at the pool.

e. Yes. It<u>'s going to snow.</u> It's a football game, and it's December.

f. We<u>'re going</u> to go to the hockey game.

EXERCISE 2

2. is going to be
3. is going to attend
4. is going to invite
5. is going to take
6. are going to film
7. are going to bring
8. is going to win
9. is going to play

EXERCISE 3

2. is going to finish
3. aren't going to win
4. are going to win
5. is not going to lose
6. is not going to win
7. is going to win
8. is not going to finish

EXERCISE 4

Dear Kathy,

I hope you're going ^to^ be in town Sunday evening. Josh and I are ^going to^ have a little party to watch the big game on TV. We are going ^to^ have pizza and dessert. We ~~be~~ ^are^ going to start the meal about 5:00. I think the game ~~are~~ ^is^ going to start at 6:00. Please come if you can. But can you let us know? We ^are^ going to be out of town until Tuesday. Call after that, OK?
Amanda

EXERCISE 5

A. They win the game.
B. 2. T   **3.** F   **4.** F   **5.** T   **6.** NI   **7.** T   **8.** T

EXERCISE 6

A. 1. A: I think it's <u>going to</u> rain.
   B: I don't think so.
   A: It is(going to)rain. Believe me!
2. A: My team is <u>going to</u> win the game.
   B: No, it isn't.
   A: Yes, it is. It's(going to)win.
3. A: This traffic is terrible. We're not(going to)make it on time.
   B: Don't worry. We're <u>going to</u> make it. We still have 20 minutes.
4. A: I don't think I'm(going to)pass this course.
   B: Of course you're <u>going to</u> pass it! Stop worrying.

UNIT 32 (pages 307–313)

AFTER YOU READ

C. 2. a big part   **4.** national TV   **6.** a program
3. a producer   **5.** awesome
D.

2. It's ^not^ going to start right away.

3. The producer wants Jessica to have a ~~small~~ ^big^ part in it.

4. ~~Jeremy~~ ^Ben^ is unhappy about Jessica's new job.

5. Tim asks, "Are you going to ~~make~~ ^travel^ a lot ~~of money~~?"

6. Ben asks, "How are you going to ~~cook for us~~ ^take me to soccer practice^?"

EXERCISE 1

1. do; b
2. begin; c
3. travel; d
4. get; a

EXERCISE 2

2. 're working, worked, Are . . . going to work
3. had, 're having, Are . . . going to have, are going to have
4. wear, wore, 're wearing, Are . . . going to wear
5. watched, are . . . watching, 'm going to watch

EXERCISE 3

A. 2. Is it going to mean a lot of work
   3. Am I really going to have a big part
   4. Are the children going to be OK
   5. Is Tim going to spend more time at home
B. 6. How often is Jessica going to be away from home
   7. When are we going to have time together
   8. When is the show going to begin
   9. Who is going to help when I'm away on business
   10. What is Jessica's new job going to do to our marriage

EXERCISE 4

2. Hi, honey. I forgot my date book. ~~Is~~ *Are* Fred and Janet going to meet us at 8:00 or 8:30? Please call.

3. This message is for Jessica Olson. This is George Selig. When is the conference going *to* start?

4. Hi Mom. I'm not going to be home until 9:00. Al and I ~~am~~ *are* going to study together.

5. Hi, Jessica. This is Meg Smith. What time *is* the meeting going to be? Please call me at 989-555-0007.

6. Hi, Jess. This is Dan. Watch the news tonight at 6:00 on Channel 2. I *'m* going to be on it.

EXERCISE 5

A. b
B. 1. b   2. a   3. b   4. a
C. you guys going to start a collection for me

EXERCISE 6

B. 2. /p/   4. /v/   6. /b/   8. /v/
   3. /f/   5. /p/   7. /f/
C. 2. producer
   3. big part
   4. part-time, bank
   5. very famous
   6. party, be
   7. buy, furniture, baby

EXERCISE 7

Possible answers:

The man and woman in the car are going to play tennis. They are going to get a parking ticket. The pickpocket is going to steal the woman's wallet. The people in the line are going to see a movie. The mother and child are going to see the cartoon.

Single-User License Agreement

THESE TERMS APPLY TO ALL LICENSED SOFTWARE ON THE DISK EXCEPT THAT THE TERMS FOR USE OF ANY SHAREWARE OR FREEWARE ON THE DISKETTES ARE AS SET FORTH IN THE ELECTRONIC LICENSE LOCATED ON THE DISK:

1. **GRANT OF LICENSE AND OWNERSHIP:** The enclosed computer programs ("Software") are licensed, not sold, to you by Pearson Education, Inc. ("We" or the "Company") and in consideration of your payment of the license fee, which is part of the price you paid, and your agreement to these terms. We reserve any rights not granted to you. You own only the disk(s) but we and/or our licensors own the Software itself. This license allows you to use and display your copy of the Software on a single computer (i.e., with a single CPU) at a single location, so long as you comply with the terms of this Agreement. You may make one copy for back up, or transfer your copy to another CPU, provided that the Software is usable on only one computer.

2. **RESTRICTIONS:** You may not transfer or distribute the Software or documentation to anyone else. Except for backup, you may not copy the documentation or the Software. You may not network the Software or otherwise use it on more than one computer or computer terminal at the same time. You may not reverse engineer, disassemble, decompile, modify, adapt, translate, or create derivative works based on the Software or the Documentation. You may be held legally responsible for any copying or copyright infringement which is caused by your failure to abide by the terms of these restrictions.

3. **TERMINATION:** This license is effective until terminated. This license will terminate automatically without notice from the Company if you fail to comply with any provisions or limitations of this license. Upon termination, you shall destroy the Documentation and all copies of the Software. All provisions of this Agreement as to limitation and disclaimer of warranties, limitation of liability, remedies or damages, and our ownership rights shall survive termination.

4. **LIMITED WARRANTY AND DISCLAIMER OF WARRANTY:** Company warrants that for a period of 30 days from the date you purchase this Software, the Software, when properly installed and used in accordance with the Documentation, will operate in substantial conformity with the description of the Software set forth in the Documentation, and that for a period of 30 days the disk(s) on which the Software is delivered shall be free from defects in materials and workmanship under normal use. The Company does not warrant that the Software will meet your requirements or that the operation of the Software will be uninterrupted or error-free. Your only remedy and the Company's only obligation under these limited warranties is, at the Company's option, return of the disk for a refund of any amounts paid for it by you or replacement of the disk. THIS LIMITED WARRANTY IS THE ONLY WARRANTY PROVIDED BY THE COMPANY AND ITS LICENSORS, AND THE COMPANY AND ITS LICENSORS DISCLAIM ALL OTHER WARRANTIES, EXPRESS OR IMPLIED, INCLUDING WITHOUT LIMITATION, THE IMPLIED WARRANTIES OF MERCHANTABILITY AND FITNESS FOR A PARTICULAR PURPOSE. THE COMPANY DOES NOT WARRANT, GUARANTEE OR MAKE ANY REPRESENTATION REGARDING THE ACCURACY, RELIABILITY, CURRENTNESS, USE, OR RESULTS OF USE, OF THE SOFTWARE.

5. **LIMITATION OF REMEDIES AND DAMAGES:** IN NO EVENT, SHALL THE COMPANY OR ITS EMPLOYEES, AGENTS, LICENSORS, OR CONTRACTORS BE LIABLE FOR ANY INCIDENTAL, INDIRECT, SPECIAL, OR CONSEQUENTIAL DAMAGES ARISING OUT OF OR IN CONNECTION WITH THIS LICENSE OR THE SOFTWARE, INCLUDING FOR LOSS OF USE, LOSS OF DATA, LOSS OF INCOME OR PROFIT, OR OTHER LOSSES, SUSTAINED AS A RESULT OF INJURY TO ANY PERSON, OR LOSS OF OR DAMAGE TO PROPERTY, OR CLAIMS OF THIRD PARTIES, EVEN IF THE COMPANY OR AN AUTHORIZED REPRESENTATIVE OF THE COMPANY HAS BEEN ADVISED OF THE POSSIBILITY OF SUCH DAMAGES. IN NO EVENT SHALL THE LIABILITY OF THE COMPANY FOR DAMAGES WITH RESPECT TO THE SOFTWARE EXCEED THE AMOUNTS ACTUALLY PAID BY YOU, IF ANY, FOR THE SOFTWARE OR THE ACCOMPANYING TEXTBOOK. BECAUSE SOME JURISDICTIONS DO NOT ALLOW THE LIMITATION OF LIABILITY IN CERTAIN CIRCUMSTANCES, THE ABOVE LIMITATIONS MAY NOT ALWAYS APPLY TO YOU.

6. **GENERAL:** This agreement shall be construed in accordance with the laws of the United States of America and the State of New York, applicable to contracts made in New York, and shall benefit the Company, its affiliates and assignees. This agreement is the complete and exclusive statement of the agreement between you and the Company and supersedes all proposals or prior agreements, oral, or written, and any other communications between you and the Company or any representative of the Company relating to the subject matter of this agreement. If you are a U.S. government user, this Software is licensed with "restricted rights" as set forth in subparagraphs (a)-(d) of the Commercial Computer-Restricted Rights clause at FAR 52.227-19 or in subparagraphs (c)(1)(ii) of the Rights in Technical Data and Computer Software clause at DFARS 252.227-7013, and similar clauses, as applicable. Should you have any questions concerning this agreement or if you wish to contact the Company for any reason, please contact in writing: Customer Service, Pearson Education, Inc., 10 Bank Street, White Plains, NY 10606.

System Requirements

WINDOWS®	MACINTOSH®	BOTH
• Windows XP/Vista/7	• Mac OS X (10.4 & 10.5)	• 256 MB RAM minimum (512+ MB recommended)
• Intel Pentium processor 1GHz or higher	• PowerPC & Intel processor 1GHz or higher	• Monitor resolution of 1024 x 768 or higher
• Internet Explorer® 7.0 or higher OR Firefox® 2.0 or higher	• Safari® 2.0 or higher OR Firefox® 2.0 or higher	• Sound card and speakers or headphones
		• 500 MB hard disk space
		• 10X CD-ROM drive or higher
		• Adobe Flash 8 plug-in or higher
		• Internet Connection: DSL, Cable/Broadband, T1, or other high-speed connection
		• Microsoft® PowerPoint Viewer

Installation Instructions

WINDOWS®

• Insert the CD-ROM into the CD-ROM drive of your computer. On most computers, the program will begin automatically.

If the program does not begin automatically:

• Open "My Computer."

• Right-click on the CD-ROM icon.

• Click on Open.

• Double-click on the "Start" file. Leave the CD-ROM in the computer while using the program.

MACINTOSH®

• Insert the CD-ROM into the CD-ROM drive of your computer.

• Double-click on the CD-ROM icon on your desktop.

• Double click on the "Start" file. Leave the CD-ROM in the computer while using the program.

Note: The original CD-ROM must be in the CD-ROM drive when you use the program.

TECHNICAL SUPPORT

For Technical Product Support, please visit our support website at www.PearsonLongmanSupport.com. You can search our **Knowledgebase** for frequently asked questions, instantly **Chat** with an available support representative, or **Submit a Ticket/Request** for assistance.